The Constitution of
The State of Louisiana:
A Quick Reference Guide

Bootblack Budget Books
Copyright 2018 ©
ISBN-13: 978-1986357364
ISBN-10: 1986357368

Contents:

PREAMBLE – Page 29

ARTICLE I: DECLARATION OF RIGHTS – Page 30

Section 1. Origin and Purpose of Government

Section 2. Due Process of Law

Section 3. Right to Individual Dignity

Section 4. Right to Property

Section 5. Right to Privacy

Section 6. Freedom from Intrusion

Section 7. Freedom of Expression

Section 8. Freedom of Religion

Section 9. Right of Assembly and Petition

Section 10. Right to Vote; Disqualification from seeking or holding an elective office

Section 11. Right to Keep and Bear Arms

Section 12. Freedom from Discrimination

Section 13. Rights of the Accused

Section 14. Right to Preliminary Examination

Section 15. Initiation of Prosecution

Section 16. Right to a Fair Trial

Section 17. Jury Trial in Criminal Cases; Joinder of Felonies; Mode of Trial

Section 18. Right to Bail

Section 19. Right to Judicial Review

Section 20. Right to Humane Treatment

Section 21. Writ of Habeas Corpus

Section 22. Access to Courts

Section 23. Prohibited Laws

Section 24. Unenumerated Rights

Section 25. Rights of a Victim

Section 26. State Sovereignty

Section 27. Freedom to Hunt, Fish and Trap

ARTICLE II: DISTRIBUTION OF POWERS – Page 43

Section 1. Three Branches

Section 2. Limitations on Each Branch

ARTICLE III: LEGISLATIVE BRANCH – Page 44

Section 1. Legislative Power; Composition; Continuous Body

Section 2. Sessions

Section 3. Size

Section 4. Qualifications; Residence and Domicile Requirements; Term; Election Limitations; Vacancies

Section 5. Taking Office

Section 6. Legislative Reapportionment; Reapportionment by Supreme Court; Procedure

Section 7. Judging Qualifications and Elections; Procedural Rules; Discipline; Expulsion; Subpoenas; Contempt; Officers

Section 8. Privileges and Immunities

Section 9. Conflict of Interest

Section 10. Quorum; Compulsory Attendance; Journal; Adjournment With Consent of Other House

Section 11. Legislative Auditor

Section 12. Prohibited Local and Special Laws

Section 13. Local or Special Laws; Notice of Intent; Publication

Section 14. Style of Laws; Enacting Clause

Section 15. Passage of Bills

Section 16. Appropriations

Section 17. Signing of Bills; Delivery to Governor

Section 18. Gubernatorial Action on Bills; Sign, Failure to Sign, Veto; Veto Session

Section 19. Effective Date of Laws

Section 20. Suspension of Laws

ARTICLE IV: EXECUTIVE BRANCH – Page 61

Section 1. Composition; Number of Departments; Reorganization

Section 2. Qualifications

Section 3. Election; Term

Section 4. Compensation

Section 5. Governor; Powers and Duties

Section 6. Lieutenant Governor; Powers and Duties

Section 7. Secretary of State; Powers and Duties

Section 8. Attorney General; Powers and Duties

Section 9. Treasurer; Powers and Duties

Section 10. Commissioner of Agriculture; Powers and Duties

Section 11. Commissioner of Insurance; Powers and Duties

Section 12. Commissioner of Election; Powers and Duties

Section 13. First Assistants; Appointment

Section 14. Vacancy in Office of Governor

Section 15. Vacancy in Office of Lieutenant Governor

Section 16. Vacancies in Other Statewide Elective Offices

Section 17. Declaration of Inability by Statewide Elected Officials

Section 18. Determination of Inability of Statewide Elected Official

Section 19. Temporary Absences

Section 20. Appointment of Officials; Merger, Consolidation of Offices and Departments

Section 21. Public Service Commission

Section 22. Term Limits; Certain Boards and Commissions

ARTICLE V: JUDICIAL BRANCH – Page 77

Section 1. Judicial Power

Section 2. Habeas Corpus, Needful Writs, Orders and Process; Contempt

Section 3. Supreme Court; Composition; Judgments; Terms

Section 4. Supreme Court; Districts

Section 5. Supreme Court; Jurisdiction; Rule-Making Power; Assignment of Judges

Section 6. Supreme Court; Chief Justice

Section 7. Supreme Court; Personnel

Section 8. Courts of Appeal; Circuits; Panels; Judgments; Terms

Section 9. Courts of Appeal; Circuits and Districts

Section 10. Courts of Appeal; Jurisdiction

Section 11. Courts of Appeal; Certification

Section 12. Courts of Appeal; Chief Judge

Section 13. Courts of Appeal; Personnel

Section 14. District Courts; Judicial Districts

Section 15. Courts; Retention; Jurisdiction; Judicial District Changes; Terms

Section 16. District Courts; Jurisdiction

Section 17. District Courts; Chief Judge

Section 18. Juvenile and Family Courts; Jurisdiction

Section 19. Special Juvenile Procedures

Section 20. Mayors' Courts; Justice of the Peace Courts

Section 21. Judges; Decrease in Terms and Compensation Prohibited

Section 22. Judges; Election; Vacancy

Section 23. Judges; Retirement

Section 24. Judges; Qualifications

Section 25. Judiciary Commission

Section 26. District Attorneys

Section 27. Sheriffs

Section 28. Clerks of Court

Section 29. Coroners

Section 30. Vacancies

Section 31. Reduction of Salaries and Benefits Prohibited

Section 32. Orleans Parish Courts, Officials

Section 33. Jurors

Section 34. Grand Jury

ARTICLE VI: LOCAL GOVERNMENT – Page 93

PART I. GENERAL PROVISIONS

Section 1. Parishes

Section 2. Municipalities

Section 3. Classification

Section 4. Existing Home Rule Charters and Plans of Government

Section 5. Home Rule Charter

Section 6. Home Rule Charter or Plan of Government; Action by Legislature Prohibited

Section 7. Powers of Other Local Governmental Subdivisions

Section 8. Home Rule Parish; Incorporation of Cities, Towns, and Villages

Section 9. Limitations of Local Governmental Subdivisions

Section 10. Codification of Ordinances

Section 11. Local Officials

Section 12. Local Officials; Compensation

Section 13. Vacancies

Section 14. Increasing Financial Burden of Political Subdivisions

Section 15. Local Governmental Subdivisions; Control Over Agencies

Section 16. Special Districts and Local Public Agencies

Section 17. Land Use; Zoning; Historic Preservation

Section 18. Industrial Areas

Section 19. Special Districts; Creation

Section 20. Intergovernmental Cooperation

Section 21. Assistance to Local Industry

Section 22. Procedure for Certain Special Elections

Section 23. Acquisition of Property

Section 24. Servitudes of Way; Acquisition by Prescription

Section 25. Courts Not Affected

PART II. FINANCE

Section 26. Parish Ad Valorem Tax

Section 27. Municipal Ad Valorem Tax

Section 28. Local Governmental Subdivisions; Occupational License Tax

Section 29. Local Governmental Subdivisions and School Boards; Sales Tax

Section 30. Political Subdivisions; Taxing Power

Section 30.1. Bonding and Taxing Authority of Certain Political Subdivisions and Other Public Entities

Section 31. Taxes; Ratification

Section 32. Special Taxes; Authorization

Section 33. Political Subdivisions; General Obligation Bonds

Section 34. Limitations on Bonded Indebtedness

Section 35. Contesting Political Subdivision Bonds

Section 36. Local Improvement Assessments

Section 37. Revenue-Producing Property

PART III. LEVEE DISTRICTS

Section 38. Levee Districts

Section 39. Levee District Taxes

Section 40. Bond Issues

Section 41. Cooperation with Federal Government

Section 42. Compensation for Property Used or Destroyed; Tax

PART IV. PORT COMMISSIONS AND DISTRICTS

Section 43. Port Commissions and Districts

PART V. DEFINITIONS

Section 44. Terms Defined

ARTICLE VII: REVENUE AND FINANCE – Page 122

PART I. GENERAL PROVISIONS

Section 1. Power to Tax; Public Purpose

Section 2. Power to Tax; Limitation

Section 2.1. Fees and Civil Fines; Limitation

Section 2.2. Power to Tax; Sales and Use Tax; Limitation

Section 3. Collection of Taxes

Section 4. Income Tax; Severance Tax; Political Subdivisions

Section 5. Motor Vehicle License Tax

Section 6. State Debt; Full Faith and Credit Obligations

Section 7. State Debt; Interim Emergency Board

Section 8. State Bond Commission

Section 9. State Funds

Section 10. Expenditure of State Funds

Section 10-A. Wildlife and Fisheries; Conservation Fund

Section 10.1. Quality Trust Fund; Education

Section 10.2. Wetlands Conservation and Restoration Fund

Section 10.3. Budget Stabilization Fund

Section 10.4. Higher Education Louisiana Partnership Fund; Program

Section 10.5. Mineral Revenue Audit and Settlement Fund

Section 10.6. Oilfield Site Restoration Fund

Section 10.7. Oil Spill Contingency Fund

Section 10.8. Millennium Trust

Section 10.9. Louisiana Fund

Section 10.10. Millennium Leverage Fund

Section 10.11. Artificial Reef Development Fund

Section 10.12. Farmers and fishermen assistance programs; Agricultural and Seafood Products Support Fund

Section 10.13. Hospital stabilization formula and assessment; Hospital Stabilization Fund

Section 10.14. Louisiana Medical Assistance Trust Fund

Section 10.15. Louisiana Medical Assistance Trust Fund

Section 10.16. Dedications of Mineral Revenues

Section 11. Budgets

Section 12. Reports and Records

Section 13. Investment of State Funds

Section 14. Donation, Loan, or Pledge of Public Credit

Section 15. Release of Obligations to State, Parish, or Municipality

Section 16. Taxes; Prescription

Section 17. Legislation to Obtain Federal Aid

PART II. PROPERTY TAXATION

Section 18. Ad Valorem Taxes

Section 19. State Property Taxation; Rate Limitation

Section 20. Homestead Exemption

Section 21. Other Property Exemptions

Section 22. No Impairment of Existing Taxes or Obligations

Section 23. Adjustment of Ad Valorem Tax Millages

Section 24. Tax Assessors

Section 25. Tax Sales

PART III. REVENUE SHARING

Section 26. Revenue Sharing Fund

PART IV. TRANSPORTATION

Section 27. Transportation Trust Fund

ARTICLE VIII: EDUCATION – Page 230

Preamble

Section 1. Public Educational System

Section 2. State Superintendent of Education

Section 3. State Board of Elementary and Secondary Education

Section 4. Approval of Private Schools

Section 5. Board of Regents

Section 6. Board of Supervisors for the University of Louisiana System

Section 7. Board of Supervisors of Louisiana State University and Agricultural and Mechanical College; Board of Supervisors of Southern University and Agricultural and Mechanical College

Section 7.1. Board of Supervisors of Community and Technical Colleges

Section 8. Boards; Membership; Compensation

Section 9. Parish School Boards; Parish Superintendents

Section 10. Existing Boards and Systems Recognized; Consolidation

Section 11. Appropriations; State Boards

Section 12. Appropriations; Higher Education

Section 13. Funding; Apportionment

Section 14. Tulane University

Section 15. Members of State Board of Elementary and Secondary Education; beginning and endof terms

Section 16. Public Hospitals

ARTICLE IX: NATURAL RESOURCES – Page 247

Section 1. Natural Resources and Environment; Public Policy

Section 2. Natural Gas

Section 3. Alienation of Water Bottoms

Section 4. Reservation of Mineral Rights; Prescription

Section 5. Public Notice; Public Bidding Requirements

Section 6. Tidelands Ownership

Section 7. Wildlife and Fisheries Commission

Section 8. Forestry

Section 9. First Use Tax Trust Fund

Section 10. Louisiana Investment Fund for Enhancement

ARTICLE X: PUBLIC OFFICIALS AND EMPLOYEES – Page 256

PART I. STATE AND CITY CIVIL SERVICE

Section 1. Civil Service Systems

Section 2. Classified and Unclassified Service

Section 3. State Civil Service Commission

Section 4. City Civil Service Commission

Section 5. Removal

Section 6. Department of Civil Service; Directors

Section 7. Appointments; Promotions

Section 8. Appeals

Section 9. Prohibitions Against Political Activities

Section 10. Rules; Investigations; Wages and Hours

Section 11. Penalties

Section 12. Appeal

Section 13. Appropriations

Section 14. Acceptance of Act; Other Cities, Parishes, City and Parish Governed Jointly

Section 15. City, Parish Civil Service System; Creation; Prohibition

PART II. FIRE AND POLICE CIVIL SERVICE

Section 16. Establishment of System

Section 17. Appointments and Promotions

Section 18. Prior Provisions

Section 19. Exclusion

Section 20. Political Activities

PART III. OTHER PROVISIONS

Section 21. Code of Ethics

Section 22. Dual Employment and Dual Officeholding

Section 23. Compensation of Elected Public Officials; Reduction

Section 24. Impeachment

Section 25. Removal by Suit; Officials Subject

Section 25.1. Removal by Suit; State, District, Parochial, Ward, or Municipal Employees

Section 26. Recall

Section 27. Filling of Vacancies

Section 28. Definition of Vacancy

Section 29. Retirement and Survivor's Benefits

Section 29.1. Part-time Public Officials

Section 30. Oath of Office

PART IV. STATE POLICE SERVICE

Section 41. State Police Service

Section 42. Classified and Unclassified Service

Section 43. State Police Commission

Section 44. Director

Section 45. Appointments; Promotions

Section 46. Appeals

Section 47. Prohibitions Against Political Activities

Section 48. Rules; Investigations; Wages and Hours

Section 49. Penalties

Section 50. Appeal

Section 51. Appropriations

ARTICLE XI: ELECTIONS – Page 290

Section 1. Election Code

Section 2. Secret Ballot; Absentee Voting; Preservation of Ballot

Section 3. Privilege from Arrest

Section 4. Prohibited Use of Public Funds

Section 5. Registrar of Voters

ARTICLE XII: GENERAL PROVISIONS – Page 292

Section 1. State Capital

Section 2. Civilian-Military Relations

Section 3. Right to Direct Participation

Section 4. Preservation of Linguistic and Cultural Origins

Section 5. Successions; Forced Heirship and Trusts

Section 6. Lotteries; Gaming, Gambling, or Wagering

Section 7. State Penal Institutions; Reimbursement of Parish Expense

Section 8. Welfare, Unemployment Compensation, and Health

Section 8.1. Worker's Compensation

Section 9. Exemptions From Seizure and Sale

Section 10. Suits Against the State

Section 11. Continuity of Government

Section 12. Corporations; Perpetual or Indefinite Duration; Dissolution;Perpetual Franchises or Privileges

Section 13. Prescription Against State

Section 14. Administrative Agency Codes

Section 15. Defense of Marriage

ARTICLE XIII: CONSTITUTIONAL REVISION – Page 305

Section 1. Amendments

Section 2. Constitutional Convention

Section 3. Laws Effectuating Amendments

ARTICLE XIV. TRANSITIONAL PROVISIONS – Page 308

PART I.

Section 1. Board of Regents

Section 2. Board of Supervisors of Louisiana State University and Agricultural and Mechanical College

Section 3. Board of Supervisors of Southern University

Section 4. State Board of Elementary and Secondary Education; Board of Trustees for State Colleges and Universities

Section 5. Boards; New Appointments

Section 6. Mandatory Reorganization of State Government

Section 7. Legislative Sessions

Section 8. Civil Service Commission; State; Cities

Section 9. Civil Service Officers; Employees; State; Cities

Section 10. Offshore Mineral Revenues; Use of Funds

Section 11. Prescription; Tidelands Taxes

Section 12. Forfeitures Prior to 1880

Section 13. Effective Date of Property Tax Provisions

PART II.

Section 14. Limitation on Transitional Provisions

Section 15. Existing Officials

Section 16. Provisions of 1921 Constitution Made Statutory

Section 17. Repealed.

Section 18. Existing Laws

Section 19. Ports; Transition to Statutes

Section 20. Public Service Commission

PART III.

Section 21. References to 1921 Constitution

Section 22. Effect of Titles

Section 23. Continuation of Actions and Rights

Section 24. Protection of Existing Taxes

Section 25. Impairment of Debt Obligations Prohibited

Section 26. Constitution Not Retroactive

Section 27. Legislative Provisions

Section 28. Judiciary Commission

Section 29. Repealed.

Section 30. Commissioner of Elections

Section 31. Pardon Board

Section 32. Levee Districts; Compensation for Property

Section 33. Suits Against the State; Effective Date

Section 34. Exemption from Seizure and Sale

Section 35. Effective Date

Section 36. Effect of Adoption

Section 37. Severability Clause

PREAMBLE

We, the people of Louisiana, grateful to Almighty God for the civil, political, economic, and religious liberties we enjoy, and desiring to protect individual rights to life, liberty, and property; afford opportunity for the fullest development of the individual; assure equality of rights; promote the health, safety, education, and welfare of the people; maintain a representative and orderly government; ensure domestic tranquility; provide for the common defense; and secure the blessings of freedom and justice to ourselves and our posterity, do ordain and establish this constitution.

ARTICLE I: DECLARATION OF RIGHTS

Section 1. Origin and Purpose of Government

All government, of right, originates with the people, is founded on their will alone, and is instituted to protect the rights of the individual and for the good of the whole. Its only legitimate ends are to secure justice for all, preserve peace, protect the rights, and promote the happiness and general welfare of the people. The rights enumerated in this Article are inalienable by the state and shall be preserved inviolate by the state.

Section 2. Due Process of Law

No person shall be deprived of life, liberty, or property, except by due process of law.

Section 3. Right to Individual Dignity

No person shall be denied the equal protection of the laws. No law shall discriminate against a person because of race or religious ideas, beliefs, or affiliations. No law shall arbitrarily, capriciously, or unreasonably discriminate against a person because of birth, age, sex, culture, physical condition, or political ideas or affiliations. Slavery and involuntary servitude are prohibited, except in the latter case as punishment for crime.

Section 4. Right to Property.

(A) Every person has the right to acquire, own, control, use, enjoy, protect, and dispose of private property. This right is subject to reasonable statutory restrictions and the reasonable exercise of the police power.

(B)(1) Property shall not be taken or damaged by the state or its political subdivisions except for public purposes and with just compensation paid to the owner or into court for his benefit. Except as specifically authorized by Article VI, Section 21 of this Constitution property shall not be taken or damaged by the state or its political subdivisions:

(a) for predominant use by any private person or entity; or
(b) for transfer of ownership to any private person or entity.

(2) As used in Subparagraph (1) of this Paragraph and in Article VI, Section 23 of this Constitution, "public purpose" shall be limited to the following:

(a) A general public right to a definite use of the property.

(b) Continuous public ownership of property dedicated to one or more of the following objectives and uses:

(i) Public buildings in which publicly funded services are administered, rendered, or provided.

(ii) Roads, bridges, waterways, access to public waters and lands, and other public transportation, access, and navigational systems available to the general public.

(iii) Drainage, flood control, levees, coastal and navigational protection and reclamation for the benefit of the public generally.

(iv) Parks, convention centers, museums, historical buildings and recreational facilities generally open to the public.

(v) Public utilities for the benefit of the public generally.

(vi) Public ports and public airports to facilitate the transport of goods or persons in domestic or international commerce.

(c) The removal of a threat to public health or safety caused by the existing use or disuse of the property.

(3) Neither economic development, of tax revenue, or any incidental benefit to the public shall be considered in determining whether the taking or damaging of property is for a public purpose pursuant to Subparagraph (1) of this Paragraph or Article VI, Section 23 of this Constitution.

(4) Property shall not be taken or damaged by any private entity authorized by law to expropriate, except for a public and necessary purpose and with just compensation paid to the owner; in such proceedings, whether the purpose is public and necessary shall be a judicial question.

(5) In every expropriation or action to take property pursuant to the provisions of this Section, a party has the right to trial by jury to determine whether the compensation is just, and the owner shall be compensated to the full extent of his loss. Except as otherwise provided in this Constitution, the full extent of loss shall include, but not be limited to, the appraised value of the property and all costs of relocation, inconvenience, and any other damages actually incurred by the owner because of the expropriation.

(6) No business enterprise or any of its assets shall be taken for the purpose of operating that enterprise or halting competition with a government enterprise. However, a municipality may expropriate a utility within its jurisdiction.

(C) Personal effects, other than contraband, shall never be taken.

(D) But the following property may be forfeited and disposed of in a civil proceeding, as provided by law: contraband drugs; property derived in whole or in part from contraband drugs; property used in the distribution, transfer, sale, felony possession, manufacture, or transportation of contraband drugs; property furnished or intended to be furnished in exchange for contraband drugs; property used or intended to be used to facilitate any of the above conduct; or other property because the above described property has been rendered unavailable.

(E) This Section shall not apply to appropriation of property necessary for levee and levee drainage purposes.

(F) Further, the legislature may place limitations on the extent of recovery for the taking of, or loss or damage to, property rights affected by coastal wetlands conservation, management, preservation, enhancement, creation, or restoration activities.

(G) Compensation paid for the taking of, or loss or damage to, property rights for the construction, enlargement, improvement, or modification of federal or non-federal hurricane protection projects, including mitigation related thereto, shall not exceed the compensation required by the Fifth Amendment of the Constitution of the United States of America. However, this Paragraph shall not apply to compensation paid for a building or structure that was destroyed or damaged by an event for which a presidential declaration of major disaster or emergency was issued, if the taking occurs within three years of such event. The legislature by law may provide procedures and definitions for the provisions of this Paragraph.

(H)(1) Except for the removal of a threat to public health or safety caused by the existing use or disuse of the property, and except for leases or operation agreements for port facilities, highways, qualified transportation facilities or airports, the state or its political subdivisions shall not sell or lease property which has been expropriated and held for not more than thirty years without first offering the property to the original owner or his heir, or, if there is no heir, to the successor in title to the owner at the time of expropriation at the current fair market value, after which the property can be transferred only by competitive bid open to the general public. After thirty years have passed from the date the property was expropriated, the state or political subdivision may sell or otherwise transfer the property as provided by law.

(2) Within one year after the completion of the project for which the property was expropriated, the state or its political subdivision which expropriated the property shall identify all property which is not necessary for the public purpose of the project and declare the property as surplus property.

(3) All expropriated property identified as surplus property shall be offered for sale to the original owner or his heir, or, if there is no heir, to the successor in title to the owner at the time of expropriation at the current fair market value, within two years after completion of the project. If the original owner, heir, or other successor in title refuses or fails to purchase the surplus property within three years from completion of the project, then the surplus property may be offered for sale to the general public by competitive bid.

(4) After one year from the completion of the project for which property was expropriated, the original owner or his heir, or, if there is no heir, the successor in title to the owner at the time of expropriation may petition the state or its political subdivision which expropriated the property to have all or any portion of his property declared surplus. If the state or its political subdivision refuses or fails to identify all or any portion of the expropriated property as surplus, the original owner or the successor in title may petition any court of competent jurisdiction to have the property declared surplus.

Section 5. Right to Privacy

Every person shall be secure in his person, property, communications, houses, papers, and effects against unreasonable searches, seizures, or invasions of privacy. No warrant shall issue without probable cause supported by oath or affirmation, and particularly describing the place to be searched, the persons or things to be seized, and the lawful purpose or reason for the search. Any person adversely affected by a search or seizure conducted in violation of this Section shall have standing to raise its illegality in the appropriate court.

Section 6. Freedom from Intrusion

No person shall be quartered in any house without the consent of the owner or lawful occupant.

Section 7. Freedom of Expression

No law shall curtail or restrain the freedom of speech or of the press. Every person may speak, write, and publish his sentiments on any subject, but is responsible for abuse of that freedom.

Section 8. Freedom of Religion

No law shall be enacted respecting an establishment of religion or prohibiting the free exercise thereof.

Section 9. Right of Assembly and Petition

No law shall impair the right of any person to assemble peaceably or to petition government for a redress of grievances.

Section 10. Right to Vote; Disqualification from Seeking or Holding an Elective Office

(A) Right to Vote

Every citizen of the state, upon reaching eighteen years of age, shall have the right to register and vote, except that this right may be suspended while a person is interdicted and judicially declared mentally incompetent or is
under an order of imprisonment for conviction of a felony.

(B) Disqualification

The following persons shall not be permitted to qualify as a candidate for elective public office or take public elective office or appointment of honor, trust, or profit in this state:

(1) A person who has been convicted within this state of a felony and who has exhausted all legal remedies, or who has been convicted under the laws of any other state or of the United States or of any foreign government or country of a crime which, if committed in this state, would be a felony and who has exhausted all legal remedies and has not afterwards been pardoned either by the governor of this state or by the officer of the state, nation, government or country having such authority to pardon in the place where the person was convicted and sentenced.

(2) A person actually under an order of imprisonment for conviction of a felony.

(C) Exception

Notwithstanding the provisions of Paragraph (B) of this Section, a person who desires to qualify as a candidate for or hold an elective office, who has been convicted of a felony and who has served his sentence, but has not been pardoned for such felony, shall be permitted to qualify as a candidate for or hold such office if the date of his qualifying for such office is more than fifteen years after the date of the completion of his original sentence.

Section 11. Right to Keep and Bear Arms

The right of each citizen to keep and bear arms is fundamental and shall not be infringed. Any restriction on this right shall be subject to strict scrutiny.

Section 12. Freedom from Discrimination

In access to public areas, accommodations, and facilities, every person shall be free from discrimination based on race, religion, or national ancestry and from arbitrary, capricious, or unreasonable discrimination based on age, sex, or physical condition.

Section 13. Rights of the Accused

When any person has been arrested or detained in connection with the investigation or commission of any offense, he shall be advised fully of the reason for his arrest or detention, his right to remain silent, his right against self incrimination, his right to the assistance of counsel and, if indigent, his right to court appointed counsel. In a criminal prosecution, an accused shall be informed of the nature and cause of the accusation against him. At each stage of the proceedings, every person is entitled to assistance of counsel of his choice, or appointed by the court if he is indigent and charged with an offense punishable by imprisonment. The legislature shall provide for a uniform system for securing and compensating qualified counsel for indigents.

Section 14. Right to Preliminary Examination

The right to a preliminary examination shall not be denied in felony cases except when the accused is indicted by a grand jury.

Section 15. Initiation of Prosecution

Prosecution of a felony shall be initiated by indictment or information, but no person shall be held to answer for a capital crime or a crime punishable by life imprisonment except on indictment by a grand jury. No person shall be twice placed in jeopardy for the same offense, except on his application for a new trial, when a mistrial is declared, or when a motion in arrest of judgment is sustained.

Section 16. Right to a Fair Trial

Every person charged with a crime is presumed innocent until proven guilty and is entitled to a speedy, public, and impartial trial in the parish where the offense or an element of the offense occurred, unless venue is changed in accordance with law. No person shall be compelled to give evidence against himself. An accused is entitled to confront and cross-examine the witnesses against him, to compel the attendance of witnesses, to present a defense, and to testify in his own behalf. However, nothing in this Section or any other section of this constitution shall prohibit the legislature from enacting a law to require a trial court to instruct a jury in a criminal trial that the governor is empowered to grant a reprieve, pardon, or commutation of sentence following conviction of a crime, that the governor in exercising such authority may commute or modify a sentence of life imprisonment without benefit of parole to a lesser sentence which includes the possibility of parole, may commute a sentence of death to a lesser sentence of life imprisonment without benefit of parole, or may allow the release of an offender either by reducing a life imprisonment or death sentence to the time already served by the offender or by granting the offender a pardon.

Section 17. Jury Trial in Criminal Cases; Joinder of Felonies; Mode of Trial

(A) Jury Trial in Criminal Cases

A criminal case in which the punishment may be capital shall be tried before a jury of twelve persons, all of whom must concur to render a verdict. A case in which the punishment is necessarily confinement at hard labor shall be tried before a jury of twelve persons, ten of whom must concur to render a verdict. A case in which the punishment may be confinement at hard labor or confinement without hard labor for more than six months shall be tried before a jury of six persons, all of whom must concur to render a verdict. The accused shall have a right to full voir dire examination of prospective jurors and to challenge jurors peremptorily. The number of challenges shall be fixed by law. Except in capital cases, a defendant may knowingly and intelligently waive his right to a trial by jury but no later than forty-five days prior to the trail date and the waiver shall be irrevocable.

(B) Joinder of Felonies; Mode of Trial

Notwithstanding any provision of law to the contrary, offenses in which punishment is necessarily confinement at hard labor may be charged in the same indictment or information with offenses in which the punishment may be confinement at hard labor; provided, however, that the joined offenses are of the same or similar character or are based on the same act or transaction or on two or more acts or transactions connected together or constituting parts of a common scheme or plan; and provided further, that cases so joined shall be tried by a jury composed of twelve jurors, ten of whom must concur to render a verdict.

Section 18. Right to Bail

(A) Excessive bail shall not be required. Before and during a trial, a person shall be bailable by sufficient surety, except when he is charged with a capital offense and the proof is evident and the presumption of guilt is great. After conviction and before sentencing, a person shall be bailable if the maximum sentence which may be imposed is imprisonment for five years or less; and the judge may grant bail if the maximum sentence which may be imposed is imprisonment exceeding five years. After sentencing and until final judgment, a person shall be bailable if the sentence actually imposed is five years or less; and the judge may grant bail if the sentence actually imposed exceeds imprisonment for five years.

(B) However, a person charged with a crime of violence as defined by law or with production, manufacture, distribution, or dispensing or possession with intent to produce, manufacture, distribute, or dispense a controlled dangerous substance as defined by the Louisiana Controlled Dangerous Substances Law, and the proof is evident and the presumption of guilt is great, shall not be bailable if, after a contradictory hearing, the judge or magistrate finds by clear and convincing evidence that there is a substantial risk that the person may flee or poses an imminent danger to any other person or the community.

Section 19. Right to Judicial Review

No person shall be subjected to imprisonment or forfeiture of rights or property without the right of judicial review based upon a complete record of all evidence upon which the judgment is based. This right may be intelligently waived. The cost of transcribing the record shall be paid as provided by law.
Section 20. Right to Humane Treatment Section 20. No law shall subject any person to euthanasia, to torture, or to cruel, excessive, or unusual punishment. Full rights of citizenship shall be restored upon termination of state and federal supervision following conviction for any offense.

Section 21. Writ of Habeas Corpus

The writ of habeas corpus shall not be suspended.

Section 22. Access to Courts

All courts shall be open, and every person shall have an adequate remedy by due process of law and justice, administered without denial, partiality, or unreasonable delay, for injury to him in his person, property, reputation, or other rights. Section 23. Prohibited Laws Section 23. No bill of attainder, ex post facto law, or law impairing the obligation of contracts shall be enacted.

Section 24. Unenumerated Rights

The enumeration in this constitution of certain rights shall not deny or disparage other rights retained by the individual citizens of the state.

Section 25. Rights of a Victim

Any person who is a victim of crime shall be treated with fairness, dignity, and respect, and shall be informed of the rights accorded under this Section. As defined by law, a victim of crime shall have the right to reasonable notice and to be present and heard during all critical stages of preconviction and postconviction proceedings; the right to be informed upon the release from custody or the escape of the accused or the offender; the right to confer with the prosecution prior to final disposition of the case; the right to refuse to be interviewed by the accused or a representative of the accused; the right to review and comment upon the presentence report prior to imposition of sentence; the right to seek restitution; and the right to a reasonably prompt conclusion of the case. The legislature shall enact laws to implement this Section. The evidentiary and procedural laws of this state shall be interpreted in a manner consistent with this Section. Nothing in this Section shall be construed to inure to the benefit of an accused or to confer upon any person the right to appeal or seek supervisory review of any judicial decision made in a criminal proceeding. Nothing in this Section shall be the basis for an award of costs or attorney fees, for the appointment of counsel for a victim, or for any cause of action for compensation or damages against the state of Louisiana, a political subdivision, a public agency, or a court, or any officer, employee, or agent thereof. Remedies to enforce the rights enumerated in this Section shall be provided by law.

Section 26. State Sovereignty

The people of this state have the sole and exclusive right of governing themselves as a free and sovereign state; and do, and forever hereafter shall, exercise and enjoy every power, jurisdiction, and right, pertaining thereto, which is not, or may not hereafter be, by them expressly delegated to the United States of America in congress assembled.

Section 27. Freedom to Hunt, Fish and Trap

The freedom to hunt, fish, and trap wildlife, including all aquatic life, traditionally taken by hunters, trappers and anglers, is a valued natural heritage that shall be forever preserved for the people. Hunting, fishing and trapping shall be managed by law and regulation consistent with Article IX, Section I of the Constitution of Louisiana to protect, conserve and replenish the natural resources of the state. The provisions of this Section shall not alter the burden of proof requirements otherwise established by law for any challenge to a law or regulation pertaining to hunting, fishing or trapping the wildlife of the state, including all aquatic life. Nothing contained herein shall be construed to authorize the use of private property to hunt, fish, or trap without the consent of the owner of the property.

ARTICLE II: DISTRIBUTION OF POWERS

Section 1. Three Branches

The powers of government of the state are divided into three separate branches: legislative, executive, and judicial.

Section 2. Limitations on Each Branch

Except as otherwise provided by this constitution, no one of these branches, nor any person holding office in one of them, shall exercise power belonging to either of the others.

ARTICLE III: LEGISLATIVE BRANCH

Section 1. Legislative Power; Composition; Continuous Body

(A) Legislative Power of State

The legislative power of the state is vested in a legislature, consisting of a Senate and a House of Representatives. The Senate shall be composed of one senator elected from each senatorial district. The House of Representatives shall be composed of one representative elected from each representative district.

(B) Continuous Body

The legislature is a continuous body during the term for which its members are elected; however, a bill or resolution not finally passed in any session shall be withdrawn from the files of the legislature.

Section 2. Sessions

(A) Annual Session

(1) The legislature shall meet annually in regular session for a limited number of legislative days in the state capital. A legislative day is a calendar day on which either house is in session.

(2)(a) No member of the legislature may introduce more than five bills that were not prefiled, except as provided in the joint rules of the legislature.

(2)(b) Except as provided in Sub-subparagraph

(2)(c) of this Subparagraph, any bill that is to be prefiled for introduction in either house shall be prefiled no later than five o'clock in the evening of the tenth calendar day prior to the first day of a regular session. (c) Any bill to effect any change in laws relating to any retirement system for public employees that is to be prefiled for introduction in either house shall be prefiled no later than five o'clock in the evening of the forty-fifth calendar day prior to the first day of a regular session.

(2)(d) The legislature is authorized to provide by joint rule for the procedures for passage of duplicate or companion instruments.

(3)(a) All regular sessions convening in even numbered years shall be general in nature and shall convene at noon on the second Monday in March. The legislature shall meet in such a session for not more than sixty legislative days during a period of eighty-five calendar days. No such session shall continue beyond six o'clock in the evening of the eighty-fifth calendar day after convening. No new matter intended to have the effect of law shall be introduced or received by either house after six o'clock in the evening of the twenty-third calendar day. No matter intended to have the effect of law, except a measure proposing a suspension of law, shall be considered on third reading and final passage in either house after six o'clock in the evening of the fifty-seventh legislative day or the eighty-second calendar day, whichever occurs first, except by a favorable record vote of two-thirds of the elected members of each house.

(3)(b) No measure levying or authorizing a new tax by the state or by any statewide political subdivision whose boundaries are coterminous with the state; increasing an existing tax by the state or by any statewide political subdivision whose boundaries are coterminous with the state; or legislating with regard to tax exemptions, exclusions, deductions or credits shall be introduced or enacted during a regular session held in an even-numbered year.

(4)(a) All regular sessions convening in odd numbered years shall convene at noon on the second Monday in April. The legislature shall meet in such a session for not more than forty-five legislative days in a period of sixty calendar days. No such session shall continue beyond six o'clock in the evening of the sixtieth calendar day after convening. No new matter intended to have the effect of law shall be introduced or received by either house after six o'clock in the evening of the tenth calendar day. No matter intended to have the effect of law, except a measure proposing a suspension of law, shall be considered on third reading and final passage in either house after six o'clock in the evening of the forty-second legislative day or fifty-seventh calendar day, whichever occurs first, except by a favorable record vote of two-thirds of the elected members of each house.

(4)(b) During any session convening in an odd numbered year, no matter intended to have the effect of law, including any suspension of law, shall be introduced or considered unless its object is to enact the General Appropriation Bill; enact the comprehensive capital budget; make an appropriation; levy or authorize a new tax; increase an existing tax; levy, authorize, increase, decrease, or repeal a fee; dedicate revenue; legislate with regard to tax exemptions, exclusions, deductions, reductions, repeals, or credits; or legislate with regard to the issuance of bonds. In addition, a matter intended to have the effect of law, including a measure proposing a suspension of law, which is not within the subject matter restrictions provided in this Subparagraph may be considered at any such session if:

(i) It is prefiled no later than the deadline provided in Subparagraph (2) of this Paragraph, provided that the member shall not prefile more than five such matters pursuant to this Sub-sub-paragraph; or

(ii) Its object is to enact a local or special law which is required to be and has been advertised in accordance with Section 13 of this Article and which is not prohibited by the provisions of Section 12 of this Article. (B) Extraordinary Session. The legislature may be convened at other times by the governor and shall be convened by the presiding officers of both houses upon written petition of a majority of the elected members of each house. The form of the petition shall be provided by law. At least seven calendar days prior to convening the legislature in extraordinary session, the governor or the presiding officers, as the case may be, shall issue a proclamation stating the objects of the extraordinary session, the date on which it shall convene, and the number of days for which it is convened. The power to legislate shall be limited, under penalty of nullity, to the objects specifically enumerated in the proclamation. The session shall be limited to the number of days stated therein, which shall not exceed thirty calendar days.

(4)(C) Emergency Session. The governor may convene the legislature in extraordinary session without prior notice or proclamation in the event of public emergency caused by epidemic, enemy attack, or public catastrophe.

(4)(D) Organizational Session. The legislature shall meet in an organizational session in the state capitol to be convened at ten o'clock in the morning on the day the members are required to take office. No such session shall exceed three legislative days. The session shall be for the primary purpose of judging the qualifications and elections of the members, taking the oath of office, organizing the two houses, and selecting officers. No matter intended to have the effect of law shall be introduced at an organizational session.

Section 3. Size

The number of members of the legislature shall be provided by law, but the number of senators shall not exceed thirty-nine and the number of representatives, one hundred five.

Section 4. Qualifications; Residence and Domicile Requirements; Term; Election Limitations; Vacancies; Temporary Successors; Salary.

(A) Age; Residence; Domicile

An elector who at the time of qualification as a candidate has attained the age of eighteen years, resided in the state for the preceding two years, and been actually domiciled for the preceding year in the legislative district from which he seeks election is eligible for membership in the legislature.

(B) Domicile; Special Provisions

However, at the next regular election for members of the legislature following legislative reapportionment, an elector may qualify as a candidate from any district created in whole or in part from a district existing prior to reapportionment if he was domiciled in that prior district for at least one year immediately preceding his qualification and was a resident of the state for the two years preceding his qualification. The seat of any member who changes his domicile from the district he represents or, if elected after reapportionment, whose domicile is not within the district he represents at the time he is sworn into office, shall be vacated thereby, any declaration of retention of domicile to the contrary notwithstanding.

(C) Term

A member of the legislature shall be elected for a four-year term.

(D) Vacancy

A vacancy in the legislature shall be filled for the remainder of the term only by election by the electors of the respective district as provided by law.

(E) Election Limitation

No person who has been elected to serve as a member of the Senate for more than two and one-half terms in three consecutive terms, that service being during a term of office that began on or after January 8, 1996, shall be elected to the Senate for the succeeding term. No person who has been elected to serve as a member of the House of Representatives for more than two and one-half terms in three consecutive terms, that service being during a term of office that began on or after January 8, 1996, shall be elected to the House of Representatives for the succeeding term.

(F) Temporary Successors

The legislature shall provide by law for the prompt and temporary succession to the powers and duties of a member of the legislature if the incumbent member is unavailable to perform his functions or duties due to being ordered to active duty in the armed services of the United States.

(G) Salary limitation

Any increase in salary of any member of the legislature shall not become effective until the commencement of the subsequent term for that office following the adoption or enactment of the increase.

Section 5. Taking Office

A) Full Term

Members of the legislature shall take office on the same day as the governor and other officials elected statewide.

(B) Filling Vacancy

A person elected to fill the remainder of an unexpired legislative term shall take office within thirty days after the secretary of state promulgates the election returns.

Section 6. Legislative Reapportionment; Reapportionment by Supreme Court; Procedure

(A) Reapportionment by Legislature

By the end of the year following the year in which the population of this state is reported to the president of the United States for each decennial federal census, the legislature shall reapportion the representation in each house as equally as practicable on the basis of population shown by the census.

(B) Reapportionment by Supreme Court

If the legislature fails to reapportion as required in Paragraph (A), the supreme court, upon petition of any elector, shall reapportion the representation in each house as provided in Paragraph (A).

(C) Procedure

The procedure for review and for petition shall be provided by law.

Section 7. Judging Qualifications and Elections; Procedural Rules; Discipline; Expulsion; Subpoenas; Contempt; Officers

(A) Judging Qualifications and Elections; Procedural Rules; Discipline; Expulsion

Each house shall be the judge of the qualifications and elections of its members; shall determine its rules of procedure, not inconsistent with the provisions of this constitution; may punish its members for disorderly conduct or contempt; and may expel a member with concurrence of two-thirds of its elected members. Expulsion creates a vacancy in the office.

(B) Subpoena Power; Contempt

Each house may compel the attendance and testimony of witnesses and the production of books and papers before it, before any committee thereof, or before joint committees of the houses and may punish those in willful disobedience of its orders for contempt.

(C) Officers

Each house shall choose its officers, including a permanent presiding officer selected from its membership. The presiding officers shall be the president of the Senate and the speaker of the House of Representatives. The clerical officers shall be the clerk of the House of Representatives and the secretary of the Senate, each of whom may administer oaths.

Section 8. Privileges and Immunities

A member of the legislature shall be privileged from arrest, except for felony, during his attendance at sessions and committee meetings of his house and while going to and from them. No member shall be questioned elsewhere for any speech in either house.

Section 9. Conflict of Interest

Legislative office is a public trust, and every effort to realize personal gain through official conduct is a violation of that trust. The legislature shall enact a code of ethics prohibiting conflict between public duty and private interests of members of the legislature.

Section 10. Quorum; Compulsory Attendance; Journal; Adjournment With Consent of Other House

(A) Quorum

Not less than a majority of the elected members of each house shall form a quorum to transact business, but a smaller number may adjourn from day-to-day and may compel the attendance of absent members.

(B) Journal

Each house shall keep a journal of its proceedings and have it published immediately after the close of each session. The journal shall accurately reflect the proceedings of that house, including all record votes. A record vote is a vote by yeas and nays, with each member's vote published in the journal.

(C) Adjournment

When the legislature is in session, neither house shall adjourn for more than three days or to another place without consent of the other house.

Section 11. Legislative Auditor

There shall be a legislative auditor responsible solely to the legislature. He shall serve as a fiscal advisor to it and shall perform the duties and functions provided by law related to auditing fiscal records of the state, its agencies, and political subdivisions. He shall be elected by the concurrence of a majority of the elected members of each house and may be removed by the concurrence of two-thirds of the elected members of each house.

Section 12. Prohibited Local and Special Laws

(A) Prohibitions

Except as otherwise provided in this constitution, the legislature shall not pass a local or special law:

(1) For the holding and conducting of elections, or fixing or changing the place of voting.

(2) Changing the names of persons; authorizing the adoption or legitimation of children or the emancipation of minors; affecting the estates of minors or persons under disabilities; granting divorces; changing the law of descent or succession; giving effect to informal or invalid wills or deeds or to any illegal disposition of property.

(3) Concerning any civil or criminal actions, including changing the venue in civil or criminal cases, or regulating the practice or jurisdiction of any court, or changing the rules of evidence in any judicial proceeding or inquiry before courts, or providing or changing methods for the collection of debts or the enforcement of judgments, or prescribing the effects of judicial sales.

(4) Authorizing the laying out, opening, closing, altering, or maintaining of roads, highways, streets, or alleys; relating to ferries and bridges, or incorporating bridge or ferry companies, except for the erection of bridges crossing streams which form boundaries between this and any other state; authorizing the constructing of street passenger railroads in any incorporated town or city.

(5) Exempting property from taxation; extending the time for the assessment or collection of taxes; relieving an assessor or collector of taxes from the performance of his official duties or of his sureties from liability; remitting fines, penalties, and forfeitures; refunding moneys legally paid into the treasury.

(6) Regulating labor, trade, manufacturing, or agriculture; fixing the rate of interest.

(7) Creating private corporations, or amending, renewing, extending, or explaining the charters thereof; granting to any private corporation, association, or individual any special or exclusive right, privilege, or immunity.

(8) Regulating the management of parish or city public schools, the building or repairing of parish or city schoolhouses, and the raising of money for such purposes.

(9) Legalizing the unauthorized or invalid acts of any officer, employee, or agent of the state, its agencies, or political subdivisions.

(10) Defining any crime.

(B) Additional Prohibition

The legislature shall not indirectly enact special or local laws by the partial repeal or suspension of a general law.

Section 13. Local or Special Laws; Notice of Intent; Publication

(A) Except as otherwise provided in this Section, no local or special law shall be enacted unless notice of the intent to introduce a bill to enact such a law has been published on two separate days, without cost to the state, in the official journal of the locality where the matter to be affected is situated. The last day of publication shall be at least thirty days prior to introduction of the bill. The notice shall state the substance of the contemplated law, and every such bill shall recite that notice has been given.

(B) No local or special law relative to the creation of a special district, the primary purpose of which includes aiding in crime prevention and adding to the security of district residents by providing for an increased presence of law enforcement personnel in the district or otherwise promoting and encouraging security in the district, shall be enacted unless notice of the intent to introduce such bill has been published on three separate days, without cost to the state, in the official journal of the locality where the special district is to be situated. The last day of publication shall be at least thirty days prior to introduction of the bill. The notice shall state the substance of the contemplated law, and shall specifically disclose whether the governing authority of the special district would be authorized by the contemplated law to impose and collect a parcel fee within the district, whether the parcel fee will be imposed or may be increased without an election, and the maximum amount of the parcel fee if a maximum amount is set forth in the contemplated law. Every such bill shall recite that the required notice has been given.

Section 14. Style of Laws; Enacting Clause

The style of a law enacted by the legislature shall be, "Be it enacted by the Legislature of Louisiana." It shall be unnecessary to repeat the enacting clause after the first section of an act.

Section 15. Passage of Bills

(A) Introduction; Title; Single Object; Public Meetings

The legislature shall enact no law except by a bill introduced during that session, and propose no constitutional amendment except by a joint resolution introduced during that session, which shall be processed as a bill. Every bill, except the general appropriation bill and bills for the enactment, rearrangement, codification, or revision of a system of laws, shall be confined to one object. Every bill shall contain a brief title indicative of its object. Action on any matter intended to have the effect of law shall be taken only in open, public meeting.

(B) No General Reference

A bill enacting, amending, or reviving a law shall set forth completely the provisions of the law enacted, amended, or revived. No system or code of laws shall be adopted by general reference to it.

(C) Germane Amendments

No bill shall be amended in either house to make a change not germane to the bill as introduced.

(D) Three Readings

Each bill shall be read at least by title on three separate days in each house. No bill shall be considered for final passage unless a committee has held a public hearing and reported on the bill.

(E) Rejected bills; Reconsideration

No bill rejected by either house may again be introduced or considered during the same session by the house which rejected it without the consent of a majority of the members elected to that house.

(F) Concurrence in Amendments

No amendment to a bill by one house shall be concurred in by the other, and no conference committee report shall be concurred in by either house except by the same vote required for final passage of the bill. The vote thereon shall be by record vote.

(G) Majority Vote; Record Vote

No bill shall become law without the favorable vote of at least a majority of the members elected to each house. Final passage of a bill shall be by record vote. In either house, a record vote shall be taken on any matter upon the request of one-fifth of the elected members.

Section 16. Appropriations

(A) Specific Appropriation for One Year

Except as otherwise provided by this constitution, no money shall be withdrawn from the state treasury except through specific appropriation, and no appropriation shall be made under the heading of contingencies or for longer than one year.

(B) Origin in House of Representatives

All bills for raising revenue or appropriating money shall originate in the House of Representatives, but the Senate may propose or concur in amendments, as in other bills.

(C) General Appropriation Bill; Limitations

The general appropriation bill shall be itemized and shall contain only appropriations for the ordinary operating expenses of government, public charities, pensions, and the public debt or interest thereon.

(D) Specific Purpose and Amount

All other bills for appropriating money shall be for a specific purpose and amount.

(E) Extraordinary Session

Except for expenses of the legislature, a bill appropriating money in an extraordinary session convened after final adjournment of the regular session in the last year of the term of office of a governor shall require the favorable vote of three-fourths of the elected members of each house.

Section 17. Signing of Bills; Delivery to Governor

(A) Signing; Delivery.

A bill passed by both houses shall be signed by the presiding officers and delivered to the governor within three days after passage.

(B) Resolutions

No joint, concurrent, or other resolution shall require the signature or other action of the governor to become effective.

Section 18. Gubernatorial Action on Bills; Sign, Failure to Sign, Veto; Veto Session

(A) Gubernatorial Action

If the governor does not approve a bill, he may veto it. A bill, except a joint resolution, shall become law if the governor signs it or if he fails to sign or veto it within ten days after delivery to him if the legislature is in session on the tenth day after such delivery, or within twenty days after delivery if the tenth day after delivery occurs after the legislature is adjourned.

(B) Veto Message

If the governor vetoes a bill, he shall return it to the legislature, with his veto message within twelve days after delivery to him if the legislature is in session. If the governor returns a vetoed bill after the legislature adjourns, he shall return it, with his veto message, as provided by law.

(C) Veto Session

(1) A bill vetoed and returned and subsequently approved by two-thirds of the elected members of each house shall become law. The legislature shall meet in veto session in the state capital at noon on the fortieth day following final adjournment of the most recent session, to consider all bills vetoed by the governor. If the fortieth day falls on Sunday, the session shall convene at noon on the succeeding Monday. No veto session shall exceed five calendar days, and any veto session may be finally adjourned prior to the end of the fifth day upon a vote of two-thirds of the elected members of each house.

(2) No veto session shall be held if a majority of the elected members of either house declare in writing that a veto session is unnecessary. The declaration must be received by the presiding officer of the respective houses at least five days prior to the day on which the veto session is to convene.

Section 19. Effective Date of Laws

All laws enacted during a regular session of the legislature shall take effect on August first of the calendar year in which the regular session is held and all laws enacted during an extraordinary session of the legislature shall take effect on the sixtieth day after final adjournment of the extraordinary session in which they were enacted. All laws shall be published prior thereto in the official journal of the state as provided by law. However, any bill may specify an earlier or later effective date.

Section 20. Suspension of Laws

Only the legislature may suspend a law, and then only by the same vote and, except for gubernatorial veto and time limitations for introduction, according to the same procedures and formalities required for enactment of that law. After the effective date of this constitution, every resolution suspending a law shall fix the period of suspension, which shall not extend beyond the sixtieth day after final adjournment of the next regular session.

ARTICLE IV: EXECUTIVE BRANCH

Section 1. Composition; Number of Departments; Reorganization

(A) Composition

The executive branch shall consist of the governor, lieutenant governor, secretary of state, attorney general, treasurer, commissioner of agriculture, commissioner of insurance, superintendent of education, commissioner of elections, and all other executive offices, agencies, and instrumentalities of the state.

(B) Number of Departments

Except for the offices of governor and lieutenant governor, all offices, agencies, and other instrumentalities of the executive branch and their functions, powers, duties, and responsibilities shall be allocated according to function within not more than twenty departments. The powers, functions, and duties allocated by this constitution to any executive office or commission shall not be affected or diminished by the allocation provided herein except as authorized by Section 20 of this Article.

(C) Reorganization

Reallocation of the functions, powers, and duties of all departments, offices, agencies, and other instrumentalities of the executive branch, except those functions, powers, duties, and responsibilities allocated by this constitution, shall be as provided by law.

Section 2. Qualifications

To be eligible for any statewide elective office, a person, by the date of his qualification as a candidate, shall have attained the age of twenty-five years, be an elector, and have been a citizen of the United States and of this state for at least the preceding five years. In addition, the attorney general shall have been admitted to the practice of law in the state for at least the five years preceding his election. During his tenure in office, a statewide elected official shall hold no other public office except by virtue of his elected office.

Section 3. Election; Term

(A) Election

Except as provided in Section 20 of this Article, the governor, lieutenant governor, secretary of state, attorney general, treasurer, commissioner of agriculture, commissioner of insurance, superintendent of education, and commissioner of elections each shall be elected for a term of four years by the electors of the state at the time and place of voting for members of the legislature. The term of each such official shall begin at noon on the second Monday in January next following the election.

(B) Limitation on Governor

A person who has served as governor for more than one and one-half terms in two consecutive terms shall not be elected governor for the succeeding term.

(C) Additional Limitation

Except as provided by this constitution, no official shall be elected statewide.

(D) Notwithstanding any other provision of this constitution or of law to the contrary, statewide elected officials and members of the legislature elected in 1987 shall hold office from and after the second Monday in March, 1988. These statewide elected officials and any successor elected to the unexpired term of any of them shall serve for terms which shall expire at noon on January 13, 1992. These members of the legislature and any successor elected to the unexpired term of any of them shall serve for terms which shall expire at ten o'clock a.m. on January 13, 1992. Thereafter, statewide elected officials and members of the legislature shall be elected for terms of four years. For purposes of retirement, the statewide elected officials and members of the legislature elected in 1987 shall be deemed to be elected for a four-year term.

Section 4. Compensation

Except as otherwise provided by this constitution, the compensation of each statewide elected official shall be provided by law. An increase in the salary of a statewide elected official shall not become effective until the commencement of the subsequent term for that office following the adoption or enactment of the increase.

Section 5. Governor; Powers and Duties

(A) Executive Authority

The governor shall be the chief executive officer of the state. He shall faithfully support the constitution and laws of the state and of the United States and shall see that the laws are faithfully executed.

(B) Legislative Reports and Recommendations

The governor shall, at the beginning of each regular session, and may, at other times, make reports and recommendations and give information to the legislature concerning the affairs of state, including its complete financial condition.

(C) Departmental Reports and Information

When requested by the governor, a department head shall provide him with reports and information, in writing or otherwise, on any subject relating to the department, except matters concerning investigations of the governor's office.

(D) Operating and Capital Budget

The governor shall submit to the legislature an operating budget and a capital budget, as provided by Article VII, Section 11 of this constitution.

(E) Pardon, Commutation, Reprieve, and Remission; Board of Pardons

(1) The governor may grant reprieves to persons convicted of offenses against the state and, upon favorable recommendation of the Board of Pardons, may commute sentences, pardon those convicted of offenses against the state, and remit fines and forfeitures imposed for such offenses. However, a first offender convicted of a non-violent crime, or convicted of aggravated battery, second degree battery, aggravated assault, mingling harmful substances, aggravated criminal damage to property, purse snatching, extortion, or illegal use of weapons or dangerous instrumentalities never previously convicted of a felony shall be pardoned automatically upon completion of his sentence, without a recommendation of the Board of Pardons and without action by the governor.

(2) The Board of Pardons shall consist of five electors appointed by the governor, subject to confirmation by the Senate. Each member of the board shall serve a term concurrent with that of the governor appointing him.

(F) Receipt of Bills from the Legislature

The date and hour when a bill finally passed by the legislature is delivered to the governor shall be endorsed thereon.

(G) Item Veto

(1) Except as otherwise provided by this constitution, the governor may veto any line item in an appropriation bill. Any item vetoed shall be void unless the veto is overridden as prescribed for the passage of a bill over a veto.

(2) The governor shall veto line items or use means provided in the bill so that total appropriations for the year shall not exceed anticipated revenues for that year.

(H) Appointments

(1) The governor shall appoint, subject to confirmation by the Senate, the head of each department in the executive branch whose election or appointment is not provided by this constitution and the members of each board and commission in the executive branch whose election or appointment is not provided by this constitution or by law.

(2) Should the legislature be in regular session, the governor shall submit for confirmation by the Senate the name of an appointee within forty-eight hours after the appointment is made. Failure of the Senate to confirm the appointment, prior to the end of the session, shall constitute rejection.

(3) If the legislature is not in regular session, the governor may make interim appointments, which shall expire at the end of the next regular session, unless submitted to and confirmed by the Senate during that session.

(4) A person not confirmed by the Senate shall not be appointed to the same office during any recess of the legislature.

(I) Removal Power

The governor may remove from office a person he appoints, except a person appointed for a term fixed by this constitution or by law.

(J) Commander-in-Chief

The governor shall be commander-in-chief of the armed forces of the state, except when they are called into service of the federal government. He may call out these forces to preserve law and order, to suppress insurrection, to repel invasion, or in other times of emergency.

(K) Other Powers and Duties

The governor shall have other powers and perform other duties authorized by this constitution or provided by law.

Section 6. Lieutenant Governor; Powers and Duties

The lieutenant governor shall serve ex officio as a member of each committee, board, and commission on which the governor serves. He shall exercise the powers delegated to him by the governor and shall have other powers and perform other duties in the executive branch authorized by this constitution or provided by law.

Section 7. Secretary of State; Powers and Duties

There shall be a Department of State. The secretary of state shall head the department and shall be the chief election officer of the state. He shall prepare and certify the ballots for all elections, promulgate all election returns, and administer the election laws, except those relating to voter registration and custody of voting machines. He shall administer the state corporation and trademark laws; serve as keeper of the Great Seal of the State of Louisiana and attest therewith all official laws, documents, proclamations, and commissions; administer and preserve the official archives of the state; promulgate and publish all laws enacted by the legislature and retain the originals thereof; and countersign and keep an official registry of all commissions. He may administer oaths, and shall have other powers and perform other duties authorized by this constitution or provided by law.

Section 8. Attorney General; Powers and Duties

There shall be a Department of Justice, headed by the attorney general, who shall be the chief legal officer of the state. The attorney general shall be elected for a term of four years at the state general election. The assistant attorneys general shall be appointed by the attorney general to serve at his pleasure. As necessary for the assertion or protection of any right or interest of the state, the attorney general shall have authority

(1) to institute, prosecute, or intervene in any civil action or proceeding;

(2) upon the written request of a district attorney, to advise and assist in the prosecution of any criminal case; and

(3) for cause, when authorized by the court which would have original jurisdiction and subject to judicial review,

(a) to institute, prosecute, or intervene in any criminal action or proceeding, or

(b) to supersede any attorney representing the state in any civil or criminal action. The attorney general shall exercise other powers and perform other duties authorized by this constitution or by law.

Section 9. Treasurer; Powers and Duties

There shall be a Department of the Treasury. The treasurer shall head the department and shall be responsible for the custody, investment, and disbursement of the public funds of the state, except as otherwise provided by this constitution. He shall report annually to the governor and to the legislature at least one month before each regular session on the financial condition of the state, and shall have other powers and perform other duties authorized by this constitution or provided by law.

Section 10. Commissioner of Agriculture; Powers and Duties

There shall be a Department of Agriculture. The commissioner of agriculture shall head the department and shall exercise all functions of the state relating to the promotion, protection, and advancement of agriculture, except research and educational functions expressly allocated by this constitution or by law to other state agencies. The department shall exercise such functions and the commissioner shall have other powers and perform other duties authorized by this constitution or provided by law.

Section 11. Commissioner of Insurance; Powers and Duties

There shall be a Department of Insurance, headed by the commissioner of insurance. The department shall exercise such functions and the commissioner shall have powers and perform duties authorized by this constitution or provided by law.

Section 12. Commissioner of Elections; Powers and Duties

There shall be a Department of Elections and Registration. The commissioner of elections shall head the department and shall administer the laws relating to custody of voting machines and voter registration. He shall have other powers and perform other duties authorized by this constitution or provided by law.

Section 13. First Assistants; Appointment

Each statewide elected official except the governor and lieutenant governor shall appoint a first assistant, subject to public confirmation by the Senate, and may remove him at his pleasure. The official shall submit the appointment to the Senate in the manner and subject to the procedures and limitations applicable to appointments submitted by the governor. The first assistant shall possess the qualifications required for election to the office.

Section 14. Vacancy in Office of Governor

When a vacancy occurs in the office of governor, the order of succession shall be

(1) the elected lieutenant governor,

(2) the elected secretary of state,

(3) the elected attorney general,

(4) the elected treasurer,

(5) the presiding officer of the Senate,

(6) the presiding officer of the House of Representatives, and then

(7) as provided by law. The successor shall serve the remainder of the term for which the governor was elected.

Section 15. Vacancy in Office of Lieutenant Governor

Should a vacancy occur in the office of lieutenant governor, the governor shall nominate a lieutenant governor, who shall take office upon confirmation by a majority vote of the elected members of each house of the legislature. If the unexpired term exceeds one year, such person shall serve as lieutenant governor only until the office is filled as provided in Section 16(B) of this Article.

Section 16. Vacancies in Other Statewide Elective Offices

(A) A vacancy in a statewide elective office other than that of governor or lieutenant governor shall be filled by the first assistant. If the unexpired term exceeds one year, the first assistant shall serve only until the person elected as provided in Paragraph (B) of this Section takes office.

(B) If the unexpired term exceeds one year, the office shall be filled by election at the next regularly scheduled congressional or statewide election; however, if no such election date is available within one year of the vacancy, the office shall be filled by election at a special election called by the governor for such purpose.

Section 17. Declaration of Inability by Statewide Elected Officials

When a statewide elected official transmits to the presiding officers of the Senate and House of Representatives a written declaration of his inability to discharge the powers and duties of his office, and until he transmits to them a written declaration to the contrary, the person who would succeed to the office when a vacancy occurs shall assume the powers and duties of the office as acting official.

Section 18. Determination of Inability of Statewide Elected Official

(A) Declaration and Counter-Declaration

When a majority of the statewide elected officials determine that any other such official is unable to discharge the powers and duties of his office, they shall transmit a written declaration to this effect to the presiding officer of each house and to the official, and shall file a copy of the declaration in the office of the secretary of state. Thereafter, the constitutional successor shall assume the office as acting official unless, within forty-eight hours after the declaration is filed in the office of the secretary of state, the elected official files in that office and transmits to the presiding officer of each house his written counter-declaration of his ability to exercise the powers and perform the duties of his office.

(B) Determination by the Legislature

The legislature shall convene at noon on the third calendar day after the filing of any counter-declaration, which may be filed by the official at any time. Should two-thirds of the elected members of each house fail to adopt a resolution within seventy-two hours declaring probable justification for the determination that inability exists, the official shall continue in or resume office.

(C) Assumption of Office by Constitutional Successor

If two-thirds of the elected members of each house adopt a resolution declaring that probable justification exists for the declaration of inability, the constitutional successor shall assume the powers and duties of the office and a copy of the resolution shall be transmitted forthwith to the supreme court.

(D) Determination by Supreme Court

By preference and with priority over all other matters, the supreme court shall determine the issue of inability after due notice and hearing, by a majority vote of members elected to the court, under such rules as it may adopt.

(E) Reconsideration by Supreme Court

A judgment of the supreme court affirming inability may be reconsidered by the court, after due notice and hearing, either upon its own motion or upon the application of the official. Upon proper showing and by majority vote of its elected members, the court may determine that no inability then exists, whereupon the official shall immediately resume the powers and duties of his office.

Section 19. Temporary Absences

When the governor is temporarily absent from the state, the lieutenant governor shall act as governor. When any other statewide elected official is temporarily absent from the state, the appointed first assistant shall act in his absence.

Section 20. Appointment of Officials; Merger, Consolidation of Offices and Departments

After the first election of state officials following the effective date of this constitution, the legislature may provide, by law enacted by two-thirds of the elected members of each house, for appointment, in lieu of election, of the commissioner of agriculture, the commissioner of insurance, the superintendent of education, the commissioner of elections, or any of them. In that event, the legislature shall prescribe qualifications and method of appointment and by similar vote, may provide by law for the merger or consolidation of any such office, its department, and functions with any other office or department in the executive branch. No action of the legislature pursuant hereto shall reduce the term or compensation of any incumbent elected official. By law enacted by two-thirds of the elected members of each house, the legislature may reestablish any such office as elective and, in that event, shall prescribe qualifications.

Section 21. Public Service Commission

(A) Composition; Term; Domicile

(1) There shall be a Public Service Commission in the executive branch. It shall consist of five members, who shall be elected for overlapping terms of six years at the time fixed for congressional elections from single member districts established by law. The commission annually shall elect one member as chairman. It shall be domiciled at the state capital, but may meet, conduct investigations, and render orders elsewhere in this state.

(2) No person who has served as a member of the commission for more than two and one-half terms in three consecutive terms shall be elected to the commission for the succeeding term. This Subparagraph shall not apply to any person elected to the commission prior to the effective date of this Subparagraph, except that it shall apply to any term of service of any such person that begins after such date.

(B) Powers and Duties

The commission shall regulate all common carriers and public utilities and have such other regulatory authority as provided by law. It shall adopt and enforce reasonable rules, regulations, and procedures necessary for the discharge of its duties, and shall have other powers and perform other duties as provided by law.

(C) Limitation

The commission shall have no power to regulate any common carrier or public utility owned, operated, or regulated on the effective date of this constitution by the governing authority of one or more political subdivisions, except by the approval of a majority of the electors voting in an election held for that purpose; however, a political subdivision may reinvest itself with such regulatory power in the manner in which it was surrendered. This Paragraph shall not apply to safety regulations pertaining to the operation of such utilities.

(D) Applications, Petitions, and Schedules; Protective Bond and Security

(1) Within twenty days after a common carrier or public utility files a proposed rate schedule which would result in a change in rates, it shall give notice thereof by publication in the official state journal and in the official journal of each parish within the geographical area in which the schedule would become applicable.

(2) Within twelve months after the effective filing date, the commission shall render a full decision on each application, petition, and proposed rate schedule.

(3) After the effective filing date of any proposed schedule by a public utility which would result in a rate increase, the commission may permit the proposed schedule to be put into effect, in whole or in part, pending its decision on the application for rate increase and subject to protective bond or security approved by the commission. If no decision is rendered on the application within twelve months after such filing date, the proposed increase may be put into effect, but only if and as provided by law and subject to protective bond or security requirements, until final action by a court of last resort.

(4) If a proposed increase which has been put into effect is finally disallowed, in whole or in part, the utility shall make full refund, with legal interest thereon, within the time and in the manner prescribed by law.

(E) Appeals

Appeal may be taken in the manner provided by law by any aggrieved party or intervenor to the district court of the domicile of the commission. A right of direct appeal from any judgment of the district court shall be allowed to the supreme court. These rights of appeal shall extend to any action by the commission, including but not limited to action taken by the commission or by a public utility under the provisions of Subparagraph (3) of Paragraph (D) of this Section.

(F) Salary limitation

Any increase in salary provided by law for the commission shall not become effective for a member of the commission until the commencement of the term of office for the member of the commission following the enactment of the increase.

Section 22. Term Limits; Certain Boards and Commissions

(A) A person who has served as a member of any one or more of the following boards or commissions for more than two and one-half terms in three consecutive terms combined shall not serve as a member of any of the following boards or commissions for a period of at least two years after the completion of such consecutive terms of service:

(1) The Public Service Commission.

(2) The State Board of Elementary and Secondary Education.

(3) The Board of Regents.

(4) The Board of Supervisors for the University of Louisiana System.

(5) The Board of Supervisors of Louisiana State University and Agricultural and Mechanical College.

(6) The Board of Supervisors of Southern University and Agricultural and Mechanical College.

(7) The Board of Supervisors of Community and Technical Colleges.

(8) The Forestry Commission.

(9) The State Civil Service Commission.

(10) The State Police Commission.

(B) This Section shall not apply to any person who is serving on any such board or commission on the effective date of this Section, except that it shall apply to any term of service of any such person that begins after such date.

ARTICLE V: JUDICIAL BRANCH

Section 1. Judicial Power

The judicial power is vested in a supreme court, courts of appeal, district courts, and other courts authorized by this Article.

Section 2. Habeas Corpus, Needful Writs, Orders and Process; Contempt

A judge may issue writs of habeas corpus and all other needful writs, orders, and process in aid of the jurisdiction of his court. Exercise of this authority by a judge of the supreme court or of a court of appeal is subject to review by the whole court. The power to punish for contempt of court shall be limited by law.

Section 3. Supreme Court; Composition; Judgments; Terms

The supreme court shall be composed of a chief justice and six associate justices, four of whom must concur to render judgment. The term of a supreme court judge shall be ten years.

Section 4. Supreme Court; Districts

The state shall be divided into at least six supreme court districts, and at least one judge shall be elected from each. The districts and the number of judges assigned to each on the effective date of this constitution are retained, subject to change by law enacted by two-thirds of the elected members of each house of the legislature.

Section 5. Supreme Court; Jurisdiction; Rule-Making Power; Assignment of Judges

(A) Supervisory Jurisdiction; Rule-Making Power; Assignment of Judges

The supreme court has general supervisory jurisdiction over all other courts. It may establish procedural and administrative rules not in conflict with law and may assign a sitting or retired judge to any court. The supreme court shall have sole authority to provide by rule for appointments of attorneys as temporary or ad hoc judges of city, municipal, traffic, parish, juvenile, or family courts.

(B) Original Jurisdiction

The supreme court has exclusive original jurisdiction of disciplinary proceedings against a member of the bar.

(C) Scope of Review

Except as otherwise provided by this constitution, the jurisdiction of the supreme court in civil cases extends to both law and facts. In criminal matters, its appellate jurisdiction extends only to questions of law.

(D) Appellate Jurisdiction

In addition to other appeals provided by this constitution, a case shall be appealable to the supreme court if

(1) a law or ordinance has been declared unconstitutional or

(2) the defendant has been convicted of a capital offense and a penalty of death actually has been imposed.

(E) Additional Jurisdiction until July 1, 1982

In addition to the provisions of Section 5(D) and notwithstanding the provisions of Section 5(D), or Sections 10(A)(3) and 10(C), the supreme court shall have exclusive appellate jurisdiction to decide criminal appeals where the defendant has been convicted of a felony or a fine exceeding five hundred dollars or imprisonment exceeding six months actually has been imposed, but only when an order of appeal has been entered prior to July 1, 1982 and shall have exclusive supervisory jurisdiction of all criminal writ applications filed prior to July 1, 1982 and of all criminal writ applications relating to convictions and sentences imposed prior to July 1, 1982.

(F) Appellate Jurisdiction; Civil Cases; Extent

Subject to the provisions in Paragraph (C), the supreme court has appellate jurisdiction over all issues involved in a civil action properly before it.

Section 6. Supreme Court; Chief Justice

The judge oldest in point of service on the supreme court shall be chief justice. He is the chief administrative officer of the judicial system of the state, subject to rules adopted by the court.

Section 7. Supreme Court; Personnel

The supreme court may select a judicial administrator, its clerks, and other personnel and prescribe their duties.

Section 8. Courts of Appeal; Circuits; Panels; Judgments; Terms

(A) Circuits; Panels

The state shall be divided into at least four circuits, with one court of appeal in each. Each court shall sit in panels of at least three judges selected according to rules adopted by the court.

(B) Judgments

A majority of the judges sitting in a case shall concur to render judgment. However, in civil matters only, when a judgment of a district court or an administrative agency determination in a workers' compensation claim is to be modified or reversed and one judge dissents, the case shall be reargued before a panel of at least five judges prior to rendition of judgment, and a majority shall concur to render judgment.

(C) Terms

The term of a court of appeal judge shall be ten years.

Section 9. Courts of Appeal; Circuits and Districts

Each circuit shall be divided into at least three districts, and at least one judge shall be elected from each. The circuits and districts and the number of judges as elected in each circuit on the effective date of this constitution are retained, subject to change by law enacted by two-thirds of the elected members of each house of the legislature.

Section 10. Courts of Appeal; Jurisdiction

(A) Jurisdiction

Except as otherwise provided by this constitution, a court of appeal has appellate jurisdiction of

(1) all civil matters, including direct review of administrative agency determinations in worker's compensation matters as heretofore or hereafter provided by law,

(2) all matters appealed from family and juvenile courts, and

(3) all criminal cases triable by a jury, except as provided in Section 5, Paragraph (D)(2) of this Article. It has supervisory jurisdiction over cases which arise within its circuit.

(B) Scope of Review

Except as limited to questions of law by this constitution, or as provided by law in the review of administrative agency determinations, appellate jurisdiction of a court of appeal extends to law and facts. In the review of an administrative agency determination in a worker's compensation matter, a court of appeal may render judgment as provided by law, or, in the interest of justice, remand the matter to the administrative agency for further proceedings. In criminal cases its appellate jurisdiction extends only to questions of law.

(C) Other Criminal Matters. In all criminal cases not provided for in Paragraph (D)(2) or Paragraph (E) of Section 5 or Paragraph (A)(3) of this Section, a defendant has a right of appeal or review, as provided by law.

Section 11. Courts of Appeal; Certification

A court of appeal may certify any question of law before it to the supreme court, and the supreme court then may give its binding instruction or decide the case upon the whole record.

Section 12. Courts of Appeal; Chief Judge

The judge oldest in point of service on each court of appeal shall be chief judge of that court and shall administer the court subject to rules adopted by it.

Section 13. Courts of Appeal; Personnel

Each court of appeal may select its clerk and other personnel and prescribe their duties.

Section 14. District Courts; Judicial Districts

The state shall be divided into judicial districts, each composed of at least one parish and served by at least one district judge.

Section 15. Courts; Retention; Jurisdiction; Judicial District Changes; Terms.

(A) Court Retention; Trial Courts of Limited Jurisdiction

The district, family, juvenile, parish, city, and magistrate courts existing on the effective date of this constitution are retained. Subject to the limitations in Sections 16 and 21 of this Article, the legislature by law may abolish or merge trial courts of limited or specialized jurisdiction. The legislature by law may establish trial courts of limited jurisdiction with parishwide territorial jurisdiction and subject matter jurisdiction which shall be uniform throughout the state. Effective January 1, 2007, the legislature by law may establish new judgeships for district courts and establish the new divisions with limited or specialized jurisdiction within the territorial jurisdiction of the district court and subject matter jurisdiction over family or juvenile matters as provided by law. The office of city marshal is continued until the city court he serves is abolished.

(B) Judicial Districts

The judicial districts existing on the effective date of this constitution are retained. Subject to the limitations in Section 21 of this Article, the legislature by law may establish, divide, or merge judicial districts with approval in a referendum in each district and parish affected.

(C) Term

The term of a district, parish, or city court judge shall be six years.

(D) Number of Judges

The legislature may change the number of judges in any judicial district by law enacted by two-thirds of the elected members of each house.

Section 16. District Courts; Jurisdiction

(A) Original Jurisdiction

(1) Except as otherwise authorized by this constitution or except as heretofore or hereafter provided by law for administrative agency determinations in worker's compensation matters, a district court shall have original jurisdiction of all civil and criminal matters.

(2) It shall have exclusive original jurisdiction of felony cases and of cases involving title to immovable property, except as provided in (3) below; the right to office or other public position; civil or political right; probate and succession matters; except for administrative agency determination provided for in (1) above, the state, a political corporation, or political subdivisions, or a succession, as a defendant; and the appointment of receivers or liquidators for corporations or partnerships.

(3) The legislature may provide by law that a family court has jurisdiction of cases involving title to movable and immovable property when those cases relate to the partition of community property and the settlement of claims arising from matrimonial regimes when such action arises as a result of divorce or annulment of marriage.

(B) Appellate Jurisdiction

A district court shall have appellate jurisdiction as provided by law.

Section 17. District Courts; Chief Judge

Each district court shall elect from its members a chief judge who shall exercise, for a term designated by the court, the administrative functions prescribed by rule of court.

Section 18. Juvenile and Family Courts; Jurisdiction

Notwithstanding any contrary provision of Section 16 of this Article, juvenile and family courts shall have jurisdiction as provided by law.

Section 19. Special Juvenile Procedures

The determination of guilt or innocence, the detention, and the custody of a person who is alleged to have committed a crime prior to his seventeenth birthday shall be pursuant to special juvenile procedures which shall be provided by law. However, the legislature may

(1) by a two-thirds vote of the elected members of each house provide that special juvenile procedures shall not apply to juveniles arrested for having committed first or second degree murder, manslaughter, aggravated rape, armed robbery, aggravated burglary, aggravated kidnapping, attempted first degree murder, attempted second degree murder, forcible rape, simple rape, second degree kidnapping, a second or subsequent aggravated battery, a second or subsequent aggravated burglary, a second or subsequent offense of burglary of an inhabited dwelling, or a second or subsequent felony-grade violation of Part X or X-B of Chapter 4 of Title 40 of the Louisiana Revised Statutes of 1950, involving the manufacture, distribution, or possession with intent to distribute controlled dangerous substances, and

(2) by two-thirds vote of the elected members of each house lower the maximum ages of persons to whom juvenile procedures shall apply, and

(3) by two-thirds vote of the elected members of each house establish a procedure by which the court of original jurisdiction may waive special juvenile procedures in order that adult procedures shall apply in individual cases. The legislature, by a majority of the elected members of each house, shall make special provisions for detention and custody of juveniles who are subject to the jurisdiction of the district court pending determination of guilt or innocence.

Section 20. Mayors' Courts; Justice of the Peace Courts

Mayors' courts and justice of the peace courts existing on the effective date of this constitution are continued, subject to change by law.

Section 21. Judges; Decrease in Terms and Compensation Prohibited

The term of office, retirement benefits, and compensation of a judge shall not be decreased during the term for which he is elected.

Section 22. Judges; Election; Vacancy

(A) Election

Except as otherwise provided in this Section, all judges shall be elected. Election shall be at the regular congressional election.

(B) Vacancy

A newly-created judgeship or a vacancy in the office of a judge shall be filled by special election called by the governor and held within twelve months after the day on which the vacancy occurs or the judgeship is established, except when the vacancy occurs in the last twelve months of an existing term. Until the vacancy is filled, the supreme court shall appoint a person meeting the qualifications for the office, other than domicile, to serve at its pleasure. The appointee shall be ineligible as a candidate at the election to fill the vacancy or the newly-created judicial office. No person serving as an appointed judge, other than a retired judge, shall be eligible for retirement benefits provided for the elected judiciary.

(C) End of Term

A judge serving on the effective date of this constitution shall serve through December thirty-first of the last year of his term or, if the last year of his term is not in the year of a regular congressional election, then through December thirty-first of the following year. The election for the next term shall be held in the year in which the term expires, as provided above.

Section 23. Judges; Retirement

(A) Retirement System

Within two years after the effective date of this constitution, the legislature shall provide for a retirement system for judges which shall apply to a judge taking office after the effective date of the law enacting the system and in which a judge in office at that time may elect to become a member, with credit for all prior years of judicial service and without contribution therefor. The retirement benefits and judicial service rights of a judge in office or retired on the effective date of this constitution shall not be diminished, nor shall the benefits to which a surviving spouse is entitled be reduced.

(B) Mandatory Retirement

Except as otherwise provided in this Section, a judge shall not remain in office beyond his seventieth birthday. A judge who attains seventy years of age while serving a term of office shall be allowed to complete that term of office.

Section 24. Judges; Qualifications

(A) A judge of the supreme court, a court of appeal, district court, family court, parish court, or court having solely juvenile jurisdiction shall have been domiciled in the respective district, circuit, or parish for one year preceding election and shall have been admitted to the practice of law in the state for at least the number of years specified as follows:

(1) For the supreme court or a court of appeals ten years.

(2) For a district court, family court, parish court, or court having solely juvenile jurisdiction - eight years.

(B) He shall not practice law.

Section 25. Judiciary Commission

(A) Composition

The judiciary commission shall consist of

(1) one court of appeal judge and two district court judges selected by the supreme court;

(2) two attorneys admitted to the practice of law for at least ten years and one attorney admitted to the practice of law for at least three years but not more than ten years, selected by the Conference of Court of Appeal Judges or its successor. They shall not be judges, active or retired, or public officials, other than notaries public; and

(3) three citizens, not lawyers, judges active or retired, or public officials, selected by the Louisiana District Judges' Association or its successor.

(B) Term; Vacancy

A member of the commission shall serve a four-year term and shall be ineligible to succeed himself. His term shall end upon the occurrence of any event which would have made him ineligible for appointment. When a vacancy occurs, a successor shall be appointed for a four-year term by the authority which appointed his predecessor.

(C) Powers

On recommendation of the judiciary commission, the supreme court may censure, suspend with or without salary, remove from office, or retire involuntarily a judge for willful misconduct relating to his official duty, willful and persistent failure to perform his duty, persistent and public conduct prejudicial to the administration of justice that brings the judicial office into disrepute, conduct while in office which would constitute a felony, or conviction of a felony. On recommendation of the judiciary commission, the supreme court may disqualify a judge from exercising any judicial function, without loss of salary, during pendency of proceedings in the supreme court. On recommendation of the judiciary commission, the supreme court may retire involuntarily a judge for disability that seriously interferes with the performance of his duties and that is or is likely to become permanent. The supreme court shall make rules implementing this Section and providing for confidentiality and privilege of commission proceedings.

(D) Other Disciplinary Action

Action against a judge under this Section shall not preclude disciplinary action against him concerning his license to practice law.

Section 26. District Attorneys

(A) Election; Qualifications; Assistants

In each judicial district a district attorney shall be elected for a term of six years. He shall have been admitted to the practice of law in the state for at least five years prior to his election and shall have resided in the district for the two years preceding election. A district attorney may select assistants as authorized by law, and other personnel.

(B) Powers

Except as otherwise provided by this constitution, a district attorney, or his designated assistant, shall have charge of every criminal prosecution by the state in his district, be the representative of the state before the grand jury in his district, and be the legal advisor to the grand jury. He shall perform other duties provided by law.

(C) Prohibition

No district attorney or assistant district attorney shall appear, plead, or in any way defend or assist in defending any criminal prosecution or charge. A violation of this Paragraph shall be cause for removal.

Section 27. Sheriffs

In each parish a sheriff shall be elected for a term of four years. He shall be the chief law enforcement officer in the parish, except as otherwise provided by this constitution, and shall execute court orders and process. He shall be the collector of state and parish ad valorem taxes and such other taxes and license fees as provided by law. This Section shall not apply to Orleans Parish.

Section 28. Clerks of Court

(A) Powers and Duties; Deputies

In each parish a clerk of the district court shall be elected for a term of four years. He shall be ex officio notary public and parish recorder of conveyances, mortgages, and other acts and shall have other duties and powers provided by law. The clerk may appoint deputies with duties and powers provided by law and, with the approval of the district judges, he may appoint minute clerks with duties and powers provided by law.

(B) Office Hours

The legislature shall establish uniform statewide office hours for clerks of the district courts.

Section 29. Coroners

In each parish a coroner shall be elected for a term of four years. He shall be a licensed physician and possess the other qualifications and perform the duties provided by law. The requirement that he be a licensed physician shall be inapplicable in any parish in which no licensed physician will accept the office.

Section 30. Vacancies

When a vacancy occurs in the following offices, the duties of the office, until it is filled by election as provided by law, shall be assumed by the persons herein designated:

(1) sheriff, by the chief criminal deputy;

(2) district attorney, by the first assistant;

(3) clerk of a district court, by the chief deputy;

(4) coroner, by the chief deputy. If there is no such person to assume the duties when the vacancy occurs, the governing authority or authorities of the parish or parishes concerned shall appoint a qualified person to assume the duties of the office until filled by election.

Section 31. Reduction of Salaries and Benefits Prohibited

The salary and retirement benefits of an attorney general, district attorney, sheriff, coroner, or clerk of the district court shall not be diminished during his term of office.

Section 32. Orleans Parish Courts, Officials

Except for provisions relating to terms of office as provided elsewhere in this Article, and notwithstanding any other contrary provision of this constitution, the following courts and officers in Orleans Parish are continued, subject to change by law; the civil and criminal district courts; the city, municipal, traffic, and juvenile courts; the clerks of the civil and criminal district courts; the civil and criminal sheriffs; the constables and the clerks of the first and second city courts; the register of conveyances; and the recorder of mortgages.

Section 33. Jurors

(A) Qualifications

A citizen of the state who has reached the age of majority is eligible to serve as a juror within the parish in which he is domiciled. The legislature may provide additional qualifications.

(B) Exemptions

Persons who are seventy years of age or older shall be exempt from jury service and may decline to serve as jurors, but may elect to serve as jurors if they meet the other qualifications for service as jurors. The supreme court shall provide by rule for other grounds for the exemption of jurors.

Section 34. Grand Jury

(A) Grand Jury

There shall be a grand jury or grand juries in each parish, whose qualifications, duties, and responsibilities shall be provided by law. The secrecy of the proceedings, including the identity of witnesses, shall be provided by law.

(B) Right to Counsel

The legislature may establish by law terms and conditions under which a witness may have the right to the advice of counsel while testifying before the grand jury.

ARTICLE VI: LOCAL GOVERNMENT

PART I. GENERAL PROVISIONS

Section 1. Parishes

(A) Parishes and Boundaries Ratified

Parishes and their boundaries as established on the effective date of this constitution are recognized and ratified.

(B) Creation; Dissolution; Merger; Boundaries

The legislature by law may establish and organize new parishes, dissolve and merge parishes, and change parish boundaries if approved by two-thirds of the electors in each parish affected voting thereon at an election held for that purpose.

(C) Change of Parish Seat

The governing authority of a parish may call an election on the question of changing the parish seat. The parish seat shall be changed if approved by two-thirds of the electors voting thereon.

(D) Adjustment of Assets and Liabilities

When a parish is enlarged or established from contiguous territory, it shall be entitled to a just proportion of the property and assets and shall be liable for a just proportion of the existing debts and liabilities of the parish or parishes from which the territory is taken.

Section 2. Municipalities

The legislature shall provide by general law for the incorporation, consolidation, merger, and government of municipalities. No local or special law shall create a municipal corporation or amend, modify, or repeal a municipal charter. However, a special legislative charter existing on the effective date of this constitution may be amended, modified, or repealed by local or special law.

Section 3. Classification

The legislature may classify parishes or municipalities according to population or on any other reasonable basis related to the purpose of the classification. Legislation may be limited in its effect to any of such class or classes.

Section 4. Existing Home Rule Charters and Plans of Government

Every home rule charter or plan of government existing or adopted when this constitution is adopted shall remain in effect and may be amended, modified, or repealed as provided therein. Except as inconsistent with this constitution, each local governmental subdivision which has adopted such a home rule charter or plan of government shall retain the powers, functions, and duties in effect when this constitution is adopted. If its charter permits, each of them also shall have the right to powers and functions granted to other local governmental subdivisions.

Section 5. Home Rule Charter

(A) Authority to Adopt; Commission

Subject to and not inconsistent with this constitution, any local governmental subdivision may draft, adopt, or amend a home rule charter in accordance with this Section. The governing authority of a local governmental subdivision may appoint a commission to prepare and propose a charter or an alternate charter, or it may call an election to elect such a commission.

(B) Petition to Elect Commission

The governing authority shall call an election to elect such a commission when presented with a petition signed by not less than ten percent of the electors or ten thousand electors, whichever is fewer, who live within the boundaries of the affected subdivision, as certified by the registrar of voters.

(C) Adoption; Amendment; Repeal

A home rule charter shall be adopted, amended, or repealed when approved by a majority of the electors voting thereon at an election held for that purpose.

(D) Adoption by Two or More Local Governmental Subdivisions

Two or more local governmental subdivisions within the boundaries of one parish may adopt a home rule charter under this Section if approved by a majority of the electors in each affected local governmental subdivision voting thereon in an election held for that purpose. The legislature shall provide by law the method of appointment or election of a commission to prepare and propose a charter consistent with Paragraph (A) of this Section and the method by which the electors may petition for an election consistent with Paragraph (B) of this Section. However, at least one member of the commission shall be elected or appointed from each affected local governmental subdivision.

(E) Structure and Organization; Powers; Functions

A home rule charter adopted under this Section shall provide the structure and organization, powers, and functions of the government of the local governmental subdivision, which may include the exercise of any power and performance of any function necessary, requisite, or proper for the management of its affairs, not denied by general law or inconsistent with this constitution.

(F) Additional Powers and Functions

Except as prohibited by its charter, a local governmental subdivision adopting a home rule charter under this Section shall have the additional powers and functions granted to local governmental subdivisions by other provisions of this constitution.

(G) Parish Officials and School Boards Not Affected

No home rule charter or plan of government shall contain any provision affecting a school board or the offices of district attorney, sheriff, assessor, clerk of a district court, or coroner, which is inconsistent with this constitution or law.

Section 6. Home Rule Charter or Plan of Government; Action by Legislature Prohibited

The legislature shall enact no law the effect of which changes or affects the structure and organization or the particular distribution and redistribution of the powers and functions of any local governmental subdivision which operates under a home rule charter.

Section 7. Powers of Other Local Governmental Subdivisions

(A) Powers and Functions

Subject to and not inconsistent with this constitution, the governing authority of a local governmental subdivision which has no home rule charter or plan of government may exercise any power and perform any function necessary, requisite, or proper for the management of its affairs, not denied by its charter or by general law, if a majority of the electors voting in an election held for that purpose vote in favor of the proposition that the governing authority may exercise such general powers. Otherwise, the local governmental subdivision shall have the powers authorized by this constitution or by law.

(B) Parish Officials and School Boards Not Affected

Nothing in this Section shall affect the powers and functions of a school board or the offices of district attorney, sheriff, assessor, clerk of a district court, or coroner.

Section 8. Home Rule Parish; Incorporation of Cities, Towns, and Villages

No parish plan of government or home rule charter shall prohibit the incorporation of a city, town, or village as provided by general law.

Section 9. Limitations of Local Governmental Subdivisions

(A) Limitations

No local governmental subdivision shall

(1) define and provide for the punishment of a felony; or

(2) except as provided by law, enact an ordinance governing private or civil relationships.

(B) Police Power Not Abridged

Notwithstanding any provision of this Article, the police power of the state shall never be abridged.

Section 10. Codification of Ordinances

Within two years after the effective date of this constitution, the governing authority of each political subdivision shall have a code prepared containing all of its general ordinances. When the code is prepared, the governing authority shall make copies available for public distribution. All general ordinances adopted after the approval of the code shall be amendments or additions to the code.

Section 11. Local Officials

The electors of each local governmental subdivision shall have the exclusive right to elect their governing authority. Nothing herein shall be construed to prohibit the election of the members from single-member districts.

Section 12. Local Officials; Compensation

The compensation or method of fixing the compensation of an elected official of any local governmental subdivision which operates under a home rule charter or plan of government, as provided in Sections 4 and 5 of this Article, shall be provided in its charter. The compensation or method of fixing the compensation of an elected official of any other local governmental subdivision shall be provided by law. Compensation of a local official shall not be reduced during the term for which he is elected.

Section 13. Vacancies

(A) Vacancy; Appointment

Except as otherwise provided by this constitution, a vacancy in any local office filled by election wholly within the boundaries of a local governmental subdivision or a school district shall be filled by appointment by the particular governing authority of the local governmental subdivision or school district in which the vacancy occurs, until it is filled by election as provided by law.

(B) Exception

This Section shall apply to each local governmental subdivision unless otherwise provided by its home rule charter or plan of government.

Section 14. Increasing Financial Burden of Political Subdivisions

(A)(1) No law or state executive order, rule, or regulation requiring increased expenditures for any purpose shall become effective within a political subdivision until approved by ordinance enacted, or resolution adopted, by the governing authority of the affected political subdivision or until, and only as long as, the legislature appropriates funds for the purpose to the affected political subdivision and only to the extent and amount that such funds are provided, or until a law provides for a local source of revenue within the political subdivision for the purpose and the affected political subdivision is authorized by ordinance or resolution to levy and collect such revenue and only to the extent and amount of such revenue. This Paragraph shall not apply to a school board.

(2) This Paragraph shall not apply to:

(a) A law requested by the governing authority of the affected political subdivision.
(b) A law defining a new crime or amending an existing crime.

(c) A law enacted and effective prior to the adoption of the amendment of this Section by the electors of the state in 1991.

(d) A law enacted, or state executive order, rule, or regulation promulgated, to comply with a federal mandate.

(e) A law providing for civil service, minimum wages, hours, working conditions, and pension and retirement benefits, or vacation or sick leave benefits for firemen and municipal policemen.

(f) Any instrument adopted or enacted by two-thirds of the elected members of each house of the legislature and any rule or regulation adopted to implement such instrument or adopted pursuant thereto.

(g) A law having insignificant fiscal impact on the affected political subdivision.

(B)(1) No law requiring increased expenditures within a city, parish, or other local public school system for any purpose shall become effective within such school system only as long as the legislature appropriates funds for the purpose to the affected school system and only to the extent and amount that such funds are provided, or until a law provides for a local source of revenue within the school system for the purpose and the affected school board is authorized by ordinance or resolution to levy and collect such revenue and only to the extent and amount of such revenue. This Paragraph shall not apply to any political subdivision to which Paragraph (A) of this Section applies.

(2) This Paragraph shall not apply to:

(a) A law requested by the school board of the affected school system.

(b) A law defining a new crime or amending an existing crime.

(c) A law enacted and effective prior to the adoption of the amendment of this Section by the electors of the state in 2006.

(d) A law enacted to comply with a federal mandate.

(e) Any instrument adopted or enacted by two-thirds of the elected members of each house of the legislature.

(f) A law having insignificant fiscal impact on the affected school system.

(g) The formula for the Minimum Foundation Program of education as required by Article VIII, Section 13(B) of this constitution, nor to any instrument adopted or enacted by the legislature approving such formula.

(h) Any law relative to the implementation of the state school and district accountability system.

Section 15. Local Governmental Subdivisions; Control Over Agencies

The governing authority of a local governmental subdivision shall have general power over any agency heretofore or hereafter created by it, including, without limitation, the power to abolish the agency and require prior approval of any charge or tax levied or bond issued by the agency.

Section 16. Special Districts and Local Public Agencies

(A) Consolidation

A local governmental subdivision may consolidate and merge into itself any special district or local public agency, except a school district, situated and having jurisdiction entirely within the boundaries of the local governmental subdivision. Upon the consolidation and merger, the local governmental subdivision shall succeed to and be vested with all of the rights, revenues, resources, jurisdiction, authority, and powers of the special district or local public agency. A consolidation and merger shall become effective only if approved by a majority of the electors voting thereon in the local governmental subdivision as a whole and by a majority of the electors voting thereon in the affected special district. A local public agency shall be consolidated and merged only if approved by a majority of the electors voting thereon in an election held for that purpose in the local governmental subdivision in which the agency is located.

(B) Assumption of Debt

If the special district or local public agency which is consolidated and merged has outstanding indebtedness, the authority provided by this Section shall not be exercised unless provision is made for the assumption of the indebtedness by the governing authority of the local governmental subdivision involved.

Section 17. Land Use; Zoning; Historic Preservation

Subject to uniform procedures established by law, a local governmental subdivision may

(1) adopt regulations for land use, zoning, and historic preservation, which authority is declared to be a public purpose;

(2) create commissions and districts to implement those regulations;

(3) review decisions of any such commission; and

(4) adopt standards for use, construction, demolition, and modification of areas and structures. Existing constitutional authority for historic preservation commissions is retained.

Section 18. Industrial Areas

(A) Authorization

The legislature by law may authorize parishes to create and define industrial areas within their boundaries in accordance with procedures and subject to regulations which it determines. An industrial area shall not be a political subdivision of the state.

(B) Access by Public Road; Police Protection

When an industrial area is so created, provision shall be made for access by public road to each entrance to the premises of every plant in the area, which is provided for use by employees of the company, or for use by employees of independent contractors working on the premises, or for delivery of materials or supplies, other than by rail or water transportation, to the premises. Police protection provided by any plant in an industrial area shall be confined to the premises of that plant.

Section 19. Special Districts; Creation

Subject to and not inconsistent with this constitution, the legislature by general law or by local or special law may create or authorize the creation of special districts, boards, agencies, commissions, and authorities of every type, define their powers, and grant to the special districts, boards, agencies, commissions, and authorities so created such rights, powers, and authorities as it deems proper, including, but not limited to, the power of taxation and the power to incur debt and issue bonds.

Section 20. Intergovernmental Cooperation

Except as otherwise provided by law, a political subdivision may exercise and perform any authorized power and function, including financing, jointly or in cooperation with one or more political subdivisions, either within or without the state, or with the United States or its agencies.

Section 21. Assistance to Local Industry

(A) Authorization

In order to:

(1) induce and encourage the location of or addition to industrial enterprises therein which would have economic impact upon the area and thereby the state,

(2) provide for the establishment and furnishing of such industrial plant,

(3) facilitate the operation of public ports, or

(4) provide movable or immovable property, or both, for pollution control facilities, the legislature by law may authorize, subject to restrictions it may impose, any political subdivision, public port commission, or public port, harbor, and terminal district to:

(a) issue bonds, subject to approval by the State Bond Commission or its successor, and use the funds derived from the sale of the bonds to acquire and improve industrial plant sites and other property necessary to the purposes thereof;

(b) acquire, through purchase, donation, exchange, and expropriation, and improve industrial plant buildings and industrial plant equipment, machinery, furnishings, and appurtenances, including public port facilities and operations which relate to or facilitate the transportation of goods in domestic and international commerce; and

(c) sell, lease, lease-purchase, or demolish all or any part of the foregoing.

(B) Property Expropriated; Sale to Aliens Prohibited

No property expropriated under the authority of this Section shall ever, directly or indirectly, be sold or donated to any foreign power, any alien, or any corporation in which the majority of the stock is controlled by any foreign power, alien corporation, or alien.

(C) Exception

This Section shall not apply to a school board.

(D) Property excepted

The bona fide homestead, as defined by Article VII, Section 20(A)(1), shall not be subject to expropriation pursuant to this Section.

Section 22. Procedure for Certain Special Elections

When an election is required in a political subdivision under the provisions of this constitution which require submission to the electors of a proposition or question, the election shall be called, conducted, and the returns thereof canvassed, in accordance with the procedures established by the law then in effect pertaining to elections for incurring bonded indebtedness and special taxes relative to local finance, or as may be otherwise provided by law.

Section 23. Acquisition of Property

Subject to and not inconsistent with this constitution and subject to restrictions provided by general law, political subdivisions may acquire property for any public purpose by purchase, donation, expropriation, exchange, or otherwise.

Section 24. Servitudes of Way; Acquisition by Prescription

The public, represented by local governmental subdivisions, may acquire servitudes of way by prescription in the manner prescribed by law.

Section 25. Courts Not Affected

Notwithstanding any provision of this Article, courts and their officers may be established or affected only as provided in Article V of this constitution.

PART II. FINANCE

Section 26. Parish Ad Valorem Tax

A) Parish Tax for General Purposes; Millage Limits; Increase

The governing authority of a parish may levy annually an ad valorem tax for general purposes not to exceed four mills on the dollar of assessed valuation. However, in Orleans Parish the limitation shall be seven mills, and in Jackson Parish the limitation shall be five mills. Millage rates may be increased in any parish when approved by a majority of the electors voting thereon in an election held for that purpose.

(B) Millage Increase Not for General Purposes

When the millage increase is for other than general purposes, the proposition shall state the specific purpose or purposes for which the tax is to be levied and the length of time the tax is to remain in effect. All proceeds of the tax shall be used solely for the purpose or purposes set forth in the proposition.

(C) Parish Tax in Municipality

The amount of the parish tax for general purposes which any parish, except Orleans Parish, may levy, without a vote of the electors, on property located wholly within any municipality which has a population exceeding one thousand inhabitants according to the last federal decennial census, or other census authorized by law, and which provides and maintains a system of street paving, shall not exceed one-half the tax levy for general purposes.

(D) Withdrawal from Parish Taxing Authority

This Section shall not affect the withdrawal of property in a municipality from parish taxing authority, in whole or in part, by a provision of the legislative charter of a municipality in effect on the effective date of this constitution.

(E) Additional Taxes for Orleans Parish

(1) In addition to any millage authorized by Paragraph (A) of this Section, the governing authority of Orleans Parish may levy annually an additional ad valorem tax for fire protection not to exceed ten mills on the dollar of assessed valuation and an additional ad valorem tax for police protection not to exceed ten mills on the dollar of assessed valuation. Notwithstanding the provisions of Article VII, Section 20(A), the homestead exemption shall not extend to such additional ad valorem taxes. The additional revenues generated by these fire and police millages shall not displace, replace, or supplant funding by the city of New Orleans for fire and police protection for calendar year 2013 nor shall the level of funding for such purposes by the city for that calendar year be decreased below such level in any subsequent calendar year. Furthermore, the revenues generated by these fire and police protection services that directly contribute to the safety of the residents of Orleans Parish. In the event of either of the above, the authorization for such fire and police millages herein shall be null, void, and of no effect. This provision shall mean that no appropriation for any calendar year from such additional revenues shall be made for any purpose for which a city appropriation was made in the previous year unless the total appropriations for that calendar year from the city for such purpose exceed city appropriations for the previous year. This provision shall in no way limit city appropriations in excess of the minimum amounts herein established.

(2) Any additional ad valorem tax authorized by the amendment of Subparagraph (1) of this Paragraph as approved by the voters in 2014 shall be levied only if approved by a majority of the electors of Orleans Parish who vote on a proposition authorizing the additional tax at an election held for that purpose.

Section 27. Municipal Ad Valorem Tax

(A) Municipal Tax for General Purposes; Millage Limits; Increase

The governing authority of a municipality may levy annually an ad valorem tax for general purposes not to exceed seven mills on the dollar of assessed valuation. However, if a municipality, by its charter or by law, is exempt from payment of parish taxes or, under legislative or constitutional authority, maintains its own public schools, it may levy an annual tax not to exceed ten mills on the dollar of assessed valuation. Millage rates may be increased in any municipality when approved by a majority of the electors voting thereon in an election held for that purpose.

(B) Millage Increase Not for General Purposes

When the millage increase is for other than general purposes, the proposition shall state the specific purpose or purposes for which the tax is to be levied and the length of time the tax is to remain in effect. All proceeds of the tax shall be used solely for the purpose or purposes set forth in the proposition.

(C) Exception

This Section shall not apply to the city of New Orleans.

Section 28. Local Governmental Subdivisions; Occupational License Tax

The governing authority of a local governmental subdivision may impose an occupational license tax not greater than that imposed by the state. Those who pay a municipal occupational license tax shall be exempt from a parish occupational license tax in the amount of the municipal tax. The governing authority of a local governmental subdivision may impose an occupational license tax greater than that imposed by the state when authorized by law enacted by the favorable vote of two-thirds of the elected members of each house of the legislature.

Section 29. Local Governmental Subdivisions and School Boards; Sales Tax

(A) Sales Tax Authorized

Except as otherwise authorized in a home rule charter as provided for in Section 4 of this Article, the governing authority of any local governmental subdivision or school board may levy and collect a tax upon the sale at retail, the use, the lease or rental, the consumption, and the storage for use or consumption, of tangible personal property and on sales of services as defined by law, if approved by a majority of the electors voting thereon in an election held for that purpose. The rate thereof, when combined with the rate of all other sales and use taxes, exclusive of state sales and use taxes, levied and collected within any local governmental subdivision, shall not exceed three percent.

(B) Additional Sales Tax Authorized

However, the legislature, by general or by local or special law, may authorize the imposition of additional sales and use taxes by local governmental subdivisions or school boards, if approved by a majority of the electors voting thereon in an election held for that purpose.

(C) Bonds; Security

Nothing in this Section shall affect any sales or use tax authorized or imposed on the effective date of this constitution or affect or impair the security of any bonds payable from the proceeds of the tax.

(D) Exemptions; Protection of Bonds

Except when bonds secured thereby have been authorized, the legislature may provide for the exemption or exclusion of any goods, tangible personal property, or services from sales or use taxes only pursuant to one of the following:

(1) Exemptions or exclusions uniformly applicable to the taxes of all local governmental subdivisions, school boards, and other political subdivisions whose boundaries are not coterminous with those of the state.

(2) Exemptions or exclusions applicable to the taxes of the state or applicable to political subdivisions whose boundaries are coterminous with those of the state, or both.

(3) Exemptions or exclusions uniformly applicable to the taxes of all the tax authorities in the state.

Section 30. Political Subdivisions; Taxing Power

(A) A political subdivision may exercise the power of taxation, subject to limitations elsewhere provided by this constitution, under authority granted by the legislature for parish, municipal, and other local purposes, strictly public in their nature. This Section shall not affect similar grants to political subdivisions under self-operative sections of this constitution.

(B) Notwithstanding the provisions of Paragraph (A) of this Section, or any other provision of law to the contrary, no political subdivision shall submit the same tax proposition, or a new tax proposition that includes such a tax proposition, to the electorate more than once within a six month period except in the case of an emergency as determined by the governing authority of the political subdivision.

Section 30.1. Bonding and Taxing Authority of Certain Political Subdivisions and Other Public Entities

(A) The Louisiana Recovery District shall have no power or authority, directly or indirectly, to incur debt or issue bonds after the effective date of this Section except to refund any such outstanding debt or bonds at a lower effective rate of interest. Any debt or bonds issued and outstanding on the effective date of this Section, or any debt incurred or bonds issued to refund such indebtedness or bonds as authorized by this Section shall be retired no later than the end of Fiscal Year 1998-1999. At such time as there is no debt or bonds of the Louisiana Recovery District outstanding, the Louisiana Recovery District shall cease to exist and any authority or power of the district shall be null and void. The Louisiana Recovery District shall not levy a new tax or increase any existing tax of the district.

(B) The legislature shall not grant any power of taxation or power to incur debt or issue bonds to any one or more political subdivisions, special districts, agencies, boards, commissions, or other authorities created by the legislature for the purpose of generating revenue for the state whose boundary or combined boundaries are coterminous with the state, except by law enacted by a favorable record vote of two-thirds of the elected members of each house of the legislature. This Paragraph shall not apply to the Louisiana Recovery District.

(C) Except as provided in Paragraphs (A) and (B), this Section shall not apply to any political subdivision, special district, agency, board, commission, municipality, parish, school board, levee district, port, or to any other similar authority.

Section 31. Taxes; Ratification

Any tax validly being levied by a political subdivision under prior legislative or constitutional authority on the effective date of this constitution is ratified.

Section 32. Special Taxes; Authorization

For the purpose of acquiring, constructing, improving, maintaining, or operating any work of public improvement, a political subdivision may levy special taxes when authorized by a majority of the electors in the political subdivision who vote thereon in an election held for that purpose.

Section 33. Political Subdivisions; General Obligation Bonds

(A) Authorization

Subject to approval by the State Bond Commission or its successor, general obligation bonds may be issued only after authorization by a majority of the electors voting on the proposition at an election in the political subdivision issuing the bonds. Bonds to refund outstanding indebtedness at the same or at a lower effective rate of interest, even though payable solely from ad valorem taxes, need not be authorized at an election if the indebtedness refunded is paid or cancelled at the time of the delivery of the refunding bonds, or if money, or securities made eligible for such purpose by law, are deposited in escrow in an adequate amount, with interest, to be utilized solely to retire the refunded indebtedness or bonds and to pay interest thereon and redemption premiums, if any, to the time of retirement.

(B) Full Faith and Credit

The full faith and credit of a political subdivision is hereby pledged to the payment of general obligation bonds issued by it under this constitution or the statute or proceedings pursuant to which they are issued. The governing authority of the issuing political subdivision shall levy and collect or cause to be levied and collected on all taxable property in the political subdivision ad valorem taxes sufficient to pay principal and interest and redemption premiums, if any, on such bonds as they mature.

Section 34. Limitations on Bonded Indebtedness

The legislature by law shall fix the limitation on bonded indebtedness payable solely from ad valorem taxes levied by political subdivisions.

Section 35. Contesting Political Subdivision Bonds

(A) Contesting Election; Time Limit

For sixty days after promulgation of the result of an election held to incur or assume debt, issue bonds, or levy a tax, any person in interest may contest the legality of the election, the bond issue provided for, or the tax authorized, for any cause. After that time no one shall have any cause or right of action to contest the regularity, formality, or legality of the election, tax provisions, or bond authorization, for any cause whatsoever. If the validity of any election, tax, debt assumption, or bond issue authorized or provided for is not raised within the sixty days, the authority to incur or assume debt, levy the tax, or issue the bonds, the legality thereof, and the taxes and other revenues necessary to pay the same shall be conclusively presumed to be valid, and no court shall have authority to inquire into such matters.

(B) Contesting Ordinance or Resolution; Time Limit

Every ordinance or resolution authorizing the issuance of bonds or other debt obligation by a political subdivision shall be published at least once in the official journal of the political subdivision or, if there is none, in a newspaper having general circulation therein. For thirty days after the date of publication, any person in interest may contest the legality of the ordinance or resolution and of any provision therein made for the security and payment of the bonds. After that time, no one shall have any cause of action to test the regularity, formality, legality, or effectiveness of the ordinance or resolution, and provisions thereof for any cause whatever. Thereafter, it shall be conclusively presumed that every legal requirement for the issuance of the bonds or other debt obligation, including all things pertaining to the election, if any, at which the bonds or other debt obligation were authorized, has been complied with. No court shall have authority to inquire into any of these matters after the thirty days.

Section 36. Local Improvement Assessments

(A) Authorization

The legislature shall provide by general law or by local or special law the procedures by which a political subdivision may levy and collect local or special assessments on real property for the purpose of acquiring, constructing, or improving works of public improvement.

(B) Certificates of Indebtedness; Security

Certificates of indebtedness may be issued to cover the cost of any such public improvement. They shall be secured by the pledge of the local or special assessments levied therefor and may be further secured by the pledge of the full faith and credit of the political subdivision.

(C) Exception

This Section shall not apply to a school board.

Section 37. Revenue-Producing Property

(A) Authorization

The legislature by law may authorize political subdivisions to issue bonds or other debt obligations to construct, acquire, extend, or improve any revenue-producing public utility or work of public improvement. The bonds or other debt obligations may be secured by mortgage on the lands, buildings, machinery, and equipment or by the pledge of the income and revenues of the public utility or work of public improvement. They shall not be a charge upon the other income and revenues of the political subdivision.

(B) Exception

This Section shall not apply to a school board.

PART III. LEVEE DISTRICTS AND REGIONAL FLOOD PROTECTION AUTHORITIES

Section 38. Levee Districts

(A) Retention; Reorganization; Consolidation

Levee districts as organized and constituted on January 1, 1974 shall continue to exist, except that

(1) The legislature may provide by law for the consolidation, division, or reorganization of existing levee districts , may create new levee districts, or may establish regional flood protection authorities as authorized by Section 38.1 of this Part. However, except for the board of commissioners of a regional flood protection authority the members of the board of commissioners of a district heretofore or hereafter created shall be appointed or elected from among residents of the district, as provided by law.

(2) A levee district whose flood control responsibilities are limited to and which is situated entirely within one parish may be consolidated and merged into such parish under the terms and conditions and in the manner provided in Section 16 of this Article.

(B) Obligation of Contract Affirmed

No action taken under this Section shall impair the obligation of outstanding bonded indebtedness or of any other contract of a levee district.

Section 38.1. Regional Flood Protection Authorities

(A) Establishment

(1) The legislature by law may establish regional flood protection authorities, with territorial jurisdiction limited to parishes and levee districts which are situated entirely or partially within the coastal zone as described in R.S. 49:214.24 as of the effective date of this Section, and provide for their territorial jurisdiction, governing authority, powers, duties, and functions for the purpose of constructing and maintaining levees, levee drainage, flood protection, and hurricane flood protection within the territorial jurisdiction of the authority, and for all other purposes incidental thereto. Each authority shall be governed by a board of commissioners which shall also be the governing authority of each levee district within the territorial jurisdiction of the authority.

(2) The legislature, by law, may include within territorial jurisdiction of the regional flood protection authority one or more parishes or portions of parishes which are included in one or more levee districts that are not included within territorial jurisdiction of the authority. The inclusion of such parishes or portions of parishes shall not affect the authority of the respective levee district

(a) to levy taxes in such areas nor prohibit the levy of taxes provided for in this Section in such areas,

(b) to employ and provide for its employees, or

(c) to own, construct, and maintain its property.

(B) Authority-wide Tax

In addition to the taxes authorized to be levied by any levee district situated within the territorial jurisdiction of a regional flood protection authority, the board of commissioners of the authority may levy annually a tax on the dollar of the assessed valuation of all property not exempt from taxation situated within the territorial jurisdiction of the authority. The necessity and the levy and rate of the tax, or any increase thereof, shall be subject to the provisions of Article VII, Section 20 of this Constitution and shall be subject to the provisions of Article VII, Section 21(F) of this Constitution and shall be submitted to the electors within the authority, and the tax or increase shall take effect only if approved by:

(1) A majority of the electors voting thereon within that authority, and

(2) Each of the parishes in that authority, by a majority of the electors voting thereon in each parish, in an election held for that purpose.

(C) Notwithstanding the provisions of Article VII, Section 10.2(D) of this Constitution, the legislature may appropriate up to five hundred thousand dollars annually to regional flood protection authorities from the Coastal Protection and Restoration Fund.

(D) Obligation of Contract Affirmed

No action taken under this Section shall impair the obligation of outstanding bonded indebtedness or of any other contract of a levee district.

(E) The phrase "levee district" when used in Sections 40 and 41 of this Part and in Articles VII and IX of this Constitution shall include regional flood protection authorities.

Section 39. Levee District Taxes

(A) District Tax; Millage Limit

For the purpose of constructing and maintaining levees, levee drainage, flood protection, hurricane flood protection, and for all other purposes incidental thereto, the governing authority of a levee district created prior to January 1, 2006, may levy annually a tax not to exceed five mills, except the Board of Levee Commissioners of the Orleans Levee District which may levy annually a tax not to exceed two and one-half mills on the dollar of the assessed valuation of all taxable property situated within the alluvial portions of the district subject to overflow.

(B) Millage Increase

If the necessity to raise additional funds arises in any levee district created prior to January 1, 2006, for any purpose set forth in Paragraph (A) of this Section, or for any other purpose related to its authorized powers and functions as specified by law, the tax may be increased. However, the necessity and the rate of the increase shall be submitted to the electors of the district, and the tax increase shall take effect only if approved by a majority of the electors voting thereon in an election held for that purpose.

(C) Districts Created After January 1, 2006

For any purpose set forth in Paragraph (A) of this Section, the governing authority of a levee district created after January 1, 2006, may annually levy a tax on all property not exempt from taxation situated within the alluvial portions of the district subject to overflow. However, such a district shall not levy such a tax nor increase the rate of such a tax unless the levy or the increase is approved by a majority of the electors of the district who vote in an election held for that purpose. If the district is comprised of territory in more than one parish, approval by a majority of the electors who vote in each parish comprising the district is also required for any such levy or increase.

Section 40. Bond Issues

(A) Authorization

Subject to approval by the State Bond Commission or its successor, the governing authority of a levee district may fund the proceeds of its taxes or other revenues into bonds or other evidences of indebtedness. Proceeds thus derived shall be used for the purposes mentioned in Part III of this Article or for the funding or payment of any outstanding indebtedness. (B) Sale. Bonds issued under the authority of Paragraph (A) shall be sold as provided by law concerning the issuance of bonds by levee districts.

Section 41. Cooperation with Federal Government

The governing authority of any levee district may cooperate with the federal government in constructing and maintaining levees in this state, under terms and conditions provided by the federal authorities and accepted by the governing authority.

Section 42. Compensation for Property Used or Destroyed; Tax

(A) Compensation

Notwithstanding any contrary provision of this constitution, lands and improvements thereon hereafter actually used or destroyed for levees or levee drainage purposes shall be paid for as provided by law. With respect to lands and improvements actually used or destroyed in the construction, enlargement, improvement, or modification of federal or non-federal hurricane protection projects, including mitigation related thereto, such payment shall not exceed the amount of compensation authorized under Article I, Section 4(G) of this constitution. However, nothing contained in this Paragraph with respect to compensation for lands and improvements shall apply to batture or to property the control of which is vested in the state or any political subdivision for the purpose of commerce. If the district has no other funds or resources from which the payment can be made, it shall levy on all taxable property within the district a tax sufficient to pay for property used or destroyed to be used solely in the district where collected.

(B) Appropriation

Nothing in this Section shall prevent the appropriation of such property before payment.

PART IV. PORT COMMISSIONS AND DISTRICTS

Section 43. Port Commissions and Districts

All deep-water port commissions and all deep-water port, harbor, and terminal districts as organized and constituted on January 1, 1974, including their powers and functions, structure and organization, and territorial jurisdiction, are ratified and confirmed and shall continue to exist, except that

(1) The legislature by law may grant additional powers and functions to any such commission or district and may create new port commissions or port, harbor, and terminal districts.

(2) Only by law enacted by the favorable vote of two-thirds of the elected members of each house, may the legislature consolidate or abolish any such commission or district or diminish, reduce, or withdraw from any such commission or district any of its powers and functions and affect the structure and organization, distribution, and redistribution of the powers and functions of any such commission or district, including additions to or reductions of its territorial jurisdiction.

(3) The legislature shall enact laws with respect to the membership of the commissions provided in this Section. Once the law with respect to membership is enacted, it may be changed only by law enacted by the favorable vote of two-thirds of the elected members of each house.

PART V. DEFINITIONS

Section 44. Terms Defined

As used in this Article:

(1) "Local governmental subdivision" means any parish or municipality.

(2) "Political subdivision" means a parish, municipality, and any other unit of local government, including a school board and a special district, authorized by law to perform governmental functions.

(3) "Municipality" means an incorporated city, town, or village.

(4) "Governing authority" means the body which exercises the legislative functions of the political subdivision.

(5) "General law" means a law of statewide concern enacted by the legislature which is uniformly applicable to all persons or to all political subdivisions in the state or which is uniformly applicable to all persons or to all political subdivisions within the same class.

(6) "General obligation bonds" means those bonds, the principal and interest of which are secured by and payable from ad valorem taxes levied without limitation as to rate or amount.

(7) "Deep-water port commissions" and "deep-water port, harbor, and terminal districts" mean those commissions or districts within whose territorial jurisdiction exist facilities capable of accommodating vessels of at least twenty-five feet of draft and of engaging in foreign commerce.

ARTICLE VII: REVENUE AND FINANCE

PART I. GENERAL PROVISIONS

Section 1. Power to Tax; Public Purpose

(A) Except as otherwise provided by this constitution, the power of taxation shall be vested in the legislature, shall never be surrendered, suspended, or contracted away, and shall be exercised for public purposes only.

(B) The power to tax may not be exercised by any court in the state, either by ordering the levy of a tax, an increase in an existing tax, or the repeal of an existing tax exemption or by ordering the legislature or any municipal or parish governing authority or any other political subdivision or governmental entity to do so.

Section 2. Power to Tax; Limitation

The levy of a new tax, an increase in an existing tax, or a repeal of an existing tax exemption shall require the enactment of a law by two-thirds of the elected members of each house of the legislature.

Section 2.1. Fees and Civil Fines; Limitation

(A) Any new fee or civil fine or increase in an existing fee or civil fine imposed or assessed by the state or any board, department, or agency of the state shall require the enactment of a law by a two-thirds vote of the elected members of each house of the legislature.

(B) The provisions of this Section shall not apply to any department which is constitutionally created and headed by an officer who is elected by majority vote of the electorate of the state.

Section 2.2. Power to Tax; Sales and Use Tax; Limitation

(A) Effective January 1, 2003, the sales and use tax rate imposed by the state of Louisiana or by a political subdivision whose boundaries are coterminous with those of the state shall not exceed two percent of the price of the following items:

(1) Food for home consumption, as defined in R.S. 47:305(D)(1)(n) through (r) on January 1, 2003.

(2) Natural gas, electricity, and water sold directly to the consumer for residential use.

(3) Prescription drugs.

(B) Effective July 1, 2003, the sales and use tax imposed by the state of Louisiana or by a political subdivision whose boundaries are coterminous with those of the state shall not apply to sales or purchases of the following items:

(1) Food for home consumption, as defined in R.S. 47:305(D)(1)(n) through (r) on January 1, 2003.

(2) Natural gas, electricity, and water sold directly to the consumer for residential use.

(3) Prescription drugs.

(C) As used in this Section, the term "sold directly to the consumer for residential use" includes the furnishing of natural gas, electricity, or water to single private residences, including the separate private units of apartment houses and other multiple dwellings, actually used for residential purposes, which residences are separately metered or measured, regardless of the fact that a person other than the resident is contractually bound to the supplier for the charges, actually pays the charges, or is billed for the charges. The use of electricity, natural gas, or water in hotel or motel units does not constitute residential use.

Section 2.3. Power to Tax; Limitation; Sale or Transfer of Immovable Property

No new tax or fee upon the sale or transfer of immovable property, including documentary transaction taxes or fees, or any other tax or fee, shall be levied by the state of Louisiana, by a political subdivision whose boundaries are coterminous with those of the state, or by a political subdivision, as defined in Article VI, Section 44(2) of this constitution after November 30, 2011. A documentary transaction is any transaction pursuant to any instrument, act, writing, or document which transfers or conveys immovable property. Fees for the cost of recordation, filing, or maintenance of documents, or records effectuating the sale or transfer of immovable property, impact fees for development of property, annual parcel fees, and ad valorem taxes shall not be considered taxes or fees upon the sale or transfer of immovable property.

Section 3. Collection of Taxes

(A) The legislature shall prohibit the issuance of process to restrain the collection of any tax. It shall provide a complete and adequate remedy for the prompt recovery of an illegal tax paid by a taxpayer.

(B)(1) Notwithstanding any contrary provision of this constitution, sales and use taxes levied by political subdivisions shall be collected by a single collector for each parish. On or before July 1, 1992, all political subdivisions within each parish which levy a sales and use tax shall agree between and among themselves to provide for the collection of such taxes by a single collector or a central collection commission. The legislature, by general law, shall provide for the collection of sales and use taxes, levied by political subdivisions, by a central collection commission in those parishes where a single collector or a central collection commission has not been established by July 1, 1992.

(2) The legislature, by local law enacted by two-thirds of the elected members of each house of the legislature, may establish an alternate method of providing for a single collector or a central collection commission in each parish.

(3) Except when authorized by the unanimous agreement of all political subdivisions levying a sales and use tax within a parish, only those political subdivisions levying a sales and use tax shall be authorized to act as the single collector or participate on any commission established for the collection of such taxes.

(4) The legislature shall provide for the prompt remittance to the political subdivisions identified on the taxpayers' returns of funds collected pursuant to the provisions of this Paragraph by a single collector or under any other centralized collection arrangement.

(5) The provisions of this Paragraph shall not apply in those parishes which have a single collector or a centralized collection arrangement as of July 1, 1992.

Section 4. Income Tax; Severance Tax; Political Subdivisions

(A) Income Tax

Equal and uniform taxes may be levied on net incomes, and these taxes may be graduated according to the amount of net income. However, the state individual and joint income tax schedule of rates and brackets shall never exceed the rates and brackets set forth in Title 47 of the Louisiana Revised Statutes on January 1, 2003.

Federal income taxes paid shall be allowed as a deductible item in computing state income taxes for the same period.

(B) Severance Tax

Taxes may be levied on natural resources severed from the soil or water, to be paid proportionately by the owners thereof at the time of severance. Natural resources may be classified for the purpose of taxation. Such taxes may be predicated upon either the quantity or value of the products at the time and place of severance. No further or additional tax or license shall be levied or imposed upon oil, gas, or sulfur leases or rights. No additional value shall be added to the assessment of land by reason of the presence of oil, gas, or sulfur therein or their production therefrom. However, sulfur in place shall be assessed for ad valorem taxation to the person, firm, or corporation having the right to mine or produce the same in the parish where located, at no more than twice the total assessed value of the physical property subject to taxation, excluding the assessed value of sulfur above ground, as is used in sulfur operations in such parish. Likewise, the severance tax shall be the only tax on timber; however, standing timber shall be liable equally with the land on which it stands for ad valorem taxes levied on the land.

(C) Political Subdivisions; Prohibitions

A political subdivision of the state shall not levy a severance tax, income tax, inheritance tax, or tax on motor fuel.

(D)(1) Severance Tax Allocation

One-third of the sulfur severance tax, but not to exceed one hundred thousand dollars; one-third of the lignite severance tax, but not to exceed one hundred thousand dollars; one-fifth of the severance tax on all natural resources, other than sulfur, lignite, or timber, but not to exceed five hundred thousand dollars; and three-fourths of the timber severance tax shall be remitted to the governing authority of the parish in which severance or production occurs.

(2) Effective July 1, 1999, one-third of the sulfur severance tax, but not to exceed one hundred thousand dollars; one-third of the lignite severance tax, but not to exceed one hundred thousand dollars; one-fifth of the severance tax on all natural resources, other than sulfur, lignite, or timber, but not to exceed seven hundred fifty thousand dollars; and three-fourths of the timber severance tax shall be remitted to the governing authority of the parish in which severance or production occurs.

(3) Effective July 1, 2007, one-fifth of the severance tax on all natural resources other than sulfur, lignite, or timber shall be remitted to the governing authority of the parish in which severance or production occurs. The initial maximum amount remitted to the parish in which severance or production occurs shall not exceed eight hundred fifty thousand dollars. The maximum amount remitted shall be increased each July first, beginning in 2008, by an amount equal to the average annual increase in the Consumer Price Index for all urban consumers, as published by the United States Department of Labor, for the previous calendar year, as calculated and adopted by the Revenue Estimating Conference.

(4) Effective April 1, 2012, the provisions of this Subparagraph shall be implemented if and when the last official forecast of revenues adopted for a fiscal year before the start of that fiscal year contains an estimate of severance tax revenues derived from natural resources other than sulfur, lignite, or timber in an amount which exceeds the actual severance tax revenues from such natural resources collected in Fiscal Year 2008-2009. Upon the adoption of such official forecast, the Revenue Estimating Conference shall certify that the requirements for the implementation of the provisions contained in this Subparagraph have been met. In such event, the following distributions and allocations of severance tax revenues and other revenues provided in this Subparagraph shall be effective and implemented for the fiscal year for which the official forecast was adopted, and each year thereafter. The legislature shall provide by law for the administrative procedures necessary to change the severance tax allocation to parishes from a calendar year basis to a fiscal year basis.

(a) Remittance to parishes

(i) In the first fiscal year of implementation of this Subparagraph, the maximum amount of severance tax on all natural resources other than sulfur, lignite, or timber which is remitted to the parish in which severance or production occurs shall not exceed one million eight hundred fifty thousand dollars. For all subsequent fiscal years, the maximum amount remitted to a parish shall not exceed two million eight hundred fifty thousand dollars.

(ii) On July first of each year the maximum amount remitted to the parish in which severance or production occurs, as provided in Item (i) of this Sub-sub-paragraph, shall be increased by an amount equal to the average annual increase in the Consumer Price Index for all urban consumers for the previous calendar year, as published by the United States Department of Labor, which amount shall be as calculated and adopted by the Revenue Estimating Conference.

(iii) Of the total amount of severance tax revenues remitted in a fiscal year to a parish governing authority pursuant to the provisions of this Subparagraph, any portion which is in excess of the amount of such tax revenues remitted to that parish in Fiscal Year 2011-2012 shall be known as "excess severance tax". At least fifty percent of the excess severance tax received by a parish governing authority in a fiscal year shall be expended within the parish in the same manner and for the same purposes as monies received by the parish from the Parish Transportation Fund.

(b) Deposit into the Atchafalaya Basin Conservation Fund

(i) Notwithstanding any other provision of this constitution to the contrary, after allocation of money to the Bond Security and Redemption Fund as provided in Article VII, Section 9(B) of this constitution, and after satisfying the required allocations in Sub-sub-paragraph (a) of this Subparagraph, Paragraph (E) of this Section, and Article VII, Sections 10-A and 10.2 of this constitution, an amount equal to fifty percent of the revenues received from severance taxes and royalties on state lands in the Atchafalaya Basin, but not to exceed ten million dollars each fiscal year, shall be deposited by the treasurer into the Atchafalaya Basin Conservation Fund, hereinafter referred to as the "fund", which is hereby created as a special fund in the state treasury. The monies in the fund shall be invested by the treasurer in the manner provided by law, and interest earned on the investment of these monies shall be deposited in and credited to the fund. All unexpended or unencumbered monies remaining in the fund at the end of the fiscal year shall remain in the fund.

(ii) The monies in the fund shall be used exclusively for projects contained in the state or federal Basin master plans or an annual Basin plan developed and approved by the advisory or approval board created by law specifically for that purpose, or to provide match for the Atchafalaya Basin Floodway System, Louisiana Project. Each year's plan for the expenditure of monies appropriated from the fund shall be subject to the approval of the appropriate subject matter committees of the legislature.

(iii) Of the monies appropriated in any fiscal year, eighty-five percent shall be used for water management, water quality, or access projects, and the remaining fifteen percent may be used to complete ongoing projects and for projects that are in accordance with the mission statement of the state master plan. However, no more than five percent of the monies appropriated in any fiscal year may be used for the operational costs of the program or the department.

(E) Royalties Allocation

One-tenth of the royalties from mineral leases on state-owned land, lake and river beds and other water bottoms belonging to the state or the title to which is in the public for mineral development shall be remitted to the governing authority of the parish in which severance or production occurs. A parish governing authority may fund these royalties into general obligation bonds of the parish in accordance with law. The provisions of this Paragraph shall not apply to properties comprising the Russell Sage Wildlife and Game Refuge.

Section 4.1. Cigarette Tax Rates

To ensure revenue for the dedication provided for in Article VII, Section 10.8(C)(2)(c) of this constitution, the rate of the tax levied pursuant to R.S. 47:841(B)(3) shall not be less than the rate set forth in that provision as it exists on January 1, 2012.

Section 5. Motor Vehicle License Tax

The legislature shall impose an annual license tax of not more than one dollar per each one thousand dollars of actual value on automobiles for private use based on the actual value of the vehicle, as provided by law. However, the annual license tax shall not be less than ten dollars per automobile for private use. On other motor vehicles, the legislature shall impose an annual license tax based upon carrying capacity, horsepower, value, weight, or any of these. After satisfying the requirements of Section 9(B) of this Article, and after satisfying pledges respecting that portion of the revenues attributable to the tax rates in effect at the time of such pledges for the payment of obligations for bonds or other evidences of indebtedness and upon the creation of a Transportation Trust Fund within this constitution, the revenues from the license tax on automobiles for private use shall be deposited therein. In the event no such trust fund is established in this constitution, the revenues shall be used exclusively and solely as provided by law for the construction, maintenance, and safety of the federal and state system of roads and bridges, for the parish and municipal road systems, for the operations of the office of state police, Department of Public Safety and Corrections or its successor, and for the payment of any obligation for bonds issued or indebtedness incurred in connection with any of the foregoing, which bonds may be issued as revenue bonds under Article VII, Section 6(C) of this constitution, subject to existing pledges only as to that portion of the tax collections attributable to the rates in effect at the time of such pledges for the payment of any obligations for bonds or other evidences of indebtedness outstanding on the effective date of this Section. No parish or municipality may impose a license fee on motor vehicles.

Section 6. State Debt; Full Faith and Credit Obligations

(A) Authorization

Unless otherwise authorized by this constitution, the state shall have no power, directly or indirectly, or through any state board, agency, commission, or otherwise, to incur debt or issue bonds except by law enacted by two-thirds of the elected members of each house of the legislature. The debt may be incurred or the bonds issued only if the funds are to be used to repel invasion; suppress insurrection; provide relief from natural catastrophes; refund outstanding indebtedness at the same or a lower effective interest rate; or make capital improvements, but only in accordance with a comprehensive capital budget, which the legislature shall adopt.

(B) Capital Improvements

(1) If the purpose is to make capital improvements, the nature and location and, if more than one project, the amount allocated to each and the order of priority shall be stated in the comprehensive capital budget which the legislature adopts.

(2) The estimated amount of debt service to be paid for capital improvements for the next fiscal year shall be stated as a separate item and by budget unit in the budget estimate required to be submitted by the governor in accordance with Section 11 of this Article.

(C) Full Faith and Credit

The full faith and credit of the state shall be pledged to the repayment of all bonds or other evidences of indebtedness issued by the state directly or through any state board, agency, or commission pursuant to the provisions of Paragraphs (A) and (B) hereof. The full faith and credit of the state is not hereby pledged to the repayment of bonds of a levee district, political subdivision, or local public agency. In addition, any state board, agency, or commission authorized by law to issue bonds, in the manner so authorized and with the approval of the State Bond Commission or its successor, may issue bonds which are payable from fees, rates, rentals, tolls, charges, grants, or other receipts or income derived by or in connection with an undertaking, facility, project, or any combination thereof, without a pledge of the full faith and credit of the state. Such revenue bonds may, but are not required to, be issued in accordance with the provisions of Paragraphs (A) and (B) hereof. If issued other than as provided in Paragraphs (A) and (B), such revenue bonds shall not carry the pledge of the full faith and credit of the state and the issuance of the bonds shall not constitute the incurring of state debt under this constitution. The rights granted to deep-water port commissions or deep-water port, harbor, and terminal districts under this constitution shall not be impaired by this Section.

(D) Referendum

The legislature, by law enacted by two-thirds of the elected members of each house, may propose a statewide public referendum to authorize incurrence of debt for any purpose for which the legislature is not herein authorized to incur debt.

(E) Exception

Nothing in this Section shall apply to any levee district, political subdivision, or local public agency unless the full faith and credit of the state is pledged to the payment of the bonds of the levee district, political subdivision, or local public agency.

(F) Limitation

(1) The legislature shall provide for the determination of a limit to the amount of net state tax supported debt which may be issued by the state in any fiscal year. Net state tax supported debt shall be defined by law. When enacted, such definition shall not be changed except by specific legislative instrument which receives a favorable vote of two-thirds of the elected members of each house of the legislature. The limitation shall be established so that by Fiscal Year 2003-2004 and thereafter the amount necessary to service outstanding net state tax supported debt shall not exceed six percent of the estimate of money to be received by the state general fund and dedicated funds contained in the official forecast adopted by the Revenue Estimating Conference at its first meeting after the beginning of each fiscal year and any other money required to be included in the estimate by this Paragraph. In making such estimate, the conference shall include all amounts which are to be used to service net state tax supported debt. For purposes of this Paragraph, servicing outstanding net state tax supported debt includes payments of principal, interest, and sinking fund requirements. The limitation established pursuant to this Paragraph shall not be construed to prevent the payment of debt service on net state tax supported debt.

(2) The limitation established pursuant to this Paragraph may be changed by passage of a specific legislative instrument by a favorable vote of two-thirds of the elected members of each house of the legislature. The limitation may be exceeded by passage of a specific legislative instrument for a project or related projects by a favorable vote of two-thirds of the elected members of each house of the legislature, provided that any debt service payment required for such projects shall, once bonds have been issued in connection therewith, not be impaired in any future year by application of this limitation. The limitation established pursuant to this Subparagraph shall be deemed to be increased as necessary to accommodate any projects approved to exceed this limit if approved as provided in this Paragraph, but only as long as there are bonds outstanding for the projects.

(3) Except as provided in Subparagraph (2) of this Paragraph, the State Bond Commission shall not approve the issuance of any net state tax supported debt, the debt service requirement of which would cause the limit herein established to be exceeded.

Section 7. State Debt; Interim Emergency Board

(A) Composition

The Interim Emergency Board is created. It shall be composed of the governor, lieutenant governor, state treasurer, presiding officer of each house of the legislature, chairman of the Senate Finance Committee, and chairman of the House Appropriations Committee, or their designees.

(B) Powers

Between sessions of the legislature, when the board by majority vote determines that an emergency or impending flood emergency exists, it may appropriate from the state general fund or borrow on the full faith and credit of the state an amount to meet the emergency. The appropriation may be made or the indebtedness incurred only for a purpose for which the legislature may appropriate funds and then only after the board obtains, as provided by law, the written consent of two-thirds of the elected members of each house of the legislature. For the purposes of this Paragraph, an emergency is an event or occurrence not reasonably anticipated by the legislature and an impending flood emergency shall be an anticipated situation which endangers an existing flood protection structure. The appropriation or indebtedness incurred for an impending flood emergency shall not exceed two hundred fifty thousand dollars for any one event or occurrence. For an impending emergency to qualify for funding it must be determined as such by the United States Army Corp of Engineers or the United States Coast Guard. Total funding for such impending emergencies shall not exceed twenty-five percent of the funds annually available to the Interim Emergency Board.

(C) Limits

The aggregate of indebtedness outstanding at any one time and the amount appropriated from the state general fund for the current fiscal year under the authority of this Section shall not exceed one-tenth of one percent of total state revenue receipts for the previous fiscal year.

(D) Allocation

An amount sufficient to pay indebtedness incurred during the preceding fiscal year under the authority of this Section is allocated, as a first priority, each year from the state general fund.

Section 8. State Bond Commission

(A) Creation

The State Bond Commission is created. Its membership and authority shall be determined by law.

(B) Approval of Bonds

No bonds or other obligations shall be issued or sold by the state, directly or through any state board, agency, or commission, or by any political subdivision of the state, unless prior written approval of the bond commission is obtained.

(C) Contesting State Bonds

Bonds, notes, certificates, or other evidences of indebtedness of the state (hereafter referred to as "bonds") shall not be invalid because of any irregularity or defect in the proceedings or in the issuance and sale thereof and shall be incontestable in the hands of a bona fide purchaser or holder. The issuing agency, after authorizing the issuance of bonds by resolution, shall publish once in the official journal of the state, as provided by law, a notice of intention to issue the bonds. The notice shall include a description of the bonds and the security therefor. Within thirty days after the publication, any person in interest may contest the legality of the resolution, any provision of the bonds to be issued pursuant to it, the provisions securing the bonds, and the validity of all other provisions and proceedings relating to the authorization and issuance of the bonds. If no action or proceeding is instituted within the thirty days, no person may contest the validity of the bonds, the provisions of the resolution pursuant to which the bonds were issued, the security of the bonds, or the validity of any other provisions or proceedings relating to their authorization and issuance, and the bonds shall be presumed conclusively to be legal. Thereafter no court shall have authority to inquire into such matters.

Section 9. State Funds

(A) Deposit in State Treasury

All money received by the state or by any state board, agency, or commission shall be deposited immediately upon receipt in the state treasury, except that received:

(1) as a result of grants or donations or other forms of assistance when the terms and conditions thereof or of agreements pertaining thereto require otherwise;

(2) by trade or professional associations;

(3) by the employment security administration fund or its successor;

(4) by retirement system funds;

(5) by state agencies operating under authority of this constitution preponderantly from fees and charges for the shipment of goods in international maritime trade and commerce; and

(6) by a state board, agency, or commission, but pledged by it in connection with the issuance of revenue bonds as provided in Paragraph (C) of Section 6 of this Article, other than any surplus as may be defined in the law authorizing such revenue bonds.

(B) Bond Security and Redemption Fund

Subject to contractual obligations existing on the effective date of this constitution, all state money deposited in the state treasury shall be credited to a special fund designated as the Bond Security and Redemption Fund, except money received as the result of grants or donations or other forms of assistance when the terms and conditions thereof or of agreements pertaining thereto require otherwise. In each fiscal year an amount is allocated from the bond security and redemption fund sufficient to pay all obligations which are secured by the full faith and credit of the state and which become due and payable within the current fiscal year, including principal, interest, premiums, sinking or reserve fund, and other requirements. Thereafter, except as otherwise provided by law, money remaining in the fund shall be credited to the state general fund.

(C) Exception

Nothing in this Section shall apply to a levee district or political subdivision unless the full faith and credit of the state is pledged to the payment of the bonds of the levee district or political subdivision.

Section 10. Expenditure of State Funds

(A) Revenue Estimating Conference

The Revenue Estimating Conference shall be composed of four members: the governor, or his designee, the president of the senate, or his designee, the speaker of the house or his designee, and a faculty member of a university or college in Louisiana who has expertise in forecasting revenues. Changes to the membership beyond the four members shall be made by law enacted by a favorable vote of two-thirds of the elected members of each house.

(B) Official Forecast

The conference shall prepare and publish initial and revised estimates of money to be received by the state general fund and dedicated funds for the current and next fiscal years which are available for appropriation. In each estimate, the conference shall designate the money in the estimate which is recurring and which is nonrecurring. All conference decisions to adopt these estimates shall be by unanimous vote of its members. Changes to the unanimous vote requirement shall be made by law enacted by a favorable vote of two-thirds of the elected members of each house. The most recently adopted estimate of money available for appropriation shall be the official forecast.

(C) Expenditure Limit

(1) The legislature shall provide for the determination of an expenditure limit for each fiscal year to be established during the first quarter of the calendar year for the next fiscal year. However, the expenditure limit for the 1991-1992 Fiscal Year shall be the actual appropriations from the state general fund and dedicated funds for that year except funds allocated by Article VII, Section 4, Paragraphs (D) and (E). For subsequent fiscal years, the limit shall not exceed the expenditure limit for the current fiscal year plus an amount equal to that limit times a positive growth factor. The growth factor is the average annual percentage rate of change of personal income for Louisiana as defined and reported by the United States Department of Commerce for the three calendar years prior to the fiscal year for which the limit is calculated.

(2) The expenditure limit may be changed in any fiscal year by a favorable vote of two-thirds of the elected members of each house. Any such change in the expenditure limit shall be approved by passage of a specific legislative instrument which clearly states the intent to change the limit.

(3) Beginning with the 1995-1996 Fiscal Year, the expenditure limit shall be determined in accordance with the provisions of Paragraph (J) of this Section. The redetermination of the expenditure limit for each fiscal year from the 1991-1992 Fiscal Year through the 1994-1995 Fiscal Year shall only be used in computing the expenditure limit for the 1995-1996 Fiscal Year and shall not affect the expenditure limit already computed in accordance with this Paragraph for such fiscal years.

(4) The provisions of this Paragraph shall not apply to or affect funds allocated by Article VII, Section 4, Paragraphs (D) and (E).

(D) Appropriations

(1) Except as otherwise provided by this constitution, money shall be drawn from the state treasury only pursuant to an appropriation made in accordance with law. Appropriations from the state general fund and dedicated funds except funds allocated by Article VII, Section 4, Paragraphs (D) and (E) shall not exceed the expenditure limit for the fiscal year.

(2) Except as otherwise provided in this constitution, the appropriation or allocation of any money designated in the official forecast as nonrecurring shall be made only for the following purposes:

(a) Retiring or for the defeasance of bonds in advance or in addition to the existing amortization requirements of the state.

(b)(i) Providing for payments against the unfunded accrued liability of the public retirement systems which are in addition to any payments required for the annual amortization of the unfunded accrued liability of the public retirement systems, as required by Article X, Section 29(E)(2)(c) of this constitution; however, any such payments to the public retirement systems shall not be used, directly or indirectly, to fund cost-of-living increases for such systems.

(ii) For Fiscal Years 2013-2014 and 2014-2015 the legislature shall appropriate no less than five percent of any money designated in the official forecast as nonrecurring to the Louisiana State Employees' Retirement System and the Teachers' Retirement System of Louisiana for application to the balance of the unfunded accrued liability of such systems existing as of June 30, 1988, in proportion to the balance of such unfunded accrued liability of each such system. Any such payments to the public retirement systems shall not be used, directly or indirectly, to fund cost-of-living increases for such systems.

(iii) For Fiscal Year 2015-2016 and every fiscal year thereafter the legislature shall appropriate no less than ten percent of any money designated in the official forecast as nonrecurring to the Louisiana State Employees' Retirement System and the Teachers' Retirement System of Louisiana for application to the balance of the unfunded accrued liability of such systems existing as of June 30, 1988, in proportion to the balance of such unfunded accrued liability of each such system. Any such payments to the public retirement systems shall not be used, directly or indirectly, to fund cost-of-living increases for such systems.

(c) Providing funding for capital outlay projects in the comprehensive state capital budget.

(d) Providing for allocation or appropriation for deposit into the Budget Stabilization Fund established in Article VII, **Section 10.**3 of this constitution.

(e) Providing for allocation or appropriation for deposit into the Coastal Protection and Restoration Fund established in Article VII, Section 10.2 of this constitution.

(f) Providing for new highway construction for which federal matching funds are available, without excluding highway projects otherwise eligible as capital projects under other provisions of this constitution.

(3)(a) The legislature shall provide by law for the payment by the state of supplements to the salaries of full-time local law enforcement and fire protection officers of the state. No law shall reduce any payments by the state provided as a supplement to the salaries of full-time local law enforcement and fire protection officers of the state. Beginning with the fiscal year which begins July 1, 2003, the legislature shall appropriate funds sufficient to fully fund the cost of such state supplement to the salaries of fulltime law enforcement and fire protection officers.

(b) For the purposes of this Subparagraph, local law enforcement and fire protection officers shall mean and include the same classes of officers which are eligible for such state salary supplements under the law as of July 1, 2003.

(c) Full funding as required in Sub-sub-paragraph (a) of this Subparagraph shall be equal to the amount which is required to meet the requirements of law.

(d) Neither the governor nor the legislature may reduce an appropriation made pursuant to this Subparagraph except that the governor may reduce such appropriation using means provided in the Act containing the appropriation, provided that two-thirds of the elected members of each house of the legislature consent to any such reduction in writing.

(E) Balanced Budget

Appropriations by the legislature from the state general fund and dedicated funds for any fiscal year except funds allocated by Article VII, Section 4, Paragraphs (D) and (E) shall not exceed the official forecast in effect at the time the appropriations are made.

(F) Projected Deficit

(1) The legislature by law shall establish a procedure to determine if appropriations will exceed the official forecast and an adequate method for adjusting appropriations in order to eliminate a projected deficit. Any law establishing a procedure to determine if appropriations will exceed the official forecast and methods for adjusting appropriations, including any constitutionally protected or mandated allocations or appropriations, once enacted, shall not be changed except by specific legislative instrument which receives a favorable vote of two-thirds of the elected members of each house of the legislature. Notwithstanding the provisions of Article III, Section 2 of this constitution, such law may be introduced and considered in any regular session of the legislature.

(2)(a) Notwithstanding any other provision of this constitution to the contrary, adjustments to any constitutionally protected or mandated allocations or appropriations, and transfer of monies associated with such adjustments, are authorized when state general fund allocations or appropriations have been reduced in an aggregate amount equal to at least seven-tenths of one percent of the total of such allocations and appropriations for a fiscal year. Such adjustments may not exceed five percent of the total appropriation or allocation from a fund for the fiscal year. For purposes of this Sub-sub-paragraph, reductions to expenditures required by Article VIII, Section 13(B) of this constitution shall not exceed one percent and such reductions shall not be applicable to instructional activities included within the meaning of instruction pursuant to the Minimum Foundation

Program formula. Notwithstanding any other provisions of this constitution to the contrary, monies transferred as a result of such budget adjustments are deemed available for appropriation and expenditure in the year of the transfer from one fund to another, but in no event shall the aggregate amount of any transfers exceed the amount of the deficit.

(b) Notwithstanding any other provision of this constitution to the contrary, for the purposes of the budget estimate and enactment of the budget for the next fiscal year, when the official forecast of recurring revenues for the next fiscal year is at least one percent less than the official forecast for the current fiscal year, the following procedure may be employed to avoid a budget deficit in the next fiscal year. An amount not to exceed five percent of the total appropriations or allocations for the current fiscal year from any fund established by law or this constitution shall be available for expenditure in the next fiscal year for a purpose other than as specifically provided by law or this constitution. For the purposes of this Sub-sub-paragraph, an amount not to exceed one percent of the current fiscal year appropriation for expenditures required by Article VIII, Section 13(B) of this constitution shall be available for expenditures for other purposes in the next fiscal year. Notwithstanding any other provisions of this constitution to the contrary, monies made available as authorized under this Sub-sub-paragraph may be transferred to a fund for which revenues have been forecast to be less than the revenues in the current fiscal year for such fund. Monies transferred as a result of the budget actions authorized by this Sub-sub-paragraph are deemed available for appropriation and expenditure, but in no event shall the aggregate amount of any such transfers exceed the amount of the difference between the official forecast for the current fiscal year and the next fiscal year.

(c) The legislature may provide by law for the implementation of the provisions of this Subparagraph.

(3) If within thirty days of the determination that appropriations will exceed the official forecast the necessary adjustments in appropriations are not made to eliminate the projected deficit, the governor shall call a special session of the legislature for this purpose unless the legislature is in regular session. This special session shall commence as soon as possible as allowed by the provisions of this constitution, including but not limited to Article III, Section 2(B).

(4) The provisions of Sub-paragraphs (1) and (2) of this Paragraph shall not be applicable to, nor affect:

(a) The Bond Security and Redemption Fund or any bonds secured thereby, or any other funds pledged as security for bonds or other evidences of indebtedness.

(b) The allocations provided for by Article VII, Section 4(D) and (E) of this constitution.

(c) The contributions made in accordance with Article X, Section 29(E) of this constitution.

(d) The Louisiana Education Quality Trust Fund as defined in Article VII, Section 10.1(A)(1) of this constitution.

(e) The Millennium Trust as provided in Article VII, Section 10.8 of this constitution, except for appropriations from the trust.

(f) Any monies not required to be deposited in the state treasury as provided in Article VII, Section 9 of this constitution.

(g) The Medicaid Trust Fund for the Elderly created under the provisions of R.S. 46:2691 et seq.

(h) The Revenue Stabilization Trust Fund as provided in Article VII, Section 10.15 of this constitution.

(G) Year End Deficit

If a deficit exists in any fund at the end of a fiscal year, that deficit shall be eliminated no later than the end of the next fiscal year.

(H) Publication

The legislature shall have published a regular statement of receipts and expenditures of all state money at intervals of not more than one year.

(I) Public Purpose

No appropriation shall be made except for a public purpose.

(J) Definition of Funds

For the purposes of this Article, the state general fund and dedicated funds shall be all money required to be deposited in the state treasury, except that money the origin of which is:

(1) The federal government.

(2) Self-generated collections by any entity subject to the policy and management authority established by Article VIII, Sections 5 through 7.

(3) A transfer from another state agency, board, or commission.

(4) The provisions of this Paragraph shall not apply to or affect funds allocated by Article VII, Section 4, Paragraphs (D) and (E).

Section 10-A. Wildlife and Fisheries; Conservation Fund

(A) Conservation Fund

Effective July 1, 1988, there shall be established in the state treasury, as a special fund, the Louisiana Wildlife and Fisheries Conservation Fund, hereinafter referred to as the Conservation Fund. Out of the funds remaining in the Bond Security and Redemption Fund after a sufficient amount is allocated from that fund to pay all obligations secured by the full faith and credit of the state which become due and payable within any fiscal year as required by Article VII, Section 9(B) of this constitution, the treasurer shall pay into the Conservation Fund all of the following, except as provided in Article VII, Section 9(A), and except for the amount provided in R.S. 56:10(B)(1)(a) as that provision existed on the effective date of this Section:

(1) All revenue from the types and classes of fees, licenses, permits, royalties, or other revenue paid into the Conservation Fund as provided by law on the effective date of this Section. Such revenue shall be deposited in the Conservation Fund even if the names of such fees, licenses, permits, or other revenues are changed. Any increase in the amount charged for such fees, licenses, permits, royalties, and other revenue, or any new fee, license, permit, royalty, or other revenue, enacted by the legislature after the effective date of this Section, shall be irrevocably dedicated and deposited in the Conservation Fund unless the legislature enacts a law specifically appropriating or dedicating such revenue to another fund or purpose.

(2) The balance remaining on June 30, 1988 in the Conservation Fund established pursuant to R.S. 56:10.

(3) All funds or revenues which may be donated expressly to the Conservation Fund.

(B) The monies in the Conservation Fund shall be appropriated by the legislature to the Department of Wildlife and Fisheries, or its successor, and shall be used solely for the programs and purposes of conservation, protection, preservation, management, and replenishment of the state's natural resources and wildlife, including use for land acquisition or for federal matching fund programs which promote such purposes, and for the operation and administration of the Department and the Wildlife and Fisheries Commission, or their successors.

(C) All unexpended and unencumbered monies in the Conservation Fund at the end of the fiscal year shall remain in the fund. The monies in the fund shall be invested by the treasurer in the manner provided by law. All interest earned on monies invested by the treasurer shall be deposited in the fund. The treasurer shall prepare and submit to the department on a quarterly basis a printed report showing the amount of money contained in the fund from all sources.

Section 10.1. Quality Trust Fund; Education

(A) Louisiana Education Quality Trust Fund

(1) Effective January 1, 1987, there shall be established in the state treasury as a special permanent trust fund the Louisiana Education Quality Trust Fund, hereinafter referred to as the "Permanent Trust Fund." After allocation of money to the Bond Security and Redemption Fund as provided in Article VII, Section 9(B) of this constitution, and notwithstanding Article XIV, Section 10 of this constitution, the treasurer shall deposit in and credit to the Permanent Trust Fund all money which is received after the first one hundred million dollars from the federal government under Section 1337(g) of Title 43 of the United States Code which is attributable to mineral production activity or leasing activity on the Outer Continental Shelf which has been held in escrow pending a settlement between the United States and the state of Louisiana; twenty-five percent of the recurring revenues received under Section 1337(g) of Title

43 of the United States Code which are attributable to mineral production activity or leasing activity on the Outer Continental Shelf; twenty-five percent of the interest income earned on investment of monies in the Permanent Trust Fund; seventy-five percent of the realized capital gains on investment of the Permanent Trust Fund, unless such percentage is changed by law enacted by two-thirds of the elected members of each house of the legislature; and twenty-five percent of the dividend income earned on investment of the Permanent Trust Fund. No appropriation shall be made from the Permanent Trust Fund. If any such money has been received prior to the effective date of this Section, the treasurer shall transfer from the state general fund to the Permanent Trust Fund on the effective date of this Section an amount of money which shall make the Permanent Trust Fund balance equal to the amount of such money previously received, except for the first one hundred million dollars. After six hundred million dollars has been credited to the Permanent Trust Fund, the sum of fifty million dollars shall be credited to the Coastal Environment Protection Trust Fund, as established in R.S. 30:313, from those monies received from the federal government under Section 1337(g) of Title 43 of the United States Code which is attributable to mineral production activity or leasing activity on the Outer Continental Shelf and which has been held in escrow pending a settlement between the United States and the state of Louisiana; all funds in excess of seven hundred fifty million dollars shall be credited to the Permanent Trust Fund.

(2) After allocation of money to the Bond Security and Redemption Fund as provided in Article VII, Section 9(B) of the constitution, and notwithstanding Article XIV, Section 10 of the constitution, seventy-five percent of the recurring revenues received under Section 1337(g) of Title 43 of the United States Code which are attributable to mineral production activity or leasing activity, and the percent remaining of the realized capital gains and interest income and dividend income earned on investment of the Permanent Trust Fund after the deposit required to the Permanent Trust Fund in Paragraph A(1) of this

Section shall be deposited and credited to a special fund which is hereby created in the state treasury and which shall be known as the Louisiana Quality Education Support Fund, hereinafter referred to as the "Support Fund".

(3) All recurring revenues and interest earnings shall be credited to the respective funds as provided in Sub-paragraphs (1) and (2) above until the balance in the Permanent Trust Fund equals two billion dollars. After the Permanent Trust Fund reaches a balance of two billion dollars, all interest earnings on the Permanent Trust Fund shall be credited to the Support Fund and all recurring revenues shall be credited to the State General Fund.

(B) Investment

The money credited to the Permanent Trust Fund pursuant to Paragraph (A) of this Section shall be permanently credited to the Permanent Trust Fund and shall be invested by the treasurer. Notwithstanding any provision of this constitution or other law to the contrary, a portion of money in the Permanent Trust Fund, not to exceed thirty-five percent, may be invested in stock. The legislature shall provide for procedures for the investment of such monies by law. The treasurer shall contract, subject to the approval of the State Bond Commission, for the management of such investments. The amounts in the Support Fund shall be available for appropriation to pay expenses incurred in the investment and management of the Permanent Trust Fund and for educational purposes only as provided in Paragraphs (C) and (D) of this Section.

(C) Reports; Allocation

(1) The State Board of Elementary and Secondary Education and the Board of Regents shall annually submit to the legislature and the governor not less than sixty days prior to the beginning of each regular session of the legislature a proposed program and budget for the expenditure of the monies in the Support Fund.

Proposals for such expenditures shall be designed to improve the quality of education and shall specifically designate those monies to be used for administrative costs, as defined and authorized by law.

(2) Except for appropriations to pay expenses incurred in the investment and management of the Permanent Trust Fund, the legislature shall appropriate from the Support Fund only for educational purposes provided in Paragraph (D) of this Section and shall appropriate fifty percent of the available funds for higher educational purposes and fifty percent for elementary and secondary educational purposes. Those monies to be used for administrative costs shall be expended for such purposes only if so approved and appropriated by the legislature.

(3) The legislature shall appropriate the total amount intended for higher educational purposes to the Board of Regents and the total amount intended for elementary and secondary educational purposes to the State Board of Elementary and Secondary Education which boards shall allocate the monies so appropriated to the programs as previously approved by the legislature.

(4) The monies appropriated by the legislature and disbursed from the Support Fund shall not displace, replace, or supplant appropriations from the general fund for elementary and secondary education, including implementing the Minimum Foundation Program, or displace, replace, or supplant funding for higher education. For elementary and secondary education and for higher education, this Paragraph shall mean that no appropriation for any fiscal year from the Support Fund shall be made for any purpose for which a general fund appropriation was made in the previous year unless the total appropriations for that fiscal year from the state general fund for such purpose exceed general fund appropriations for the previous year. This Paragraph shall in no way limit general fund appropriations in excess of the minimum amounts herein established.

(D) Disbursement; Higher Education and Elementary and Secondary Education

(1) The treasurer shall disburse not more than fifty percent of the monies in the Support Fund as that money is appropriated by the legislature and allocated by the Board of Regents for any or all of the following higher educational purposes to enhance economic development: (a) The carefully defined research efforts of public and private universities in Louisiana. (b) The endowment of chairs for eminent scholars. (c) The enhancement of the quality of academic, research, or agricultural departments or units within a community college, college, or university. These funds shall not be used for athletic purposes or programs. students.

(2) The treasurer shall disburse not more than fifty percent of the monies in the Support Fund as that money is appropriated by the legislature and allocated by the State Board of Elementary and Secondary Education for any or all of the following elementary and secondary educational purposes:

(a) To provide compensation to city or parish school board professional instructional employees.

(b) To insure an adequate supply of superior textbooks, library books, equipment, and other instructional materials.

(c) To fund exemplary programs in elementary and secondary schools designed to improve elementary or secondary student academic achievement or vocational-technical skill.

(d) To fund carefully defined research efforts, including pilot programs, designed to improve elementary and secondary student academic achievement.

(e) To fund school remediation programs and preschool programs.

(f) To fund the teaching of foreign languages in elementary and secondary schools.

(g) To fund an adequate supply of teachers by providing scholarships or stipends to prospective teachers in academic or vocational-technical areas where there is a critical teacher shortage.

Section 10.2. Coastal Protection and Restoration Fund

(A) There shall be established in the state treasury the Coastal Protection and Restoration Fund to provide a dedicated, recurring source of revenues for the development and implementation of a program to protect and restore Louisiana's coastal area. Of revenues received in each fiscal year by the state as a result of the production of or exploration for minerals, hereinafter referred to as mineral revenues from severance taxes, royalty payments, bonus payments, or rentals, and excluding such revenues received by the state as a result of grants or donations when the terms or conditions thereof require otherwise, the treasurer shall make the following allocations:

(1) To the Bond Security and Redemption Fund as provided in Article VII, Section 9(B) of this constitution.

(2) To the political subdivisions of the state as provided in Article VII, Sections 4(D) and (E) of this constitution.

(3) As provided by the requirements of Article VII, Sections 10-A and 10.1 of this constitution.

(B)(1) After making the allocations provided for in Paragraph (A), the treasurer shall then deposit in and credit to the Coastal Protection and Restoration Fund any amount of mineral revenues that may be necessary to insure that a total of five million dollars is deposited into such fund for the fiscal year from this source; provided that the balance of the fund which consists of mineral revenues from severance taxes, royalty payments, bonus payments, or rentals shall not exceed an amount provided by law, but in no event shall the amount provided by law be less than five hundred million dollars.

(2) After making the allocations and deposits provided for in Paragraphs (A) and (B)(1) of this Section, the treasurer shall deposit in and credit to the Coastal Protection and Restoration Fund as follows:

(a) Ten million dollars of the mineral revenues in excess of six hundred million dollars which remain after the allocations provided for in Paragraph (A) are made by the treasurer.

(b) Ten million dollars of the mineral revenues in excess of six hundred fifty million dollars which remain after the allocations provided in Paragraph (A) are made by the treasurer. However, the balance of the fund which consists of mineral revenues from severance taxes, royalty payments, bonus payments, or rentals shall not exceed an amount provided by law, but in no event shall the amount provided by law be less than five hundred million dollars.

(C) The money in the fund shall be invested as provided by law and any earnings realized on investment of money in the fund shall be deposited in and credited to the fund. Money from other sources, such as donations, appropriations, or dedications, may be deposited in and credited to the fund; however, the balance of the fund which consists of mineral revenues from severance taxes, royalty payments, bonus payments, or rentals shall not exceed an amount provided by law, but in no event shall the amount provided by law be less than five hundred million dollars. Any unexpended money remaining in the fund at the end of the fiscal year shall be retained in the fund.

(D) The money in the fund may be appropriated for purposes consistent with the Coastal Protection Plan developed by the Coastal Protection and Restoration Authority, or its successor. No appropriation shall be made from the fund inconsistent with the purposes of the plan.

(E)(1) Subject to Article VII, Sections 9(B) and 10.1 of this constitution, in each fiscal year, the federal revenues that are received by the state generated from Outer Continental Shelf oil and gas activity and eligible, as provided by federal law, to be used for the purposes of this Paragraph shall be deposited and credited by the treasurer to the Coastal Protection and Restoration Fund.

(2) Federal revenues credited to the Coastal Protection and Restoration Fund pursuant to this Paragraph shall be used only for the purposes of coastal protection, including conservation, coastal restoration, hurricane protection, and infrastructure directly impacted by coastal wetland losses.

(3) The fund balance limitations provided for in Paragraph (B) of this Section relative to the mineral revenues deposited to this fund shall not apply to revenues deposited pursuant to the provisions of this Paragraph.

(F)(1) Notwithstanding the provisions of Article VII, Section 10, Article VII, Section 10.3, Article VII, Section 10.8, or any other provision of this constitution to the contrary, if, after July 1, 2006, the state securitizes any portion of the revenues received from the Master Settlement Agreement executed November 23, 1998, and approved by Consent Decree and Final Judgment entered in the case "Richard P. Ieyoub, Attorney General, ex rel. State of Louisiana v. Philip Morris, Incorporated, et al.," bearing Number 98-6473 on the docket of the Fourteenth Judicial District for the parish of Calcasieu, state of Louisiana, the treasurer shall transfer to the fund established in Paragraph A of this Section twenty percent in the aggregate of the revenues received as a result of the securitization occurring after July 1, 2006.

(2) The legislature may appropriate up to twenty percent of the funds deposited into the fund pursuant to Subparagraph (1) of this Paragraph to the Barrier Island Stabilization and Preservation

Fund to be used for purposes of the Louisiana Coastal Wetlands Conservation and Restoration Program.

(3) The fund balance limitations provided for in Paragraph (B) of this Section relative to the mineral revenues deposited to this fund shall not apply to revenues deposited pursuant to the provisions of this Paragraph.

Section 10.3. Budget Stabilization Fund

(A) There is hereby established in the state treasury a Budget Stabilization Fund hereinafter referred to as the fund. Money shall be deposited in the fund as follows:

(1) All money available for appropriation from the state general fund and dedicated funds in excess of the expenditure limit, except funds allocated by Article VII, Section 4, Paragraphs (D) and (E), shall be deposited in the fund.

(2)(a) All revenues received in each fiscal year by the state in excess of seven hundred fifty million dollars, hereinafter referred to as the base, as a result of the production of or exploration for minerals, hereinafter referred to as mineral revenues, including severance taxes, royalty payments, bonus payments, or rentals, and excluding such revenues designated as nonrecurring pursuant to Article VII, Section 10(B) of the constitution, any such revenues received by the state as a result of grants or donations when the terms or conditions thereof require otherwise, and revenues derived from any tax on the transportation of minerals, shall be deposited in the fund after the following allocations of said mineral revenues have been made: (i) To the Bond Security and Redemption Fund as provided by Article VII, Section 9 (B) of this constitution. (ii) To the political subdivisions of the state as provided in Article VII, Sections 4 (D) and (E) of this constitution. (iii) As provided by the requirements of Article VII, Section 10-A and 10.1 of this constitution.

(b) The base may be increased every ten years beginning in the year 2000 by a law enacted by two-thirds of the elected members of each house of the legislature. Any such increase shall not exceed fifty percent in the aggregate of the increase in the consumer price index for the immediately preceding ten years.

(3) Twenty-five percent of any money designated in the official forecast as nonrecurring as provided in Article VII, Section 10(D)(2) of this constitution shall be deposited in and credited to the fund.

(4) Any money appropriated to the fund by the legislature including any appropriation to the fund from money designated in the official forecast as provided in Article VII, Section 10(D)(2) of this constitution shall be deposited in the fund.

(B) Money in the fund shall be invested as provided by law. Earnings realized in each fiscal year on the investment of monies in the fund shall be deposited to the credit of the fund. All unexpended and unencumbered monies in the fund at the end of the fiscal year shall remain in the fund.

(C) The money in the fund shall not be available for appropriation or use except under the following conditions:

(1) If the official forecast of recurring money for the next fiscal year is less than the official forecast of recurring money for the current fiscal year, the difference, not to exceed one-third of the fund shall be incorporated into the next year's official forecast only after the consent of two-thirds of the elected members of each house of the legislature. If the legislature is not in session, the two-thirds requirement may be satisfied upon obtaining the written consent of two-thirds of the elected members of each house of the legislature in a manner provided by law.

(2) If a deficit for the current fiscal year is projected due to a decrease in the official forecast, an amount equal to one-third of the fund not to exceed the projected deficit may be appropriated after the consent of two-thirds of the elected members of each house of the legislature. Between sessions of the legislature the appropriation may be made only after the written consent of two-thirds of the elected members of each house of the legislature.

(3) In no event shall the amount included in the official forecast for the next fiscal year plus the amount appropriated in the current fiscal year exceed one-third of the fund balance at the beginning of the current fiscal year.

(4) No appropriation or deposit to the fund shall be made if such appropriation or deposit would cause the balance in the fund to exceed four percent of total state revenue receipts for the previous fiscal year.

Section 10.4. Higher Education Louisiana Partnership Fund; Program

(A) Higher Education Louisiana Partnership Fund

(1) There is hereby established a special fund in the state treasury to be known as the Higher Education Louisiana Partnership Fund, hereinafter referred to as the "fund", consisting of monies appropriated annually by the legislature, grants, gifts, and donations received by the state for the purposes of this Section, and other revenues as may be provided by law; provided that no such monies shall come from the allocations provided in Article VII, Section 4, Paragraphs (D) and (E) of this constitution.

(2) All unexpended and unencumbered monies in the Higher Education Louisiana Partnership Fund at the end of a fiscal year shall remain in such fund and be available for appropriation in the next fiscal year. The monies in the fund shall be invested by the state treasurer in accordance with state law, and interest earned on the investment of these monies shall be credited to the fund, after compliance with the requirements of Article VII, Section 9(B) of the Constitution of Louisiana, relative to the Bond Security and Redemption Fund.

(B) Higher Education Louisiana Partnership Program.

(1) Upon appropriation by the legislature, the monies in the fund shall be divided into matching grants for the Higher Education Louisiana Partnership Program which shall be administered by the Board of Regents. The Board of Regents may allocate program funds to each public or independent institution of higher education on a one to one and one-half matching basis or one twenty thousand dollar state matching grant for each thirty thousand dollars raised specifically for the purposes of participation in the Higher Education Louisiana Partnership Program by the institutions of higher education from private sources. The state matching portion shall be allocated by the Board of Regents only after it determines that an eligible institution has accumulated not less than the minimum required amount from private sources for the purposes of the Higher Education Louisiana Partnership Program.

(2)(a) No public institution of higher education shall be eligible in any given fiscal year to receive a share of program funds which is greater than that institution's proportion of the full-time equivalent number of students enrolled in public higher education in the state.

(b) No independent institution of higher education shall be eligible in any given fiscal year to receive a share of program funds which is greater than that institution's proportion of the full-time equivalent number of students enrolled in independent institutions of higher education in the state.

(c) However, if there are monies which have been appropriated to the fund but remain on March first of any fiscal year unallocated to any matching grant, then any participating institution of higher education which has raised the required funds from private sources may apply for and be awarded the number of additional matching grants for which unallocated funding is available and which the institution is able to match. Provided however, that no participating institution shall receive more than fifty percent of available funds in any fiscal year.

(d) However, the share of the program funds received annually by independent institutions of higher education shall not exceed fifteen percent in the aggregate of the total amount of program funds available for matching grants under this program.

(3) State matching funds shall be applied only to private source funds contributed after July 1, 1991, and pledged for the purposes of this Section as certified by the Board of Regents. Pledged contributions shall not be eligible for state matching funds prior to their actual collection.

(4) Each institution of higher education may establish its own Higher Education Louisiana Partnership Program fund as a depository for private contributions and state matching funds as provided herein. The state matching funds allocated by the Board of Regents shall be transferred to an institution upon notification that the institution has received and deposited the necessary private contributions in its own Higher Education Louisiana Partnership Program fund.

(5) Each institution of higher education, under the supervision and management of its board, shall have the responsibility for the administration of the Higher Education Louisiana Partnership Program at that institution and for maintenance and investment of its fund. The institution shall be responsible for soliciting and receiving gifts from private sources to be used for the purposes of this Section.

(6) State matching grants from funds allocated for the Higher Education Louisiana Partnership Program may be made for the purposes of endowed professorships totaling one hundred thousand dollars or more; endowed undergraduate scholarships totaling fifty thousand dollars or more; library acquisitions, laboratory enhancement, or research and instructional equipment acquisitions totaling fifty thousand dollars or more; or facilities construction or renovations totaling one hundred thousand dollars or more.

(7) The monies appropriated by the legislature and disbursed from the Higher Education Louisiana Partnership Fund shall not displace, replace, or supplant appropriations for higher education from the general fund or from bond proceeds. This shall mean that no disbursement from the fund for a current fiscal year shall be made for any higher education purpose for which an appropriation was made the previous year from the general fund or from bond proceeds unless the total appropriations for the current fiscal year for higher education from the state general fund or from bond proceeds exceed general fund appropriations or bond proceeds appropriations for higher education for the previous year. This requirement shall in no way limit appropriations from the general fund or from bond proceeds in excess of the minimum amounts herein established.

(C) Implementation

The legislature shall provide for the implementation of this Section.

Section 10.5. Mineral Revenue Audit and Settlement Fund Section

(A) There shall be established in the state treasury the Mineral Revenue Audit and Settlement Fund, hereinafter referred to as the "fund". Of revenues received in each fiscal year by the state through settlements or judgments which equal, in both principal and interest, five million dollars or more for each such settlement or judgment, resulting from underpayment to the state of severance taxes, royalty payments, bonus payments, or rentals, the treasurer shall make the following allocations as required:

(1) To the Bond Security and Redemption Fund as provided in Article VII, Section 9(B) of this constitution.

(2) To the political subdivisions of the state as provided in Article VII, Section 4(D) and (E) of this constitution.

(3) As provided by the requirements of Article VII, Sections 10-A, 10.1, 10.2, and 10.3 of this constitution.

(B) After making the allocations provided for in Paragraph (A), the treasurer shall then deposit in and credit to the Mineral Revenue Audit and Settlement Fund any such remaining revenues. Any revenues deposited in and credited to the fund shall be considered mineral revenues from severance taxes, royalty payments, bonus payments, or rentals for purposes of determining deposits and credits to be made in and to the Coastal Protection and Restoration Fund as provided in Article VII, Section 10.2 of this constitution. Any revenues deposited in and credited to the fund shall not be considered mineral revenues for purposes of the Budget Stabilization Fund as provided in Article VII, Section 10.3 of this constitution. Money in the fund shall be invested as provided by law. The earnings realized in each fiscal year on the investment of monies in the Mineral Revenue Audit and Settlement Fund shall be deposited in and credited to the Mineral Revenue Audit and Settlement Fund.

(C) After making the allocations provided for in Paragraph (A), the treasurer shall credit thirty-five million dollars to the Coastal Protection and Restoration Fund, and thereafter any monies credited to the fund in any fiscal year may be annually appropriated by the legislature only for the purposes of retirement in advance of maturity through redemption, purchase, or repayment of debt of the state, pursuant to a plan proposed by the State Bond Commission to maximize the savings to the state; for payments against the unfunded accrued liability of the public retirement systems which are in addition to any payments required for the annual amortization of the unfunded accrued liability of the public retirement systems, required by Article X, Section 29 of this constitution; however, any such payment to the public retirement systems shall not be used, directly or indirectly, to fund cost-of-living increases for such systems; and for deposit in the Coastal Protection and Restoration Fund.

Section 10.6. Oilfield Site Restoration Fund

(A) Oilfield Site Restoration Fund

Effective January 4, 1996, there shall be established in the state treasury, as a special fund, the Oilfield Site Restoration Fund, hereinafter referred to as the restoration fund. Out of the funds remaining in the Bond Security and Redemption Fund after a sufficient amount is allocated from that fund to pay all obligations secured by the full faith and credit of the state which become due and payable within any fiscal year as required by Article VII, Section 9(B) of this constitution, the treasurer shall pay into the restoration fund all of the following:

(1) All revenue from the types and classes of fees, penalties, other revenues, or judgments associated with site cleanup activities paid into the restoration fund as provided by law on the effective date of this Section. Such revenue shall be deposited in the restoration fund even if the names of such fees, other revenues, or penalties are changed. Any increase in the amount charged for such fees, penalties, other revenues, or judgments associated with site cleanup activities enacted by the legislature after the effective date of this Section, for the purpose of orphaned oilfield site restoration shall be irrevocably dedicated and deposited in the restoration fund.

(2) The balance remaining on January 4, 1996 in the Oilfield Site Restoration Fund established by law.

(3) All funds or revenues which may be donated expressly to the restoration fund.

(4) All site-specific trust account funds established by law.

(B) The monies in the restoration fund shall be appropriated by the legislature to the Department of Natural Resources, or its successor, and shall be used solely for the programs and purposes of oilfield site restoration as required by law.

(C) All unexpended and unencumbered monies in the restoration fund at the end of the fiscal year shall remain in the fund. The monies in the fund shall be invested by the treasurer in the manner provided by law. All interest earned on monies invested by the treasurer shall be deposited in the fund. The treasurer shall prepare and submit to the department on a quarterly basis a printed report showing the amount of money contained in the fund from all sources.

(D) The provisions of this Section shall not apply to or affect funds allocated by Article VII, Section 4, Paragraphs (D) and (E).

Section 10.7. Oil Spill Contingency Fund

(A) Oil Spill Contingency Fund

Effective January 4, 1996, there shall be established in the state treasury, as a special fund, the Oil Spill Contingency Fund, hereinafter referred to as the contingency fund. Out of the funds remaining in the Bond Security and Redemption Fund after a sufficient amount is allocated from that fund to pay all obligations secured by the full faith and credit of the state which become due and payable within any fiscal year as required by Article VII, Section 9(B) of this constitution, the treasurer shall pay into the contingency fund all of the following, on the effective date of this Section:

(1) All revenue from the types and classes of fees, taxes, penalties, judgments, reimbursements, charges, and federal funds collected or other revenue paid into the contingency fund as provided by law on the effective date of this Section. Such revenue shall be deposited in the contingency fund even if the names of such fees, taxes, penalties, judgments, reimbursements, charges, and federal funds collected or other revenues are changed. Any increase in the amount charged for such fees, taxes, penalties, judgments, reimbursements, charges, and federal funds collected or other revenue, or any new fees, taxes, penalties, judgments, reimbursements, charges, and federal funds collected or other revenue enacted by the legislature for the purposes of abatement and containment of actual or threatened unauthorized discharges of oil after the effective date of this Section, shall be irrevocably dedicated and deposited in the contingency fund.

(2) The balance remaining on January 4, 1996 in the Oil Spill Contingency Fund established by law.

(3) All funds or revenues which may be donated expressly to the contingency fund.

(B) The monies in the contingency fund shall be appropriated by the legislature to be used solely for the programs and purposes of abatement and containment of actual or threatened unauthorized discharges of oil as provided by law; and for administrative expenses associated with such programs and purposes as provided by law.

(C) All unexpended and unencumbered monies in the contingency fund at the end of the fiscal year shall remain in the fund. The monies in the fund shall be invested by the treasurer in the manner provided by law. All interest earned on monies invested by the treasurer shall be deposited in the fund. The balance of the fund shall not exceed thirty million dollars or otherwise as provided by law.

(D) The provisions of this Section shall not apply to or affect funds allocated by Article VII, Section 4, Paragraphs (D) and (E).

Section 10.8. Millennium Trust

Millennium Trust

(A) Creation

(1) There shall be established in the state treasury as a special permanent trust the "Millennium Trust". After allocation of money to the Bond Security and Redemption Fund as provided in Article VII, Section 9(B) of this constitution, the treasurer shall deposit in and credit to the Millennium Trust certain monies received as a result of the Master Settlement Agreement, hereinafter the "Settlement Agreement", executed November 23, 1998, and approved by Consent Decree and Final Judgment entered in the case "Richard P. Ieyoub, Attorney General, ex rel. State of Louisiana v. Philip Morris, Incorporated, et al.", bearing Number 98-6473 on the docket of the Fourteenth Judicial District for the parish of Calcasieu, state of Louisiana; and all dividend and interest income and all realized capital gains on investment of the monies in the Millennium Trust. The treasurer shall deposit in and credit to the Millennium Trust the following amounts of monies received as a result of the Settlement Agreement:

(a) Fiscal Year 2000-2001, forty-five percent of the total monies received that year.

(b) Fiscal Year 2001-2002, sixty percent of the total monies received that year.

(c) Fiscal Year 2002-2003 and each fiscal year thereafter, seventy-five percent of the total monies received that year. However, beginning in Fiscal Year 2011-2012 after the balance in the Millennium Trust reaches a total of one billion three hundred eighty million dollars, the monies deposited in and credited to the Millennium Trust, received as a result of the Settlement

Agreement, shall be allocated to the various funds within the Millennium Trust as provided in Sub-sub-paragraphs (2)(b), (3)(b), and (4)(b) and (c) of this Paragraph.

(d) For Fiscal Year 2000-2001, Fiscal Year 2001-2002, and Fiscal Year 2002-2003, ten percent of the total monies received in each of those years for credit to the Education Excellence Fund which, notwithstanding the provisions of Subparagraph (C)(1) of this Section, shall be appropriated for the purposes provided in Sub-sub-paragraph (d) of Subparagraph (3) of Paragraph (C) of this Section.

(2)(a) The Health Excellence Fund shall be established as a special fund within the Millennium Trust. The treasurer shall credit to the Health Excellence Fund one-third of the Settlement Agreement proceeds deposited each year into the Millennium Trust, and one-third of all investment earnings on the investment of the Millennium Trust. The treasurer shall report annually to the legislature as to the amount of Millennium Trust investment earnings credited to the Health Excellence Fund.

(b) Beginning Fiscal Year 2011-2012, and each fiscal year thereafter, the treasurer shall credit to the Health Excellence Fund one-third of all investment earnings on the investment of the Millennium Trust. The treasurer shall report annually to the legislature as to the amount of Millennium Trust investment earnings credited to the Health Excellence Fund.

(c) Beginning on July 1, 2012, after allocation of money to the Bond Security and Redemption Fund as provided in Article VII, Section 9(B) of this constitution, the state treasurer shall deposit in and credit to the Health Excellence Fund an amount equal to the revenues derived from the tax levied pursuant to R.S. 47:841(B)(3).

(3)(a) The Education Excellence Fund shall be established as a special fund within the Millennium Trust. The treasurer shall credit to the Education Excellence Fund one-third of the Settlement Agreement proceeds deposited each year into the Millennium Trust, and one-third of all investment earnings on the investment of the Millennium Trust. The treasurer shall report annually to the legislature and the state superintendent of education as to the amount of Millennium Trust investment earnings credited to the Education Excellence Fund.

(b) Beginning Fiscal Year 2011-2012, and each fiscal year thereafter, the treasurer shall credit to the Education Excellence Fund one-third of all investment earnings on the investment of the Millennium Trust. The treasurer shall report annually to the legislature and the state superintendent of education as to the amount of Millennium Trust investment earnings credited to the Education Excellence Fund.

(4)(a) The TOPS Fund shall be established as a special fund within the Millennium Trust. The treasurer shall deposit in and credit to the TOPS Fund one-third of the Settlement Agreement proceeds deposited into the Millennium Trust, and one-third of all investment earnings on the investment of the Millennium Trust. The treasurer shall report annually to the legislature as to the amount of Millennium Trust investment earnings credited to the TOPS Fund.

(b) Beginning Fiscal Year 2011-2012, and each fiscal year thereafter, the treasurer shall credit to the TOPS Fund one hundred percent of the Settlement Agreement proceeds deposited into the Millennium Trust, and one-third of all investment earnings on the investment of the Millennium Trust. The treasurer shall report annually to the legislature as to the amount of Millennium Trust Settlement Agreement proceeds and investment earnings credited to the TOPS Fund.

(c) Upon the effective date of this sub-sub-paragraph, the state treasurer shall deposit, transfer, or otherwise credit funds in an amount equal to such Settlement Agreement proceeds deposited in and credited to the Millennium Trust received by the state between April 1, 2011 and the effective date of this sub-sub-paragraph to the TOPS Fund.

(5) The amount of Settlement Agreement revenues deposited in the Millennium Trust and credited to the respective funds may be increased and the amount of such revenues deposited into the Louisiana Fund may be decreased by a specific legislative instrument which receives a favorable vote of two-thirds of the elected members of each house of the legislature.

(B) Investment. Monies credited to the Millennium Trust pursuant to Paragraph (A) of this Section shall be invested by the treasurer with the same authority and subject to the same restrictions as the Louisiana Education Quality Trust Fund. However, the portion of monies in the Millennium Trust which may be invested in stock may be increased to no more than fifty percent by a specific legislative instrument which receives a favorable vote of two-thirds of the elected members of each house of the legislature. The legislature shall provide for procedures for the investment of such monies by law. The treasurer may contract, subject to the approval of the State Bond Commission, for the management of such investments and, if a contract is entered into, amounts necessary to pay the costs of the contract shall be appropriated from the Millennium Trust.

(C) Appropriations

(1)(a) Appropriations from the Education Excellence Fund shall be limited to an annual amount not to exceed the estimated aggregate annual earnings from interest, dividends, and realized capital gains on investment of the trust allocated as provided by Paragraph (A) of this Section and as recognized by the Revenue Estimating Conference. Amounts determined to be available for appropriation shall be those aggregate investment earnings which are in excess of an inflation factor as determined by the Revenue Estimating Conference. The amount of realized capital gains on investment which may be included in the aggregate earnings available for appropriation in any year shall not exceed the aggregate of earnings from interest and dividends for that year.

(b)(i) For Fiscal Year 2011-2012, appropriations from the Health Excellence Fund shall be limited to an annual amount not to exceed the estimated aggregate annual earnings from interest, dividends, and realized capital gains on investment of the trust and credited to the Health Excellence Fund as provided by Sub-subparagraph (A)(2)(b) of this Section and as recognized by the Revenue Estimating Conference.

(ii) For Fiscal Year 2012-2013, and each fiscal year thereafter, appropriations from the Health Excellence Fund shall be limited to an annual amount not to exceed the estimated aggregate annual earnings from interest, dividends, and realized capital gains on investment of the trust and credited to the Health Excellence Fund as provided by sub-sub-paragraph (A)(2)(b) of this Section and as recognized by the Revenue Estimating Conference and the amount of proceeds credited to and deposited into the Health Excellence Fund as provided by sub-sub-paragraph (A)(2)(c) of this Section.

(c)(i) For Fiscal Year 2011-2012, appropriations from the TOPS Fund shall be limited to the amount of Settlement Agreement proceeds credited to and deposited into the TOPS Fund as provided by sub-sub-paragraphs (A)(4)(b) and (c) of this Section, and an annual amount not to exceed the estimated aggregate annual earnings from interest, dividends, and realized capital gains on investment of the trust and credited to the TOPS Fund as provided by sub-sub-paragraph (A)(4)(b) of this Section and as recognized by the Revenue Estimating Conference.

(ii) For Fiscal Year 2012-2013, and each fiscal year thereafter, appropriations from the TOPS Fund shall be limited to the amount of annual Settlement Agreement proceeds credited to and deposited into the TOPS Fund as provided in sub-sub-paragraph (A)(4)(b) of this Section, and an annual amount not to exceed the estimated aggregate annual earnings from interest, dividends, and realized capital gains on investment of the trust and credited to the TOPS Fund as provided in sub-sub-paragraph (A)(4)(b) of this Section and as recognized by the Revenue Estimating Conference.

(iii) Further, for Fiscal Year 2011-2012, and each fiscal year thereafter, amounts determined to be available for appropriation from the TOPS Fund from interest earnings shall be those aggregate investment earnings which are in excess of an inflation factor as determined by the Revenue Estimating Conference. The amount of realized capital gains on investment which may be included in the aggregate earnings available for appropriation in any year shall not exceed the aggregate of earnings from interest and dividends for that year.

(2) Appropriations from the Health Excellence Fund shall be restricted to the following purposes:

(a) Initiatives to ensure the optimal development of Louisiana's children through the provision of appropriate health care, including children's health insurance, services provided by school-based health clinics, rural health clinics, and primary care clinics, and early childhood intervention programs targeting children from birth through age four including programs to reduce infant mortality.

(b) Initiatives to benefit the citizens of Louisiana with respect to health care through pursuit of innovation in advanced health care sciences, and the provision of comprehensive chronic disease management services.

(c) Each appropriation from the Health Excellence Fund shall include performance expectations to ensure accountability in the expenditure of such monies.

(3) Appropriations from the Education Excellence Fund shall be limited as follows:

(a) Fifteen percent of monies available for appropriation in any fiscal year from the Education Excellence Fund shall be appropriated to the state superintendent of education for distribution on behalf of all children attending private elementary and secondary schools that have been approved by the State Board of Elementary and Secondary Education, both academically and as required for such school to receive money from the state.

(b) Appropriations shall be made each year to the Louisiana School for the Deaf, the Louisiana School for the Visually Impaired, the Louisiana Special Education Center in Alexandria, the Louisiana School for Math, Science and the Arts, the New Orleans Center for Creative Arts and the Louis Armstrong High School for the Arts, after such schools are operational, to provide for a payment to each school of seventy-five thousand dollars plus an allocation for each pupil equal to the average statewide per pupil amount provided each city, parish, and local school system pursuant to sub-sub-paragraphs (d) and (e) of this Subparagraph.

(c) Appropriations may be made for independent public schools which have been approved by the State Board of Elementary and Secondary Education or any city, parish, or other local school system and for alternative schools and programs which are authorized and approved by the State Board of Elementary and Secondary Education but are not subject to the jurisdiction and management of any city, parish, or local school system, to provide for an allocation for each pupil, which shall be the average statewide per pupil amount provided in each city, parish, or local school system pursuant to sub-sub-paragraphs (d) and (e) of this Subparagraph.

(d) Beginning Fiscal Year 2000-2001 and for each fiscal year through the end of Fiscal Year 20062007, of the monies available for appropriation after providing for the purposes enumerated in sub-sub-paragraphs (a), (b), and (c) of this Subparagraph, the following appropriations shall be made to the state superintendent of education for distribution as follows:

(i) Thirty percent of the funds available to be divided equally among each city, parish, and other local school system.

(ii) Seventy percent of the funds available to be divided among each city, parish, and other local school system in amounts which are proportionate to each school's share of the total state share of the Minimum Foundation Program appropriation as contained in the most recent Minimum Foundation Program budget letter approved by the State Board of Elementary and Secondary Education.

(e) Beginning Fiscal Year 2007-2008 and for each fiscal year thereafter, of the monies available for appropriation after providing for the purposes enumerated in sub-sub-paragraphs (a), (b), and (c) of this Subparagraph, one hundred percent of the monies available for appropriation in any fiscal year shall be appropriated for each city, parish, and other local school system on a pro rata basis which is based on the ratio of the student population of that school or school system to that of the total state student population as contained in the most recent Minimum Foundation Program.

(f) Monies appropriated pursuant to this Subparagraph shall be restricted to expenditure for pre-kindergarten through twelfth grade instructional enhancement for students, including early childhood education programs focused on enhancing the preparation of at-risk children for school, remedial instruction, and assistance to children who fail to achieve the required scores on any tests passage of which are required pursuant to state law or rule for advancement to a succeeding grade or other educational programs approved by the legislature. Expenditures for maintenance or renovation of buildings, capital improvements, and increases in employee salaries are prohibited. The state superintendent of education shall be responsible for allocating all money due private schools.

(g) Each recipient school or school system shall annually prepare and submit to the state Department of Education, hereinafter the "department", a prioritized plan for expenditure of funds it expects to receive in the coming year from the Education Excellence Fund. The plan shall include performance expectations to ensure accountability in the expenditure of such monies. The department shall review such plans for compliance with the requirements of this Subparagraph and to assure that the expenditure plans will support excellence in educational practice. No funds may be distributed to any school or school system until its plan has received both legislative and departmental approval as provided by law.

(h) No amount appropriated as required in this Paragraph shall displace, replace, or supplant appropriations from the general fund for elementary and secondary education, including implementing the Minimum Foundation Program. This sub-sub-paragraph shall mean that no appropriation for any fiscal year from the Education Excellence Fund shall be made for any purpose for which a general fund appropriation was made in the previous year unless the total appropriations for the fiscal year from the state general fund for such purpose exceed general fund appropriations of the previous year. Nor shall any money allocated to a city or parish school board pursuant to this Paragraph displace, replace, or supplant locally generated revenue, which means that no allocation to any city or parish school board from the investment earnings attributable to the Education Excellence Fund shall be expended for any purpose for which a local revenue source was expended for that purpose for the previous year unless the total of the local revenue amount expended that fiscal year exceeds the total of such local revenue amounts for the previous fiscal year.

(i) The treasurer shall maintain within the state treasury a record of the amounts appropriated and credited for each entity through appropriations authorized in this Subparagraph and which remain in the state treasury. Notwithstanding any other provisions of this constitution to the contrary, such amounts, and investment earnings attributable to such amounts, shall remain to the credit of each recipient entity at the close of each fiscal year.

(4) Appropriations from the TOPS Fund shall be restricted to support of state programs for financial assistance for students attending Louisiana institutions of postsecondary education.

Section 10.9. Louisiana Fund

Louisiana Fund

(A) The Louisiana Fund is established in the state treasury as a special fund. After allocation of money to the Bond Security and Redemption Fund as provided in Article VII, Section 9(B) of this constitution, the treasurer shall deposit in and credit to the Louisiana Fund all remaining monies received as a result of the Settlement Agreement after deposits into the Millennium Trust as provided in Section 10.8 of this Article, and all interest income on the investment of monies in the Louisiana Fund. Monies in the Louisiana Fund shall be invested by the treasurer in the same manner as the state general fund. B. Appropriations from the Louisiana Fund shall be restricted to the following purposes:

(1) Initiatives to ensure the optimal development of Louisiana's children through enhancement of educational opportunities and the provision of appropriate health care, which shall include but not be limited to:

(a) Early childhood intervention programs targeting children from birth through age four, including programs to reduce infant mortality.

(b) Support of state programs for children's health insurance.

(c) School-based health clinics, rural health clinics, and primary care clinics.

(2) Initiatives to benefit the citizens of Louisiana with respect to health care through pursuit of innovation in advanced health care sciences, provision of comprehensive chronic disease management services, and expenditures for capital improvements for state health care facilities.

(3) Provision of direct health care services for tobacco-related illnesses.

(4) Initiatives to diminish tobacco-related injury and death to Louisiana's citizens through educational efforts, cessation assistance services, promotion of a tobacco-free lifestyle, and enforcement of the requirements of the Settlement Agreement by the attorney general. C. Each appropriation from the Louisiana Fund shall include performance expectations to ensure accountability in the expenditure of such monies. Any unexpended and unencumbered monies in each fund at the end of a fiscal year shall remain in the respective fund.

Section 10.10. Millennium Leverage Fund

(A) Millennium Leverage Fund

Notwithstanding the provisions of Article VII, Sections 10.8 and 10.9 of this constitution, the legislature may provide, by passage of a specific legislative instrument by a favorable vote of two-thirds of the elected members of each house of the legislature, for the deposit of all or a portion of monies received by the state as a result of the Master Settlement Agreement, hereinafter the "Settlement Agreement", executed November 23, 1998, and approved by Consent Decree and Final Judgment entered in the case "Richard P. Ieyoub, Attorney General, ex rel. State of Louisiana v. Philip Morris, Incorporated, et al.", bearing Number

986473 on the docket of the Fourteenth Judicial District for the parish of Calcasieu, state of Louisiana; after satisfying the requirements of Article VII, Section 9(B) of this constitution, into the Millennium Leverage Fund which is hereby established as a special permanent trust fund in the state treasury. The Millennium Leverage Fund shall hereinafter be referred to as the "Leverage Fund".

(B) Investment

Monies deposited in the Leverage Fund shall be invested and administered by the treasurer. Notwithstanding any provision of this constitution to the contrary, a portion of the monies in the Leverage Fund, not to exceed fifty percent, may be invested in stock. The legislature shall provide for the procedure for the investment of such monies by law. The treasurer shall contract, subject to approval of the State Bond Commission, for the management of such investments. The monies in the Leverage Fund shall be available for appropriation to pay expenses incurred in the investment and management of monies in the fund.

(C) Revenue Bonds

The State Bond Commission, or its successor, may issue and sell bonds, notes, or other obligations, hereinafter the "bonds" secured by a pledge of a portion of the monies received by the state as a result of the Settlement Agreement which are otherwise to be deposited in the Leverage Fund as provided in this Section. Such bonds may be issued only in amounts authorized by the legislature by twothirds of the elected members of each house of the legislature. If settlement revenues are pledged to secure any revenue bonds issued pursuant to this Section, any portion thereof needed to pay principal, interest, or premium, if any, and other obligations incident to the issuance, security, prepayment, defeasance, and payment in respect thereof may be expended by the treasurer without the need for an appropriation, provided that the prepayment or defeasance has been approved by the legislature. Bonds so issued may also be further secured by a collateralization of all or a portion of monies in the Leverage Fund. If bonds are issued subject to such a collateralization, the treasurer may pay from the Leverage Fund any principal, interest, or premium, if any, and other obligations incident to the issuance, security, prepayment, defeasance, and payment in respect thereof without the need for an appropriation, provided that the prepayment or defeasance has been approved by the legislature. The net proceeds of any bonds issued pursuant to this Section shall be deposited in and credited to the Leverage Fund. Any revenue bonds issued under authority of this Section shall not be general obligation bonds secured by the full faith and credit of the state.

(D). Appropriations

(1) The legislature may annually appropriate the bond proceeds credited to the Leverage Fund and all earnings, income, and realized capital gains on investment of monies in the Leverage Fund as recognized as available for appropriation in the official forecast of the Revenue Estimating Conference. The Revenue Estimating Conference shall include in its forecast of monies available for appropriation only that amount of earnings, income, and realized capital gains which are in excess of inflation as determined by the conference.

(2) Appropriations may be made only for the following purposes: (a) Twenty-five percent shall be available for appropriation for the purposes as provided in the TOPS Fund. (b) Twenty-five percent shall be available for appropriation for the purposes as provided in the Health Excellence Fund. (c) Twenty-five percent shall be available for appropriation as provided in the Education Excellence Fund. (d) Twenty-five percent shall be available for appropriation as provided in the Louisiana Fund. (e) The amounts available for appropriation for each of the purposes contained in sub-paragraphs (a) through (c) of this Paragraph may be increased, and the amount available for appropriation for the purposes of sub-sub-paragraph (d) may be decreased by a specific legislative instrument which receives a favorable vote of two-thirds of the elected members of each house of the legislature.

(E) Termination.

The legislature may, by passage of a specific legislative instrument by a favorable vote of two-thirds of the elected members of each house of the legislature, provide for the termination of deposits to the Leverage Fund. Any such termination shall be made in such a manner so as to not impair the obligation, validity, or security of any bonds issued under the authority of this Section. Upon termination, the amount of any settlement revenues over and above the amount pledged for security of any bonds issued pursuant to the authority granted in this Section, shall be deposited in and credited as provided in Article VII, Sections 10.8 and 10.9 of this Constitution.

Section 10.11. Artificial Reef Development Fund

(A) Artificial Reef Development Fund

There shall be established in the state treasury, as a special fund, the Artificial Reef Development Fund. Out of the funds remaining in the Bond Security and Redemption Fund after a sufficient amount is allocated from that fund to pay all obligations secured by the full faith and credit of the state that become due and payable within any fiscal year as required by Article VII, Section 9(B) of this constitution, the treasurer shall pay into the Artificial Reef Development Fund the monies received as provided in Paragraph (B) of this Section.

(B) The secretary of the Department of Wildlife and Fisheries is authorized to accept and receive grants, donations of monies, and other forms of assistance from private and public sources that are provided to the state for the purpose of siting, designing, constructing, permitting, monitoring, and otherwise managing an artificial reef system.

(C) The monies in the Artificial Reef Development Fund shall be appropriated by the legislature to the Department of Wildlife and Fisheries, or its successor, and shall be allocated solely for the following:

(1) For the programs and purposes of siting, designing, constructing, permitting, monitoring, and otherwise managing an artificial reef system.

(2) For the salaries of personnel assigned to the Artificial Reef Development Program and for related operating expenses.

(3) An amount not to exceed ten percent of the monies deposited to the fund each year and ten percent of the interest income credited to the fund each year may be used by the department to provide funding in association with the wild seafood certification program, particularly in support of wild caught shrimp, established by the department. Such funding may be used for a subsidy granted to seafood harvesters or processors to assist in their efforts to comply with the certification program requirements and may be used for administration of the program.

(4) An amount not to exceed ten percent of the funds deposited to the fund each year and ten percent of the interest income credited to the fund each year may be used by the department to provide funding for inshore fisheries habitat enhancement projects, particularly in support of the Artificial Reef Development Program established by the department. Such funding may be used for grants to nonprofit conservation organizations working in cooperation with the department.

(D) All unexpended and unencumbered monies in the Artificial Reef Development Fund at the end of the fiscal year shall remain in the fund. The monies in the fund shall be invested by the treasurer in the manner provided by law. All interest earned on monies invested by the treasurer shall be deposited in the fund. The treasurer shall prepare and submit to the department on a quarterly basis a written report showing the amount of money contained in the fund from all sources.

Section 10.12. Farmers and fishermen assistance programs

Agricultural and Seafood Products Support Fund

A. The legislature is authorized to provide by law for programs to assist Louisiana farmers and fishermen with support and expansion of their industries.

B(1) The Agricultural and Seafood Products Support Fund is hereby established in the state treasury as a special fund, hereinafter referred to as the "fund". The source of monies in this fund shall be any monies received by the state from the licensing of trademarks or labels for use in promoting Louisiana agricultural and seafood products; grants, gifts, and donations received by the state for the purposes of this Section; any other revenues as may be provided by law; and other monies which may be appropriated by the legislature to the fund. After compliance with the requirements of Article VII, Section 9(B) of this constitution relative to the Bond Security and Redemption Fund, and prior to monies being placed in the state general fund, an amount equal to that deposited into the state treasury from the foregoing sources shall be deposited in and credited to the fund. Monies in the fund shall be subject to appropriation in accordance with Paragraph (2) of this Section. All unexpended and unencumbered monies remaining in the fund at the end of the fiscal year shall remain in the fund. The monies in the fund shall be invested by the state treasurer in the same manner as monies in the state general fund.

(2) The monies in the Agricultural and Seafood Products Support Fund may be appropriated solely for the programs and purposes as required by the Department of Economic Development for assistance to Louisiana farmers and fishermen with support and expansion of their industries. C. The provisions of this Section shall not apply to or affect funds allocated by Article VII, Section 4, Paragraphs (D) and (E).

Section 10.13. Hospital stabilization formula and assessment; Hospital Stabilization Fund

(A) Hospital Stabilization Formula

(1) The legislature may annually adopt a Hospital Stabilization Formula, hereafter referred to in this Section as "the formula", by concurrent resolution by a favorable vote of a majority of the elected members of each house. Such resolution shall be referred to the standing committees of the legislature that hear the general appropriation bill. The formula shall, to the maximum extent possible, enhance the economic viability of Louisiana hospitals and reduce shifting the cost of caring for Louisiana's needy residents to the state's insured residents.

(2)(a) The first formula established pursuant to Subparagraph (1) of this Paragraph, which shall require a favorable vote of two-thirds of the elected members of each house for adoption, shall define and establish as the base reimbursement level under the Louisiana medical assistance program provided for in Title XIX of the Social Security Act, hereafter referred to as the "Medicaid Program", to hospitals for inpatient and outpatient services in Fiscal Year 2012-2013. The formula shall also provide for the preservation and protection of rural hospitals as provided for by law. Each formula established thereafter may apply a rate of inflation, which shall not be a negative rate, to the base reimbursement level from the previous formula adopted by the legislature.

(b) Each formula shall also include and establish assessments to be paid by hospitals and the basis on which such assessments shall be calculated, provided the amount of the assessments does not exceed the nonfederal share of the reimbursement enhancements.

(c) Each formula shall also establish reimbursement enhancements under the Medicaid Program, or its successor, achieving the maximum reimbursement by federal law and resulting in distributing such reimbursement enhancements exclusively among hospitals for hospital services. Reimbursement enhancements may also be distributed for uninsured services delivered.

(d) Each formula shall also include any additional provisions necessary to the implementation of the formula. Neither the assessments nor the reimbursement enhancements established in the formula adopted by the legislature shall be implemented until each has been approved by the federal authority which administers the Medicaid Program.

(3) The base reimbursement level resulting from the formula shall not be paid from the Hospital Stabilization Fund.

(4) No additional assessment shall be collected and any assessment shall be terminated for the remainder of the fiscal year from the date on which any of the following occur:

(a) The legislature fails to adopt a formula for the subsequent fiscal year.

(b) The Department of Health and Hospitals, or its successor or contractors, reduces or does not pay reimbursement enhancements established in the current formula as adopted by the legislature.

(c) The appropriations provided for in Subparagraph (B)(2) of this Section are reduced.

(5) The treasurer shall return any monies collected after the date of termination of an assessment to the hospital from which it was collected.

(B) Appropriation

(1) The legislature shall annually appropriate an amount necessary to fund the base reimbursement level for hospitals established in the most recent formula adopted by the legislature.

(2) The legislature shall annually appropriate the balance of the Hospital Stabilization Fund solely to fund the reimbursement enhancements as provided in the most recent formula adopted by the legislature.

(3) Notwithstanding Article VII, Section 10(F) of this constitution, neither the governor nor the legislature may reduce the appropriation funding the base reimbursement level or the reimbursement enhancements to satisfy a budget deficit, except the governor may reduce the appropriation to the base reimbursement level if the following occur:

(a) Such reduction does not exceed the average reduction of those made to the appropriations and reimbursement for other providers under the Medicaid Program, or its successor; and

(b)(i) If the legislature is in session, the reduction is consented to in writing by two-thirds of the elected members of each house in a manner provided by law; or

(ii) If the legislature is not in session, the reduction is approved by two-thirds of the members of the Joint Legislative Committee on the Budget, or its successor.

(C) Hospital Stabilization Fund

There is hereby established as a special fund in the state treasury the Hospital Stabilization Fund, hereafter referred to as "the fund". After compliance with the requirements of Article VII, Section 9(B) of this constitution relative to the Bond Security and Redemption Fund, the treasurer shall deposit all proceeds from the assessment collected pursuant to the Hospital Stabilization Formula provided for in this Section. The monies in the fund shall be invested in the same manner as monies in the state general fund, and all interest earned on the investment of the fund shall be deposited in and credited to the fund. Appropriations from the fund shall be restricted to funding the reimbursement enhancements established in the Hospital Stabilization Formula adopted by the legislature for the fiscal year in which the assessment is collected.

Section 10.14. Louisiana Medical Assistance Trust Fund

(A) There is hereby established as a special fund in the state treasury the Louisiana Medical Assistance Trust Fund, hereinafter referred to as "the fund", which shall consist of monies generated by fees as provided for in law. Subject to the exceptions contained in Article VII, Section 9(A) of this constitution, and after compliance with the requirements of Article VII, Section 9(B) of this constitution relative to the Bond Security and Redemption Fund, the treasurer shall deposit all proceeds from the fees collected as provided for in laws relative to the Louisiana Medical Assistance Trust Fund into the fund. The monies in the fund shall be invested by the state treasurer in the same manner as monies in the state general fund. All interest earned from the investment of monies in the fund shall be deposited in and remain to the credit of the fund. All unexpended and unencumbered monies remaining in the fund at the close of each fiscal year shall remain in the fund.

(B) The treasurer is hereby authorized to establish a separate account within the fund for each health care provider group in which fees are collected according to law. Monies collected from each provider group, and the interest earned on those monies, shall be deposited into the account created for that provider group. Any monies deposited into the fund from sources not required by law, and the interest earned on those monies, shall be deposited into a separate account within the fund, hereafter referred to as "the general account".

(C) The legislature is authorized to appropriate monies from the fund only if the appropriation is eligible for federal financial participation under Title XIX of the Social Security Act, or its successor. The balance of each account shall be appropriated for reimbursement of services to the provider group which paid the fee into the account in any fiscal year, except monies deposited into the general account may be appropriated for any Medicaid Program expenditure.

(D) The monies appropriated from the provider accounts in the fund shall not be used to displace, replace, or supplant appropriations from the state general fund for the Medicaid Program below the amount of state general fund appropriations to the Medicaid Program for Fiscal Year 2013-2014.

(E)(1) The legislature shall annually appropriate the funds necessary to provide for Medicaid Program rates for each provider group which pays fees into the fund that is no less than the average Medicaid Program rates established for Fiscal Year 2013-2014 and which may be adjusted annually by establishing the rates of inflation, or rebasing if applicable, which rates shall not be negative, to be applied to the base rates to establish the new base rates for the next fiscal year as authorized by law. For the purpose of this Section, "Medicaid Program" shall refer to the Louisiana medical assistance program provided for in Title XIX of the Social Security Act, or its successor.

(2) Notwithstanding Article VII, Section 10(F) of this constitution, neither the governor nor the legislature may reduce the base rate as provided for in this Paragraph to satisfy a budget deficit, except the governor may reduce the appropriation for the base rate if the following occur:

(a) Such reduction does not exceed the average reduction of those made to the appropriations and reimbursement for other providers under the Medicaid Program, or its successor; and

(b)(i) If the legislature is in session, the reduction is consented to in writing by two-thirds of the elected members of each house in a manner provided by law; or

(ii) If the legislature is not in session, the reduction is approved by two-thirds of the members of the Joint Legislative Committee on the Budget, or its successor.

Section 10.15. Revenue Stabilization Trust Fund

Revenue Stabilization Trust Fund

(A) The Revenue Stabilization Trust Fund is hereby established in the state treasury as a special trust fund, hereinafter referred to as the "fund".

(B) After allocation of money to the Bond Redemption and Security Fund as provided in Article VII, Section 9(B) of the Constitution of Louisiana, the treasurer shall deposit in and credit to the fund the revenues as provided for in Paragraphs (C) and (D) of this Section.

(C) The treasurer shall deposit into the fund the amount of mineral revenues as provided in Section 10.16 of this constitution.

(D) The treasurer shall deposit into the fund the amount of revenues in excess of six hundred million dollars received each fiscal year from corporate franchise and income taxes as recognized by the Revenue Estimating Conference.

(E)(1) Except as provided for in Paragraph (F) of this Section, monies deposited into the Revenue Stabilization Trust Fund shall be permanently credited to the trust fund and shall be invested by the treasurer in a manner provided for by law.

(2) The treasurer shall deposit all interest or other income from investment generated from the fund into the state general fund.
(F)(1) Except as provided in sub-paragraphs (2) and (3) of this Paragraph, no appropriations shall be made from the Revenue Stabilization Trust Fund.

(2)(a) In any fiscal year in which the balance of the fund at the beginning of the year is in excess of five billion dollars, hereinafter referred to as the minimum fund balance, the legislature may appropriate an amount not to exceed ten percent of the fund balance, hereinafter referred to as the allowable percentage, for the following:

(i) Capital outlay projects in the comprehensive state capital budget.

(ii) Transportation infrastructure.

(b) The minimum fund balance or the allowable percentage may be changed by a law enacted by two-thirds of the elected members of each house of the legislature.

(3) In order to ensure the money in the fund is available for appropriation in an emergency, the legislature may authorize an appropriation from the fund at any time for any purpose only after the consent of two-thirds of the elected members of each house of the legislature. If the legislature is not in session, the two-thirds requirement may be satisfied upon obtaining the written consent of two-thirds of the elected members of each house of the legislature in a manner provided by law.

Section 10.16. Dedications of Mineral Revenues

(A) All mineral revenues as defined in Paragraph (D) of this Section received in each fiscal year by the state as a result of the production of or exploration for minerals, hereinafter referred to as "mineral revenues", shall be allocated as provided in this Section after the following allocations and deposits of mineral revenues have been made:

(1) To the Bond Security and Redemption Fund as provided in Article VII, Section 9 (B) of this constitution.

(2) To the political subdivisions of the state as provided in Article VII, Sections 4 (D) and (E) of this constitution.

(3) To the Louisiana Wildlife and Fisheries Conservation Fund as provided by the requirements of Article VII, Section 10-A of this constitution and as provided by law.

(4) To the Louisiana Wildlife and Fisheries Conservation Fund and the Oil and Gas Regulatory Fund as provided by law.

(5) To the Rockefeller Wildlife Refuge and Game Preserve Fund as provided by law.

(6) To the Marsh Island Operating Fund and the Russell Sage or Marsh Island Refuge Fund as provided by law.

(7) To the MC Davis Conservation Fund as provided by law.

(8) To the White Lake Property Fund as provided by law.

(9) To the Louisiana Education Quality Trust Fund and Louisiana Quality Education Support Fund as provided in Article VII, Section 10.1 of this constitution.

(10) To the Coastal Protection and Restoration Fund as provided in Article VII, Section 10.2 of this constitution and as provided by law.

(11) To the Mineral Revenue and Audit Settlement Fund as provided in Article VII, Section 10.5 of this constitution and as provided by law.

(12) To the Budget Stabilization Fund as provided in Article VII, Section 10.3 of this constitution and as provided by law.

(13) An amount equal to the state general fund deposited into the Transportation Trust Fund and the Louisiana State Transportation Infrastructure Fund as provided by law.

(B) Allocation of Mineral Revenues. After the allocations and deposits provided in Paragraph (A) of this Section, the mineral revenues received in each year in excess of six hundred sixty million dollars and less than nine hundred fifty million dollars shall be allocated as follows:

(1) Thirty percent shall be appropriated to the Louisiana State Employees' Retirement System and the Teachers' Retirement System of Louisiana for application to the balance of the unfunded accrued liability of such systems existing as of June 30, 1988, in proportion to the balance of such unfunded accrued liability of each such system, until such unfunded accrued liability has been eliminated. Any such payments to the public retirement systems shall not be used, directly or indirectly, to fund cost-of-living increases for such systems.

(2) The remainder shall be deposited into the Revenue Stabilization Trust Fund.

(C) Mineral revenues in excess of the base which would otherwise be deposited into the Budget Stabilization Fund under Subparagraph (A)(2) of Section 10.3 of this constitution, but are prohibited from being deposited into the fund under Subparagraph (C)(4) of Section 10.3 of this constitution, shall be distributed as follows:

(1) Thirty percent shall be appropriated to the Louisiana State Employees' Retirement System and the Teachers' Retirement System of Louisiana for application to the balance of the unfunded accrued liability of such systems existing as of June 30, 1988, in proportion to the balance of such unfunded accrued liability of each such system, until such unfunded accrued liability has been eliminated. Any such payments to the public retirement systems shall not be used, directly or indirectly, to fund cost-of-living increases for such systems.

(2) The remainder shall be deposited into the Revenue Stabilization Trust Fund.

(D) For purposes of this Section, "mineral revenues" shall include severance taxes, royalty payments, bonus payments, or rentals, with the following exceptions:

(1) Revenues designated as nonrecurring, pursuant to Article VII, Section 10(B) of this constitution.

(2) Revenues received by the state as a result of grants or donations when the terms or conditions thereof require otherwise.

(3) Revenues derived from any tax on the transportation of minerals.

Section 11. Budgets

(A) Budget Estimate

The governor shall submit to the legislature, at the time and in the form fixed by law, a budget estimate for the next fiscal year setting forth all proposed state expenditures. This budget shall include a recommendation for appropriations from the state general fund and from dedicated funds, except funds allocated by Article VII, Section 4, Paragraphs (D) and (E), which shall not exceed the official forecast of the Revenue Estimating Conference and the expenditure limit for the fiscal year. The recommendation shall also comply with the provisions of Article VII, Section 10(D). This budget shall include a recommendation for funding of state salary supplements for full-time law enforcement and fire protection officers of the state, as provided in Article VII, Section 10(D)(3) of this constitution.

(B) Operating Budget

The governor shall cause to be submitted a general appropriation bill for proposed ordinary operating expenditures which shall be in conformity with the recommendations for appropriations contained in the budget estimate. The governor may cause to be submitted a bill or bills to raise additional revenues with proposals for the use of these revenues.

(C) Capital Budget

The governor shall submit to the legislature, at each regular session, a proposed five-year capital outlay program and request implementation of the first year of the program. Prior to inclusion in the comprehensive capital budget which the legislature adopts, each capital improvement project shall be evaluated through a feasibility study, as defined by the legislature, which shall include an analysis of need and estimates of construction and operating costs. The legislature shall provide by law for procedures, standards, and criteria for the evaluation of such feasibility studies and shall set the schedule of submission of such feasibility studies which shall take effect not later than December thirty-first following the first regular session convening after this Paragraph takes effect. These procedures, standards, and criteria for evaluation of such feasibility studies cannot be changed or altered except by a separate legislative instrument approved by a favorable vote of two-thirds of the elected members of each house of the legislature. For those projects not eligible for funding under the provisions of Article VII, Section 27 of this constitution, the request for implementation of the first year of the program shall include a list of the proposed projects in priority order based on the evaluation of the feasibility studies submitted. Capital outlay projects approved by the legislature shall be made a part of the comprehensive state capital budget, which shall be adopted by the legislature.

Section 12. Reports and Records

Reports and records of the collection, expenditure, investment, and use of state money and those relating to state obligations shall be matters of public record, except returns of taxpayers and matters pertaining to those returns.

Section 13. Investment of State Funds

All money in the custody of the state treasurer which is available for investment shall be invested as provided by law.

Section 14. Donation, Loan, or Pledge of Public Credit

(A) Prohibited Uses

Except as otherwise provided by this constitution, the funds, credit, property, or things of value of the state or of any political subdivision shall not be loaned, pledged, or donated to or for any person, association, or corporation, public or private. Except as otherwise provided in this Section, neither the state nor a political subdivision shall subscribe to or purchase the stock of a corporation or association or for any private enterprise.

(B) Authorized Uses

Nothing in this Section shall prevent

(1) the use of public funds for programs of social welfare for the aid and support of the needy;

(2) contributions of public funds to pension and insurance programs for the benefit of public employees;

(3) the pledge of public funds, credit, property, or things of value for public purposes with respect to the issuance of bonds or other evidences of indebtedness to meet public obligations as provided by law;

(4) the return of property, including mineral rights, to a former owner from whom the property had previously been expropriated, or purchased under threat of expropriation, when the legislature by law declares that the public and necessary purpose which originally supported the expropriation has ceased to exist and orders the return of the property to the former owner under such terms and conditions as specified by the legislature;

(5) acquisition of stock by any institution of higher education in exchange for any intellectual property;

(6) the donation of abandoned or blighted housing property by the governing authority of a municipality or a parish to a nonprofit organization which is recognized by the Internal Revenue Service as a 501(c)(3) or 501(c)(4) nonprofit organization and which agrees to renovate and maintain such property until conveyance of the property by such organization;

(7) the deduction of any tax, interest, penalty, or other charges forming the basis of tax liens on blighted property so that they may be subordinated and waived in favor of any purchaser who is not a member of the immediate family of the blighted property owner or which is not any entity in which the owner has a substantial economic interest, but only in connection with a property renovation plan approved by an administrative hearing officer appointed by the parish or municipal government where the property is located;

(8) the deduction of past due taxes, interest, and penalties in favor of an owner of a blighted property, but only when the owner sells the property at less than the appraised value to facilitate the blighted property renovation plan approved by the parish or municipal government and only after the renovation is completed such deduction being canceled, null and void, and to no effect in the event ownership of the property in the future reverts back to the owner or any member of his immediate family;

(9) the donation by the state of asphalt which has been removed from state roads and highways to the governing authority of the parish or municipality where the asphalt was removed, or if not needed by such governing authority, then to any other parish or municipal governing authority, but only pursuant to a cooperative endeavor agreement between the state and the governing authority receiving the donated property;

(10) the investment in stocks of a portion of the Rockefeller Wildlife Refuge Trust and Protection Fund, created under the provisions of R.S. 56:797, and the Russell Sage or Marsh Island Refuge Fund, created under the provisions of R.S. 56:798, such portion not to exceed thirty-five percent of each fund;

(11) the investment in stocks of a portion of the state-funded permanently endowed funds of a public or private college or university, not to exceed thirty-five percent of the public funds endowed;

(12) the investment in equities of a portion of the Medicaid Trust Fund for the Elderly created under the provisions of R.S. 46:2691 et seq., such portion not to exceed thirty-five percent of the fund; or

(13) the investment of public funds to capitalize a state infrastructure bank to be utilized solely for transportation projects.

(C) Cooperative Endeavors

For a public purpose, the state and its political subdivisions or political corporations may engage in cooperative endeavors with each other, with the United States or its agencies, or with any public or private association, corporation, or individual.

(D) Prior Obligations

Funds, credit, property, or things of value of the state or of a political subdivision heretofore loaned, pledged, dedicated, or granted by prior state law or authorized to be loaned, pledged, dedicated, or granted by the prior laws and constitution of this state shall so remain for the full term as provided by the prior laws and constitution and for the full term as provided by any contract, unless the authorization is revoked by law enacted by two-thirds of the elected members of each house of the legislature prior to the vesting of any contractual rights pursuant to this Section.

(E) Surplus Property

Nothing in this Section shall prevent the donation or exchange of movable surplus property between or among political subdivisions whose functions include public safety.

Section 15. Release of Obligations to State, Parish, or Municipality

The legislature shall have no power to release, extinguish, or authorize the releasing or extinguishing of any indebtedness, liability, or obligation of a corporation or individual to the state, a parish, or a municipality. However, the legislature, by law, may establish a system under which claims by the state or a political subdivision may be compromised, and may provide for the release of heirs to confiscated property from taxes due thereon at the date of its reversion to them.

Section 16. Taxes

Prescription Taxes, except real property taxes, and licenses shall prescribe in three years after the thirty-first day of December in the year in which they are due, but prescription may be interrupted or suspended as provided by law.

Section 17. Legislation to Obtain Federal Aid

The legislature may enact laws to enable the state, its agencies, boards, commissions, and political subdivisions and their agencies to comply with federal laws and regulations in order to secure federal participation in funding capital improvement projects.

PART II. PROPERTY TAXATION

Section 18. Ad Valorem Taxes

(A) Assessments

Property subject to ad valorem taxation shall be listed on the assessment rolls at its assessed valuation, which, except as provided in Paragraphs (C) and (G), shall be a percentage of its fair market value. The percentage of fair market value shall be uniform throughout the state upon the same class of property.

(B) Classification

The classifications of property subject to ad valorem taxation and the percentage of fair market value applicable to each classification for the purpose of determining assessed valuation are as follows:

Classifications Percentages

1. Land 10%

2. Improvements for residential purposes 10%

3. Electric cooperative properties, excluding land 15%

4. Public service properties; excluding land 25

5. Other property 15% The legislature may enact laws defining electric cooperative properties and public service properties.

(C) Use Value

Bona fide agricultural, horticultural, marsh, and timber lands, as defined by general law, shall be assessed for tax purposes at ten percent of use value rather than fair market value. The legislature may provide by law similarly for buildings of historic architectural importance.

(D) Valuation

Each assessor shall determine the fair market value of all property subject to taxation within his respective parish or district except public service properties, which shall be valued at fair market value by the Louisiana Tax Commission or its successor. Each assessor shall determine the use value of property which is to be so assessed under the provisions of Paragraph (C). Fair market value and use value of property shall be determined in accordance with criteria which shall be established by law and which shall apply uniformly throughout the state.

(E) Review

The correctness of assessments by the assessor shall be subject to review first by the parish governing authority, then by the Louisiana Tax Commission or its successor, and finally by the courts, all in accordance with procedures established by law.

(F) Reappraisal

All property subject to taxation shall be reappraised and valued in accordance with this Section, at intervals of not more than four years.

(G)(1) Special Assessment Level

(a)(i) The assessment of residential property receiving the homestead exemption which is owned and occupied by any of the following and who meet all of the other requirements of this Section shall not be increased above the total assessment of that property for the first year that the owner qualifies for and receives the special assessment level, provided that such person or persons remain qualified for and receive the special assessment level:

(aa) People who are sixty-five years of age or older.

(bb) People who have a service-connected disability rating of fifty percent or more by the United States Department of Veterans Affairs.

(cc) Members of the armed forces of the United States or the Louisiana National Guard who owned and last occupied such property who are killed in action, or who are missing in action or are a prisoner of war for a period exceeding ninety days.

(dd) Any person or persons permanently totally disabled as determined by a final non-appealable judgment of a court or as certified by a state or federal administrative agency charged with the responsibility for making determinations regarding disability.

(ii) Any person or persons shall be prohibited from receiving the special assessment as provided in this Section if such person's or persons' adjusted gross income, as reported in the federal tax return for the year prior to the application for the special assessment, exceeds fifty thousand dollars. For persons applying for the special assessment whose filing status is married filing separately, the adjusted gross income for purposes of this Section shall be determined by combining the adjusted gross income on both federal tax returns. Beginning for the tax year 2001, and for each tax year thereafter, the fifty thousand dollar limit shall be adjusted annually by the Consumer Price Index as reported by the United States Government.

(iii) An eligible owner or the owner's spouse or other legally qualified representative shall apply for the special assessment level by filing a signed application establishing that the owner qualifies for the special assessment level with the assessor of the parish or, in the parish of Orleans, the assessor of the district where the property is located.

(iv) An owner who is below the age of sixty-five and who has applied for and received the special assessment level may qualify for and receive the special assessment level in the subsequent year by certifying to the assessor of the parish, or in the parish of Orleans, the assessor of the district where the property is located, that such person or persons' adjusted gross income in the prior tax year satisfied the income requirement of this Section. The provisions of this sub-sub-paragraph (a)(iv) shall not apply to an owner who has qualified for and received the special assessment level for persons sixty-five years of age or older or to such owner's surviving spouse as described in sub-sub-paragraph (a)(i) of this Subparagraph.

(b) Any millage rate applied to the special assessment level shall not be subject to a limitation.

(2) Provided such owner is qualified for and receives the special assessment level, the special assessment level shall remain on the property as long as:

(a)(i) The owner who is sixty-five years of age or older, or that owner's surviving spouse who is fifty-five years of age or older or who has minor children, remains the owner of the property.

(ii) The owner who has a service-connected disability of fifty percent or more, or that owner's surviving spouse who is forty-five years of age or older or who has minor children, remains the owner of the property.

(iii) The spouse of the owner who is killed in action remains the owner of the property.

(iv) The first day of the tax year following the tax year in which an owner who was missing in action or was a prisoner of war for a period exceeding ninety days is no longer missing in action or a prisoner of war.

(v) Even if the ownership interest of any surviving spouse or spouse of an owner who is missing in action as provided for in this Subparagraph is an interest in usufruct.

(b) The value of the property does not increase more than twenty-five percent because of construction or reconstruction.

(3) A new or subsequent owner of the property may claim a special assessment level when eligible under this Section. The new owner is not necessarily entitled to the same special assessment level on the property as when that property was owned by the previous owner.

(4)(a) The special assessment level on property that is sold shall automatically expire on the last day of December in the year prior to the year that the property is sold. The property shall be immediately revalued at fair market value by the assessor and shall be assessed by the assessor on the assessment rolls in the year it was sold at the assessment level provided for in Article VII, Section 18 of the Constitution of Louisiana.

(b) This new assessment level shall remain in effect until changed as provided by this Section or this Constitution.

(5)(a) Any owner entitled to the special assessment level set forth in this Paragraph who is unable to occupy the homestead on or before December thirty-first of a future calendar year due to damage or destruction of the homestead caused by a disaster or emergency declared by the governor shall be entitled to keep the special assessment level of the homestead prior to its damage or destruction on the repaired or rebuilt homestead provided the repaired or rebuilt homestead is reoccupied by the owner within five years from December thirty-first of the year following the disaster. The assessed value of the land and buildings on which the homestead was located prior to its damage shall not be increased above its assessed value immediately prior to the damage or destruction described in this sub-sub-paragraph. If the property owner receives a homestead exemption on another homestead during the same five-year period, the damaged or destroyed property shall not be entitled to keep the special assessment level, and the land and buildings shall be assessed in that year at the percentage of fair market value set forth in this constitution. In addition, the owner shall also maintain the homestead exemption set forth in Article VII, Section 20(A)(10) to qualify for the special assessment level in this sub-sub-paragraph.

(b) Any owner entitled to the special assessment level set forth in sub-sub-paragraph (a) of this Subparagraph who is unable to reoccupy his homestead within five years from December thirty-first of the year following the disaster shall be eligible for an extension of the special assessment level on the homestead for a period not to exceed two years. A homeowner shall be eligible for this extension only if the homeowner's damage claim is filed and pending in a formal appeal process with any federal, state, or local government agency or program offering grants or assistance for repairing or rebuilding damaged or destroyed homes as a result of the disaster, or if a homeowner has a damage claim filed and pending against the insurer of the property. The homeowner shall apply for this extension of the special assessment level with the assessor of the parish in which the homestead is located. The assessor shall require the homeowner to provide official documentation from the government agency or program evidencing the homeowner's participation in the formal appeal process or official documentation evidencing the homeowner has a damage claim filed and pending against the insurer of the damaged property, as provided by law.

(c) After expiration of the extension authorized in sub-sub-paragraph (b) of this Subparagraph, an assessor shall have the authority to grant on a case-by-case basis up to three additional one-year extensions of the special assessment level as prescribed by law.

Section 19. State Property Taxation; Rate Limitation

State taxation on property for all purposes shall not exceed an annual rate of five and three-quarter mills on the dollar of assessed valuation.

Section 20. Homestead Exemption

(A) Homeowners

(1) The bona fide homestead, consisting of a tract of land or two or more tracts of land even if the land is classified and assessed at use value pursuant to Article VII, Section 18(C) of this constitution, with a residence on one tract and a field with or without timber on it, pasture, or garden on the other tract or tracts, not exceeding one hundred sixty acres, buildings and appurtenances, whether rural or urban, owned and occupied by any person or persons owning the property in indivision, shall be exempt from state, parish, and special ad valorem taxes to the extent of seven thousand five hundred dollars of the assessed valuation. The same homestead exemption shall also fully apply to the primary residence, including a mobile home, which serves as a bona fide home and which is owned and occupied by any person or persons owning the property in indivision, regardless of whether the homeowner owns the land upon which the home or mobile home is sited; however, this homestead exemption shall not apply to the land upon which such primary residence is sited if the homeowner does not own the land.

(2) The homestead exemption shall extend and apply fully to the surviving spouse or a former spouse when the homestead is occupied by the surviving spouse or a former spouse and title to it is in the name of

(a) the surviving spouse as owner of any interest or either or both of the former spouses,

(b) the surviving spouse as usufructuary, or

(c) a testamentary trust established for the benefit of the surviving spouse and the descendants of the deceased spouse or surviving spouse, but not to more than one homestead owned by either the husband or wife, or both.

(3) The homestead exemption shall extend to property owned by a trust when the principal beneficiary or beneficiaries of the trust are the settlor or settlors of the trust and were the immediate prior owners of the homestead, and the homestead is occupied as such by a principal beneficiary. The provisions of this Subparagraph shall apply only to property which qualified for the homestead exemption immediately prior to transfer, conveyance, or donation in trust, or which would have qualified for the homestead exemption if such property were not owned in trust.

(4) The homestead exemption shall extend to property where the usufruct of the property has been granted to no more than two usufructuaries who were the immediate prior owners of the homestead and the homestead is occupied as such by a usufructuary. The provisions of this Subparagraph shall apply only to property which qualified for the homestead exemption immediately prior to the granting of such usufruct, or which would have qualified for the homestead exemption if such usufruct had not been granted.

(5) The homestead exemption shall extend only to a natural person or persons and to a trust created by a natural person or persons, in which the beneficiaries of the trust are a natural person or persons provided that the provisions of this Paragraph are otherwise satisfied.

(6) Except as otherwise provided for in this Paragraph, the homestead exemption shall apply to property owned in indivision, but shall be limited to the pro rata ownership interest of that person or persons occupying the homestead.

(7) No homestead exemption shall be granted on bond for deed property. However, any homestead exemption granted prior to June 20, 2003 on any property occupied upon the effective date of this Paragraph by a buyer under a bond for deed contract shall remain valid as long as the circumstances giving rise to the exemption at the time the exemption was granted remain applicable.

(8) Notwithstanding any provision of this Paragraph to the contrary, in no event shall more than one homestead exemption extend or apply to any person in this state.

(9) This exemption shall not extend to municipal taxes. However, the exemptions shall apply

(a) in Orleans Parish, to state, general city, school, levee, and levee district taxes and

(b) to any municipal taxes levied for school purposes.

(10)(a) Any homestead receiving the homestead exemption that is damaged or destroyed during a disaster or emergency declared by the governor whose owner is unable to occupy the homestead on or before December thirty-first of a calendar year due to such damage or destruction shall be entitled to claim and keep the exemption by filing an annual affidavit of intent to return and reoccupy the homestead within five years from December thirty-first of the year following the disaster with the assessor within the parish or district where such homestead is situated prior to December thirty-first of the year in which the exemption is claimed. In no event shall more than one homestead exemption extend or apply to any person in this state.

(b) For homesteads qualifying for the homestead exemption under the provisions of sub-sub-paragraph (a) of this Subparagraph, after expiration of the five-year period, the owner of a homestead shall be entitled to claim and keep the exemption for a period not to exceed two additional years by filing an annual affidavit of intent to return and reoccupy the homestead with the assessor within the parish where the homestead is located prior to December thirty-first of the year in which the exemption is claimed. A homeowner shall be eligible for this extension only if the homeowner's damage claim to repair or rebuild the damaged or destroyed homestead is filed and pending in a formal appeal process with any federal, state, or local government agency or program offering grants or assistance for repairing or rebuilding damaged or destroyed homes as a result of the disaster, or if a homeowner has a damage claim filed and pending against the insurer of the property. The assessor shall require the homeowner to provide official documentation from the government agency or program evidencing the homeowner's participation in the formal appeal process or official documentation evidencing the homeowners has a damage claim filed and pending against the insurer of the property as provided by law.

(c) After expiration of the extension authorized in sub-sub-paragraph (b) of this Subparagraph, an assessor shall have the authority to grant on a case-by-case basis up to three additional one-year extensions of the homestead exemption as prescribed by law.

(B) Residential Lessees

Notwithstanding any contrary provision in this constitution, the legislature may provide for tax relief to residential lessees in the form of credits or rebates in order to provide equitable tax relief similar to that granted to homeowners through homestead exemptions.

Section 21. Other Property Exemptions

In addition to the homestead exemption provided for in Section 20 of this Article, the following property and no other shall be exempt from ad valorem taxation:

(A) Public lands and other public property used for public purposes. Land or property owned by another state or owned by a political subdivision of another state shall not be exempt under this Paragraph.

(B)(1)(a)(i) Property owned by a nonprofit corporation or association organized and operated exclusively for religious, dedicated places of burial, charitable, health, welfare, fraternal, or educational purposes, no part of the net earnings of which inure to the benefit of any private shareholder or member thereof and which is declared to be exempt from federal or state income tax; and

(ii) medical equipment leased for a term exceeding five years to such a nonprofit corporation or association which owns or operates a small, rural hospital and which uses the equipment solely for health care purposes at the hospital, provided that the property shall be exempt only during the term of the lease to such corporation or association, and further provided that "small, rural hospital" shall mean a hospital which meets all of the following criteria:

(aa) It has less than fifty Medicare-licensed acute care beds.

(bb) It is located in a municipality with a population of less than ten thousand which has been classified as an area with a shortage of health manpower by the United States Health Service; and

(b) property leased to such a nonprofit corporation or association for use solely as housing for homeless persons, as defined by regulation adopted by the tax commission or its successor provided that the term of such lease shall be for at least five years, that as a condition of entering into the lease the property be in compliance with all applicable health and sanitation codes for use as housing for homeless persons, that the lease shall provide that compensation to be paid the lessor shall not exceed one dollar per year, and that such contract of lease shall recite that the property shall be used exclusively for the purpose of housing the homeless, and further provided that at such time as the property is no longer used solely as housing for homeless persons, the property shall no longer be exempt from taxation;

(2) property of a bona fide labor organization representing its members or affiliates in collective bargaining efforts; and

(3) property of an organization such as a lodge or club organized for charitable and fraternal purposes and practicing the same, and property of a nonprofit corporation devoted to promoting trade, travel, and commerce, and also property of a trade, business, industry or professional society or association, if that property is owned by a nonprofit corporation or association organized under the laws of this state for such purposes. None of the property listed in Paragraph (B) shall be exempt if owned, operated, leased, or used for commercial purposes unrelated to the exempt purposes of the corporation or association.

(C)(1) Cash on hand or deposit;

(2) stocks and bonds, except bank stocks, the tax on which shall be paid by the banking institution;

(3) obligations secured by mortgage on property located in Louisiana and the notes or other evidence thereof;

(4) loans by life insurance companies to policyholders, if secured solely by their policies;

(5) the legal reserve of domestic life insurance companies;

(6) loans by a homestead or building and loan association to its members, if secured solely by stock of the association;

(7) debts due for merchandise or other articles of commerce or for services rendered;

(8) obligations of the state or its political subdivisions;

(9) personal property used in the home or on loan in a public place;

(10) irrevocably dedicated places of burial held by individuals for purposes of burial of themselves or members of their families;

(11) agricultural products while owned by the producer, agricultural machinery and other implements used exclusively for agricultural purposes, animals on the farm, and property belonging to an agricultural fair association;

(12) property used for cultural, Mardi Gras carnival, or civic activities and not operated for profit to the owners;

(13) rights-of-way granted to the State Department of Highways;

(14) boats using gasoline as motor fuel;

(15) commercial vessels used for gathering seafood for human consumption; and

(16) ships and oceangoing tugs, towboats, and barges engaged in international trade and domiciled in Louisiana ports. However, this exemption shall not apply to harbor, wharf, shed, and other port dues or to any vessel operated in the coastal trade of the states of the United States.

(17) Materials, boiler fuels, and energy sources used by public utilities to fuel the generation of electricity.

(18) All incorporeal movables of any kind or nature whatsoever, except public service properties, bank stocks, and credit assessments on premiums written in Louisiana by insurance companies and loan and finance companies. For purposes of this Section, incorporeal movables shall have the meaning set forth in the Louisiana Civil Code of 1870, as amended.

(19) All artwork including sculptures, glass works, paintings, drawings, signed and numbered posters, photographs, mixed media, collages, or any other item which would be considered as the material result of a creative endeavor which is listed as a consignment article by an art dealer.

(D)(1) Raw materials, goods, commodities, and articles imported into this state from outside the states of the United States:

(a) so long as the imports remain on the public property of the port authority or docks of the common carrier where they first entered this state;

(b) so long as the imports (other than minerals and ores of the same kind as any mined or produced in this state and manufactured articles) are held in this state in the original form in bales, sacks, barrels, boxes, cartons, containers, or other original packages, and raw materials held in bulk as all or a part of the new material inventory of manufacturers or processors, solely for manufacturing or processing; or

(c) so long as the imports are held by an importer in any public or private storage in the original form in bales, sacks, barrels, boxes, cartons, containers, or other original packages and agricultural products in bulk. This exemption shall not apply to these imports when held by a retail merchant as part of his stock-in-trade for sale at retail.

(2) Raw materials, goods, commodities, and other articles being held on the public property of a port authority, on docks of any common carrier, or in a warehouse, grain elevator, dock, wharf, or public storage facility in this state for export to a point outside the states of the United States.

(3) Goods, commodities, and personal property in public or private storage while in transit through this state which are moving in interstate commerce through or over the territory of the state or which are in public or private storage within Louisiana, having been shipped from outside Louisiana for storage in transit to a final destination outside Louisiana, whether such destination was specified when transportation began or afterward. Property described in Paragraph (D), whether or not entitled to exemption, shall be reported to the proper taxing authority on the forms required by law.

(E) Motor vehicles used on the public highways of this state, from state, parish, municipal, and special ad valorem taxes.

(F) Notwithstanding any contrary provision of this Section, the State Board of Commerce and Industry or its successor, with the approval of the governor, may enter into contracts for the exemption from ad valorem taxes of a new manufacturing establishment or an addition to an existing manufacturing establishment, on such terms and conditions as the board, with the approval of the governor, deems in the best interest of the state. The exemption shall be for an initial term of no more than five calendar years, and may be renewed for an additional five years. All property exempted shall be listed on the assessment rolls and submitted to the Louisiana Tax Commission or its successor, but no taxes shall be collected thereon during the period of exemption. The terms "manufacturing establishment" and "addition" as used herein mean a new plant or establishment or an addition or additions to any existing plant or establishment which engages in the business of working raw materials into wares suitable for use or which gives new shapes, qualities or combinations to matter which already has gone through some artificial process.

(G) Coal or lignite stockpiled in Louisiana for use in Louisiana for industrial or manufacturing purposes or for boiler fuel, gasification, feedstock, or process purposes.

(H) Notwithstanding any contrary provision of this constitution, the State Board of Commerce and Industry or its successor, with the approval of the governor and the local governing authority and in accordance with procedures and conditions provided by law, may enter into contracts granting to a property owner, who proposes the expansion, restoration, improvement, or development of an existing structure or structures in a downtown, historic, or economic development district established by a local governing authority or in accordance with law, the right for an initial term of five years after completion of the work to pay ad valorem taxes based upon the assessed valuation of the property for the year prior to the commencement of the expansion, restoration, improvement, or development. Contracts may be renewed, subject to the same conditions, for an additional five years extending such right for a total of ten years from completion of the work.

(I)(1) Notwithstanding any contrary provision of this Section, the authority or district charged with economic development of each parish is hereby authorized to enter into contracts for the exemption from parish, municipal, and special ad valorem taxes of goods held in inventory by distribution centers. In the absence of the existence of an economic development authority or district, the parish governing authority is authorized to grant contracts of exemption as are provided for in this Paragraph.

(2) The contract for exemption shall be on such terms and to the extent, up to and including the full assessed valuation of the goods held in inventory, as the economic development authority or district deems in the best interest of the parish. However, prior to entering into each individual contract, the economic development authority or district must request and receive written approval of the contract, including its terms and an estimated fiscal impact, from each affected tax recipient body in the parish, as evidenced by a favorable vote of a majority of the members of the governing authority of the tax recipient body. Failure to receive all required approvals from the tax recipient bodies before entering into a contract shall render the contract null and void and of no effect.

(3) The term "distribution center" as used herein means an establishment engaged in the sale of products for resale or further processing for resale. The term "goods held in inventory" as used herein means goods or products which have been given new shapes, qualities, or combinations through some artificial process and does not include raw materials such as natural gas, crude oil, sulfur, or timber or goods or products held for sale to consumers.

(J)(1) Drilling rigs used exclusively for the exploration and development of minerals outside the territorial limits of the state in Outer Continental Shelf waters which are within the state for the purpose of being stored or stacked for use outside the territorial limits of the state, or for the purpose of being converted, renovated, or repaired, and any property in the state for the purpose of being incorporated in, or to be used in the operation of said drilling rigs.

(2) The exemption provided in this Paragraph shall be applicable in any parish in which the exemption has been approved by a majority of the electors of the parish voting thereon at an election called for that purpose.

(K)(1) On and after January 1, 2015, in addition to the homestead exemption authorized under the provisions of Article VII, Section 20 of this constitution, which applies to the first seven thousand five hundred dollars of the assessed valuation of property, the next seven thousand five hundred dollars of the assessed valuation of property receiving the homestead exemption that is owned and occupied by a veteran with a service-connected disability rating of one hundred percent unemployability or totally disabled by the United States Department of Veterans Affairs shall be exempt from ad valorem taxation. The surviving spouse of a deceased veteran with a service-connected disability rating of one hundred percent unemployability or totally disabled by the United States Department of Veterans Affairs shall be eligible for this exemption if the surviving spouse occupies and remains the owner of the property, whether or not the exemption was in effect on the property prior to the death of the veteran. If property eligible for the exemption provided for in this Paragraph has an assessed value in excess of fifteen thousand dollars, ad valorem property taxes shall apply to the assessment in excess of fifteen thousand dollars.

(2) Notwithstanding any provision of this constitution to the contrary, the property assessment of a property for which this exemption has been claimed, to the extent of seven thousand five hundred dollars, shall not be treated as taxable property for purposes of any subsequent reappraisals and valuation for millage adjustment purposes under Article VII, Section 23(B) of this Constitution. The decrease in the total amount of ad valorem tax collected by a taxing authority as a result of the exemption shall be absorbed by the taxing authority and shall not create any additional tax liability for other taxpayers in the taxing district as a result of any subsequent reappraisal and valuation or millage adjustment. Implementation of the exemption authorized in this Paragraph shall neither trigger nor be cause for a reappraisal of property or an adjustment of millages pursuant to the provisions of Article VII, Section 23(B) of this constitution.

(3)(a) The exemption provided for in this Paragraph shall extend and apply in a parish only if it is established through an election that shall be called by either an ordinance or a resolution from the parish governing authority. The proposition shall state that the exemption shall extend and apply in the parish and become effective only after the question of its adoption has been approved by a majority of the registered voters of the parish voting in an election held for that purpose.

(b) If a parish held an election as provided by this Subparagraph and the electors approved the exemption prior to November 4, 2014, the parish may implement the exemption as amended by the statewide electors on November 4, 2014, without holding an additional election.

(L)(1) Except as otherwise provided herein, property owned or leased by, and used by, a targeted non-manufacturing business in the operation of its facility, including buildings, improvements, equipment, and other property necessary or beneficial to such operation, according to a program and pursuant to contracts of exemption which contain such terms and conditions which shall be provided by law. Land underlying the facility and other property pertaining to the facility on which ad valorem taxes have previously been paid, inventories, consumables, and property eligible for the manufacturing exemption provided by Paragraph (F) of this Section, shall not be exempt under this Paragraph.

(2) Ad valorem taxes shall apply to the assessed valuation of the first ten million dollars or ten percent of fair market value, whichever is greater, and this amount of property shall not be exempt under this Paragraph.

(3) A targeted non-manufacturing business means at least fifty percent of such business' total annual sales from a site or sites in the state is to out-of-state customers or buyers, or to in-state customers or buyers but the product or service is resold by the purchaser to an out-of-state customer or buyer for ultimate use, or to the federal government, or any combination thereof. The legislature may provide by law for the inclusion of sales by affiliates when appropriate in making this fifty percent determination.

(4) A contract for the exemption shall be available only in parishes which have agreed to participate, in the manner provided by the legislature by law.

(M) There is hereby established an exemption from ad valorem tax for the total assessed value of the homestead of the unmarried surviving spouse of a person who died under the conditions enumerated in sub-sub-paragraph (1)(a) or (b) of this Paragraph, and if the conditions established in sub-sub-paragraph (1)(c) of this Paragraph are met.

(1)(a) For ad valorem taxes due in 2017 and thereafter, the exemption shall apply beginning in the tax year in which any of the following persons died or 2017, whichever is later:

(i) A member of the armed forces of the United States or the Louisiana National Guard who died while on active duty.

(ii) A state police officer who died while on duty.

(iii) A law enforcement or fire protection officer who qualified for the salary supplement authorized in Section 10(D)(3) of this Article who died while on duty.

(b) For ad valorem taxes due in 2018 and thereafter, the exemption shall apply beginning in the tax year in which any of the following persons died or 2018, whichever is later:

(i) An emergency medical responder, technician, or paramedic, as such terms may be defined by law, who died while performing the duties of their employment.

(ii) A volunteer firefighter, verified by the Office of the State Fire Marshal to have died while performing firefighting duties.

(iii) A law enforcement or fire protection officer who died while on duty and who would have qualified for the salary supplement authorized in Section 10(D)(3) of this Article if he had completed the first year of his employment before his death.

(c)(i) The property is eligible for the homestead exemption and the property was the residence of a person listed within sub-sub-paragraph (a) or (b) of this Subparagraph at the time of that person's death.

(ii) The surviving spouse has not remarried.

(iii) The surviving spouse annually provides evidence of their eligibility for the exemption in accordance with the requirements of Subparagraph (2) of this Paragraph.

(2) Each assessor shall establish a procedure whereby a person may annually apply for the exemption. Eligibility for the exemption shall be established by the production of documents and certification of information by the surviving spouse to the assessor as follows:

(a) In an initial application for the exemption, the surviving spouse shall produce documentation issued by their deceased spouse's employer evidencing the death.

(b) For purposes of the continuation of an existing exemption, the surviving spouse shall annually provide a sworn statement to the assessor attesting to the fact that the surviving spouse has not remarried.

(3) Once an unmarried surviving spouse has qualified for and taken the exemption, if the surviving spouse then acquires a different property which qualifies for the homestead exemption, the surviving spouse shall be entitled to an exemption on that subsequent homestead, the exemption being limited in value to the amount of the exemption claimed on the prior homestead in the last year for which the exemption was claimed. The assessor may require the submission of certain information concerning the amount of the exemption on the prior homestead for purposes of determining the extent of the exemption available for the subsequent homestead.

(N)(1) All property delivered to a construction project site for the purpose of incorporating the property into any tract of land, building, or other construction as a component part, including the type of property that may be deemed to be a component part once placed on an immovable for its service and improvement pursuant to the provisions of the Louisiana Civil Code of 1870, as amended. The exemption provided for in this Paragraph shall be applicable until the construction project for which the property has been delivered is complete. A construction project shall be deemed complete when construction is finished to the extent that the project can be used or occupied for its intended purpose. A construction project shall not be deemed complete during its inspection, testing, or commissioning stages, as defined by reasonable industry standards.

(2) Notwithstanding the provisions of Subparagraph (1) of this Paragraph, this exemption shall not apply to any of the following:

(a) Any portion of a construction project that is complete, available for its intended use, or operational on the date that property is assessed.

(b) For projects constructed in two or more distinct phases, any phase of the construction project that is complete, available for its intended use, or operational on the date the property is assessed.

(c) Any public service property, unless the public service property is otherwise eligible for an exemption provided by any other provision of this constitution.

Section 22. No Impairment of Existing Taxes or Obligations

This Part shall not be applied in a manner which will

(a) invalidate taxes authorized and imposed prior to the effective date of this constitution or

(b) impair the obligations, validity, or security of any bonds or other debt obligations authorized prior to the effective date of this constitution.

Section 23. Adjustment of Ad Valorem Tax Millages

(A) First Adjustment

Prior to the end of the third year after the effective date of this constitution, the assessors and the Louisiana Tax Commission or its successor shall complete determination of the fair market value or the use value of all property subject to taxation within each parish for use in implementing this Article. Except as provided in this Section, the total amount of ad valorem taxes collected by any taxing authority in the year in which Sections 18 and 20 of this Article are implemented shall not be increased or decreased, because of their provisions, above or below ad valorem taxes collected by that taxing authority in the year preceding implementation. To accomplish this result, it shall be mandatory for each affected taxing authority, in the year in which Sections 18 and 20 of this Article are implemented, to adjust millages upwards or downwards without regard to millage limitations contained in this constitution, and the maximum authorized millages shall be increased or decreased, without further voter approval, in proportion to the amount of the adjustment upward or downward. Thereafter, such millages shall remain in effect unless changed as permitted by this constitution.

(B) Subsequent Adjustments

Except as otherwise permitted in this Section, the total amount of ad valorem taxes collected by any taxing authority in the year in which the reappraisal and valuation provisions of Section 18, Paragraph (F) of this Article are implemented shall not be increased or decreased because of a reappraisal or valuation or increases or decreases in the homestead exemption above or below the total amount of ad valorem taxes collected by that taxing authority in the year preceding implementation of the reappraisal and valuation. To accomplish this result, the provisions of millage adjustments relative to implementation of Section 18 and Section 20 of this Article, as set forth in Paragraph (A) of this Section shall be mandatory. Thereafter, following implementation of each subsequent reappraisal and valuation required by Paragraph (F) of Section 18 of this Article, the millages as fixed in each such implementation shall remain in effect unless changed as permitted by Paragraph (C) of this Section.

(C) Increases Permitted

Nothing herein shall prohibit a taxing authority from collecting, in the year in which Sections 18 and 20 of this Article are implemented or in any subsequent year, a larger dollar amount of ad valorem taxes by

(1) levying additional or increased millages as provided by law or

(2) placing additional property on the tax rolls. Increases in the millage rate in excess of the rates established as provided by Paragraph (B) above but not in excess of the prior year's maximum authorized millage rate may be levied by two-thirds vote of the total membership of a taxing authority without further voter approval but only after a public hearing held in accordance with the open meetings law; however, in addition to any other requirements of the open meetings law, public notice of the time, place, and subject matter of such hearing shall be published on two separate days no less than thirty days before the public hearing. Such public notice shall be published in the official journal of the taxing authority, and another newspaper with a larger circulation within the taxing authority than the official journal of the taxing authority, if there is one.

(D) Application

This Section shall not apply to millages required to be levied for the payment of general obligation bonds.

Section 24. Tax Assessors

(A) Election; Term

A tax assessor shall be elected by the electors of each parish. His term of office shall be four years. His election, duties, and compensation shall be as provided by law.

(B) Orleans Parish

The assessor shall be elected at the same time as the municipal officers of New Orleans.

(C) Vacancy

When a vacancy occurs in the office of tax assessor, the duties of the office, until filled by election as provided by law, shall be assumed by the chief deputy assessor.

Section 25. Tax Sales

(A) Tax Sales

(1) There shall be no forfeiture of property for nonpayment of taxes. However, at the expiration of the year in which the taxes are due, the collector, without suit, and after giving notice to the delinquent in the manner provided by law, shall advertise for sale the property on which the taxes are due. The advertisement shall be published in the official journal of the parish or municipality, or, if there is no official journal, as provided by law for sheriffs' sales, in the manner provided for judicial sales. On the day of sale, the collector shall sell the portion of the property which the debtor points out. If the debtor does not point out sufficient property, the collector shall sell immediately the least quantity of property which any bidder will buy for the amount of the taxes, interest, and costs. The sale shall be without appraisement. A tax deed by a tax collector shall be prima facie evidence that a valid sale was made.

(2) If property located in a municipality with a population of more than four hundred fifty thousand persons as of the most recent federal decennial census fails to sell for the minimum required bid in the tax sale, the collector may offer the property for sale at a subsequent sale with no minimum required bid. The proceeds of the sale shall be applied to the taxes, interest, and costs due on the property, and any remaining deficiency shall be eliminated from the tax rolls.

(B) Redemption

(1) The property sold shall be redeemable for three years after the date of recordation of the tax sale, by paying the price given, including costs, five percent penalty thereon, and interest at the rate of one percent per month until redemption.

(2) In the city of New Orleans, when such property sold is residential or commercial property which is abandoned property as defined by R.S. 33:4720.12(1) or blighted property as defined by Act 155 of the 1984 Regular Session, it shall be redeemable for eighteen months after the date of recordation of the tax sale by payment in accordance with Subparagraph (1) of this Paragraph.

(3) In any parish other than Orleans, when such property sold is vacant residential or commercial property which has been declared blighted, as defined by R.S. 33:1374(B)(1) on January 1, 2013, or abandoned, as defined by R.S. 33:4720.59(D)(2) on January 1, 2013, it shall be redeemable for eighteen months after the date of recordation of the tax sale by payment in accordance with Subparagraph (1) of this Paragraph.

(C) Annulment

No sale of property for taxes shall be set aside for any cause, except on proof of payment of the taxes prior to the date of the sale, unless the proceeding to annul is instituted within six months after service of notice of sale. A notice of sale shall not be served until the final day for redemption has ended. It must be served within five years after the date of the recordation of the tax deed if no notice is given. The fact that taxes were paid on a part of the property sold prior to the sale thereof, or that a part of the property was not subject to taxation, shall not be cause for annulling the sale of any part thereof on which the taxes for which it was sold were due and unpaid. No judgment annulling a tax sale shall have effect until the price and all taxes and costs are paid, and until ten percent per annum interest on the amount of the price and taxes paid from date of respective payments are paid to the purchaser; however, this shall not apply to sales annulled because the taxes were paid prior to the date of sale.

(D) Quieting Tax Title

The manner of notice and form of proceeding to quiet tax titles shall be provided by law.

(E) Movables; Tax Sales

When taxes on movables are delinquent, the tax collector shall seize and sell sufficient movable property of the delinquent taxpayer to pay the tax, whether or not the property seized is the property which was assessed. Sale of the property shall be at public auction, without appraisement, after ten days advertisement, published within ten days after date of seizure. It shall be absolute and without redemption. If the tax collector can find no corporeal movables of the delinquent to seize, he may levy on incorporeal rights, by notifying the debtor thereof, or he may proceed by summary rule in the courts to compel the delinquent to deliver for sale property in his possession or under his control.

(F) Postponement of Taxes

The legislature may postpone the payment of taxes, but only in cases of overflow, general conflagration, general crop destruction, or other public calamity, and may provide for the levying, assessing, and collecting of such postponed taxes. In such case, the legislature may authorize the borrowing of money by the state on its faith and credit, by bond issue or otherwise, and may levy taxes, or apply taxes already levied and not appropriated, to secure payment thereof, in order to create a fund from which loans may be made through the Interim Emergency Board to the governing authority of the parish where the calamity occurs. The money loaned shall be applied to and shall not exceed the deficiency in revenue of the parish or a political subdivision therein or of which the parish is a part, caused by postponement of taxes. No loan shall be made to a parish governing authority without the approval of the Interim Emergency Board.

PART III. REVENUE SHARING

Section 26. Revenue Sharing Fund

(A) Creation of Fund

The Revenue Sharing Fund is created as a special fund in the state treasury.

(B) Annual Allocation

The sum of ninety million dollars is allocated annually from the state general fund to the revenue sharing fund. The legislature may appropriate additional sums to the fund.

(C) Distribution Formula

The revenue sharing fund shall be distributed annually as provided by law solely on the basis of population and number of homesteads in each parish in proportion to population and the number of homesteads throughout the state. Unless otherwise provided by law, population statistics of the last federal decennial census shall be utilized for this purpose. After deductions in each parish for retirement systems and commissions as authorized by law, the remaining funds, to the extent available, shall be distributed by first priority to the tax recipient bodies within the parish, as defined by law, to offset current losses because of homestead exemptions granted in this Article. Any balance remaining in a parish distribution shall be allocated to the municipalities and tax recipient bodies within each parish as provided by law.

(D) Distributing Officer

The funds distributed to each parish as provided in Paragraph (C) shall be distributed in Orleans Parish by the city treasurer of New Orleans and in all other parishes by the parish tax collector. The funds allocated to the Monroe City School Board or its successor shall be distributed to and by the city treasurer of Monroe.

(E) Bonded Debt

A political subdivision, as defined by Article VI of this constitution, may incur debt by issuing negotiable bonds and may pledge for the payment of all or part of the principal and interest of such bonds the proceeds derived or to be derived from that portion of the funds received by it from the revenue sharing fund, to offset current losses caused by homestead exemptions granted by this Article. Unless otherwise provided by law, no moneys allocated within any parish from the balance remaining in its distribution may be pledged to the payment of the principal or interest of any bonds. Bonds issued under this Paragraph shall be issued and sold as provided by law, and shall require approval of the State Bond Commission or its successor prior to issuance and sale.

PART IV. TRANSPORTATION

Section 27. Transportation Trust Fund

(A) Creation of fund

Effective January 1, 1990, there shall be established in the state treasury as a special permanent trust fund the Transportation Trust Fund ("the trust fund") in which shall be deposited the "excess revenues" as defined herein which are a portion of the avails received in each year from all taxes levied on gasoline and motor fuels and on special fuels (said avails being referred to as the "revenues") as provided herein. After satisfying pledges respecting that portion of the revenues attributable to the tax rates in effect at the time of such pledges for the payment of obligations for bonds or other evidences of indebtedness on the effective date of this Section, the treasurer shall allocate such portion of the revenues received in each year as necessary to pay all principal, interest, premium, if any, and other obligations incident to the issuance, security, and payment in respect of bonds as authorized in Paragraph (C) hereof. Thereafter, the portion of the revenues remaining shall be deposited in the Bond Security and Redemption Fund in the state treasury. After

(1) the payment of any obligations for bonds or other evidences of indebtedness in existence on the effective date of this Section which are secured by revenues;

(2) payments in respect of bonds authorized in Paragraph (C) hereof; and

(3) credit to the Bond Security and Redemption Fund, the treasurer shall deposit in and credit to the trust fund all of the revenues remaining (the "excess revenues") from the avails of all taxes levied on gasoline and motor fuels and on special fuels, as follows: for the fiscal year beginning July 1, 1989, the avails of twelve cents per gallon of said taxes received on and after January 1, 1990; for the fiscal year beginning on July 1, 1990, the avails of fourteen cents per gallon of said taxes; for the fiscal year beginning on July 1, 1991, and thereafter, the avails of all taxes levied on gasoline and motor fuels and on special fuels. Purchases of gasoline, diesel fuel, or special fuels which are subject to excise tax under Chapter 7 of Subtitle II of Title 47 of the Louisiana Revised Statutes of 1950 shall be exempt from the state sales tax and any sales tax levied by a political subdivision as defined by Article VI, Section 44(2). All monies appropriated by the Federal Highway Administration and the Federal Aviation Administration, or their successors, either reimbursed or paid directly, shall be paid directly or deposited in and credited to the trust fund.

(B)(1) Except as provided for in Subparagraph (2) of this Paragraph, the monies in the trust fund shall be appropriated or dedicated solely and exclusively for the costs for and associated with construction and maintenance of the roads and bridges of the state and federal highway systems, the Statewide Flood-Control Program or its successor, ports, airports, transit, state police for traffic control purposes, and the Parish Transportation Fund or its successor and for the payment of all principal, interest, premium, if any, and other obligations incident to the issuance, security, and payment in respect of bonds or other obligations payable from the trust fund as authorized in Paragraph (D) hereof. Unless pledged to the repayment of bonds authorized in Paragraphs (C) or (D) of this Section, the monies in the trust fund allocated to ports, airports, flood control, parish transportation, and state highway construction shall be appropriated annually by the legislature only pursuant to programs established by law which establish a system of priorities for the expenditure of such monies, except that the Transportation Infrastructure Model for Economic Development, which shall include only those projects enumerated in House Bill 17 of the 1989 First Extraordinary Session of the Legislature* and US Highway 61 from Thompson Creek to the Mississippi Line, in lieu of "US 61-Bains to Mississippi Line", and US Highway 165 from I-10 to Alexandria to Monroe to Bastrop and thence on US Highway 425 from Bastrop to the Arkansas Line, in lieu of "US 165-I-10 Alexandria-Monroe-Bastrop-Arkansas Line" and LA 15-Natchez, Mississippi to Chase in lieu of "LA 15-Natchez, Mississippi to Monroe", shall be funded as provided by law. The state generated tax monies appropriated for ports, Parish Transportation Fund, or its successor, and the Statewide Flood-Control Program, or its successor, and state police for traffic control purposes shall not exceed twenty percent annually of the state generated tax revenues in the trust fund; provided, however, that no less than the avails of one cent of the tax on gasoline and special fuels shall be appropriated each year to the Parish Transportation Fund, or its successor. The annual appropriation for airports shall be a sum equal to, but not greater than, the annual estimated revenue to be derived from the state taxes to be collected and received on aviation fuel. Unencumbered and unexpended balances at the end of each fiscal year shall remain in the trust fund. The earnings realized in each fiscal year on the investment of monies in the trust fund shall be deposited in and credited to the trust fund.

(2) There is hereby established in the Transportation Trust Fund a special sub-fund to be known as the "Construction Sub-fund", hereinafter referred to as "the sub-fund", in which shall be deposited the avails of any new taxes that become effective and are levied on gasoline, motor fuels, or special fuels on or after July 1, 2017. The monies in the sub-fund shall be appropriated and dedicated solely for the direct costs associated with actual project delivery, construction, and maintenance of transportation and capital transit infrastructure projects of the state and local government. The monies in the sub-fund that are appropriated by the legislature to the Department of Transportation and Development, or its successor, shall not be utilized by the department for the payment of employee wages and related benefits or employee retirement benefits.

(C) The State Bond Commission or its successor, may issue and sell bonds, notes, or other obligations ("Bonds") secured by a pledge of a portion of the revenues not to exceed the avails of four cents per gallon of the taxes on gasoline and motor fuels and on special fuels received by the state treasurer. Bonds so issued may also be secured by a pledge of all or a portion of excess revenues as additional security therefor, and if so pledged any portion thereof needed to pay principal, interest, or premium, if any, and other obligations incident to the issuance, security, and payment in respect to Bonds may be expended by the treasurer without the need for legislative appropriation. The Bonds may be issued in the manner set forth in this Section to provide for the costs for and associated with construction and maintenance of the roads and bridges of the state and federal highway systems, Statewide Flood-Control Program, ports, airports, and for any other purpose for which monies in the trust fund may be expended as provided by law. Such Bonds shall not be considered to be debt under Article VII, Section 6, unless the provisions of Article VII, Section 6, relative to incurring debt by the state are met, in which case the full faith and credit of the state may also be pledged in addition to the revenues received by the treasurer.

(D) The State Bond Commission or its successor may also issue and sell bonds, notes, or other obligations secured by a pledge of the excess revenues deposited in the trust fund, which shall otherwise be issued in the manner and for the purposes provided for in this Section, and if so pledged any portion thereof needed to pay principal, interest, or premium, if any, and other obligations incident to the issuance, security, and payment in respect thereof may be expended by the treasurer without the need for legislative appropriation.

(E) Bonds, notes, or other obligations issued pursuant to the provisions of Paragraphs (C) or (D) above may be issued in the manner provided by resolution of the State Bond Commission or its successor under the authority of said Paragraphs without compliance with any other requirement of this constitution or law. To that end, said Paragraphs (C) and (D) hereof shall be deemed self-operative.

ARTICLE VIII: EDUCATION

PREAMBLE

The goal of the public educational system is to provide learning environments and experiences, at all stages of human development, that are humane, just, and designed to promote excellence in order that every individual may be afforded an equal opportunity to develop to his full potential.

Section 1. Public Educational System

The legislature shall provide for the education of the people of the state and shall establish and maintain a public educational system.

Section 2. State Superintendent of Education

There shall be a superintendent of education for public elementary and secondary education who, subject to provisions for appointment in lieu of election set forth in Article IV, Section 20, of this constitution, shall be elected for a term of four years. If the office is made appointive, the State Board of Elementary and Secondary Education shall make the appointment. He shall be the administrative head of the Department of Education and shall implement the policies of the State Board of Elementary and Secondary Education and the laws affecting schools under its jurisdiction. The qualifications and other powers, functions, duties, and responsibilities of the superintendent shall be provided by law.

Section 3. State Board of Elementary and Secondary Education

(A) Creation; Functions

The State Board of Elementary and Secondary Education is created as a body corporate. It shall supervise and control the public elementary and secondary schools and special schools under its jurisdiction and shall have budgetary responsibility for all funds appropriated or allocated by the state for those schools, all as provided by law. The board shall have other powers, duties, and responsibilities as provided by this constitution or by law, but shall have no control over the business affairs of a city, parish, or other local public school board or the selection or removal of its officers and employees; however, the board shall have the power to supervise, manage, and operate or provide for the supervision, management, and operation of a public elementary or secondary school which has been determined to be failing, including the power to receive, control, and expend state funds appropriated and allocated pursuant to Section 13(B) of this Article, any local contribution required by Section 13 of this Article, and any other local revenue available to a school board with responsibility for a school determined to be failing in amounts that are calculated based on the number of students in attendance in such a school, all in the manner provided by and in accordance with law.

(B)(1) Membership; Terms

The board shall consist of eleven members, eight of whom shall be elected from single-member districts, which shall be determined as provided by law, and three of whom shall be appointed by the governor from the state at large, with consent of the Senate. Members shall serve terms of four years, which shall be concurrent with the term of the governor.

(2) No person who has served as a member of the board for more than two and one-half terms in three consecutive terms shall be elected or appointed to the board for the succeeding term. This Subparagraph shall not apply to any person elected or appointed to the board prior to the effective date of this Subparagraph, except that it shall apply to any term of service of any such person that begins after such date.

(C) Vacancy

A vacancy in the office of an elected member, if the remaining portion of the term is more than one year, shall be filled for the remainder of the term by election, as provided by law. Other vacancies shall be filled for the remainder of the term by appointment by the governor.

Section 4. Approval of Private Schools

Upon application by a private elementary, secondary, or proprietary school with a sustained curriculum or specialized course of study of quality at least equal to that prescribed for similar public schools, the State Board of Elementary and Secondary Education shall approve the private school. A certificate issued by an approved private school shall carry the same privileges as one issued by a state public school.

Section 5. Board of Regents

(A) Creation; Functions

The Board of Regents is created as a body corporate. It shall plan, coordinate, and have budgetary responsibility for all public postsecondary education and shall have other powers, duties, and responsibilities provided in this Section or by law.

(B)(1) Membership; Terms

The board shall be composed of fifteen members, of whom two members shall be from each congressional district and the remaining member or members shall be from the state at large appointed by the governor, with consent of the Senate, for overlapping terms of six years, following initial terms which shall be fixed by law. The board should be representative of the state's population by race and gender to ensure diversity.

(2) No person who has served as a member of the board for more than two and one-half terms in three consecutive terms shall be appointed to the board for the succeeding term. This Subparagraph shall not apply to any person appointed to the board prior to the effective date of this Subparagraph, except that it shall apply to any term of service of any such person that begins after such date.

(C) Vacancy

A vacancy occurring prior to the expiration of a term shall be filled for the remainder of the unexpired term by appointment by the governor, with consent of the Senate.

(D) Powers

The Board of Regents shall meet with the State Board of Elementary and Secondary Education at least twice a year to coordinate programs of public elementary, secondary, vocational-technical, career, and higher education. The Board of Regents shall have the following powers, duties, and responsibilities relating to public institutions of postsecondary education:

(1) To revise or eliminate an existing degree program, department of instruction, division, or similar subdivision.

(2) To approve, disapprove, or modify a proposed degree program, department of instruction, division, or similar subdivision.

(3)(a) To study the need for and feasibility of creating a new institution of postsecondary education, which includes establishing a branch of such an institution or converting any non-degree granting institution to an institution which grants degrees or converting any college or university which is limited to offering degrees of a lower rank than baccalaureate to a college or university that offers baccalaureate degrees or merging any institution of postsecondary education into any other institution of postsecondary education, establishing a new management board, and transferring a college or university from one board to another.

(b) If the creation of a new institution, the merger of any institutions, the addition of another management board, or the transfer of an existing institution of higher education from one board to another is proposed, the Board of Regents shall report its written findings and recommendations to the legislature within one year. Only after the report has been filed, or after one year from the receipt of a request for a report from the legislature if no report is filed, may the legislature take affirmative action on such a proposal and then only by law enacted by two-thirds of the elected members of each house.

(4) To formulate and make timely revision of a master plan for postsecondary education. As a minimum, the plan shall include a formula for equitable distribution of funds to the institutions of postsecondary education.

(5) To require that every postsecondary education board submit to it, at a time it specifies, an annual budget proposal for operational needs and for capital needs of each institution under the control of each board. The Board of Regents shall submit its budget recommendations for all institutions of postsecondary education in the state. It shall recommend priorities for capital construction and improvements.

(E) Powers Not Vested

Powers of management over public institutions of postsecondary education not specifically vested by this Section in the Board of Regents are reserved to the Board of Supervisors of Louisiana State University and Agricultural and Mechanical College, the Board of Supervisors of Southern University and Agricultural and Mechanical College, the Board of Trustees for State Colleges and Universities, the Board of Supervisors of Community and Technical Colleges, and any other such board created pursuant to this Article, as to the institutions under the control of each.

Section 6. Board of Supervisors for the University of Louisiana System

(A) Creation; Functions

The Board of Supervisors for the University of Louisiana System is created as a body corporate. Subject to powers vested by this Article in the Board of Regents, it shall have supervision and management of state colleges and universities not managed by a higher education board created by or under this Article.

(B)(1) Membership; Terms

The board shall be composed of fifteen members, of whom two members shall be from each congressional district and the remaining member or members shall be from the state at large, appointed by the governor with consent of the Senate. The members shall serve overlapping terms of six years, following initial terms fixed by law.

(2) No person who has served as a member of the board for more than two and one-half terms in three consecutive terms shall be appointed to the board for the succeeding term. This Subparagraph shall not apply to any person appointed to the board prior to the effective date of this Subparagraph, except that it shall apply to any term of service of any such person that begins after such date.

(C) Vacancy

A vacancy occurring prior to the expiration of a term shall be filled for the remainder of the unexpired term by appointment by the governor, with consent of the Senate.

Section 7. Board of Supervisors of Louisiana State University and Agricultural and Mechanical College; Board of Supervisors of Southern University and Agricultural and Mechanical College.

(A) Creation; Powers

The Board of Supervisors of Louisiana State University and Agricultural and Mechanical College and the Board of Supervisors of Southern University and Agricultural and Mechanical College are created as bodies corporate. Subject to powers vested by this Article in the Board of Regents, each shall supervise and manage the institutions, statewide agricultural programs, and other programs administered through its system.

(B)(1) Membership; Terms

Each board shall be composed of fifteen members, of whom two members shall be from each congressional district and the remaining member or members shall be from the state at large, appointed by the governor with consent of the Senate. The members shall serve overlapping terms of six years, following initial terms fixed by law.

(2) No person who has served as a member of either board for more than two and one-half terms in three consecutive terms shall be appointed to the board for the succeeding term. This Subparagraph shall not apply to any person appointed to either board prior to the effective date of this Subparagraph, except that it shall apply to any term of service of any such person that begins after such date.

(C) Vacancy

A vacancy occurring prior to the expiration of a term shall be filled for the remainder of the unexpired term by appointment by the governor, with consent of the Senate.

Section 7.1. Board of Supervisors of Community and Technical Colleges

(A) Creation; Powers; Institutions; Divisions

(1) The Board of Supervisors of Community and Technical Colleges is created as a body corporate to manage the Louisiana Community and Technical College System subject to powers vested by this Article in the Board of Regents. The system shall include all programs of public postsecondary vocational-technical training, and, as provided by law, institutions of higher education which offer associate degrees but not baccalaureate degrees and such programs and institutions shall be supervised and managed by the board. The system shall be comprised of two divisions, the vocational-technical division which shall include all public postsecondary vocational-technical schools and the community college division which shall include the community colleges in the system.

(2) All public institutions which exclusively or predominantly provide programs of postsecondary vocational-technical education shall be under the jurisdiction of the Board of Supervisors of Community and Technical Colleges. Such institutions may not be transferred from the Louisiana

Community and Technical College System.

(3) The provision of any program subject to the supervision and management of and offered at any institution under the jurisdiction of the Board of Supervisors of Community and Technical Colleges which is not a degree program shall require no approval beyond that of the Board of Supervisors of Community and Technical Colleges.

(B)(1) Membership; Terms; Initial Membership and Terms

The board shall be composed of fifteen members appointed by the governor, as provided by law. In addition, the board shall have two student members as provided by law. All members selected and appointed by the governor shall be appointed with the consent of the Senate. Of those members selected and appointed by the governor, there shall be two members from each congressional district and the remaining member or members from the state at large. The board should be representative of the state's population by race and gender to ensure diversity. The members selected and appointed by the governor shall serve terms of six years, except that the initial members shall serve terms as provided by law. (2) No person who has served as a member of the board for more than two and one-half terms in three consecutive terms shall be appointed to the board for the succeeding term. This Subparagraph shall not apply to any person appointed to the board prior to the effective date of this Subparagraph, except that it shall apply to any term of service of any such person that begins after such date.

(C) Vacancy

A vacancy occurring prior to the expiration of a term of a member selected and appointed by the governor shall be filled for the remainder of the unexpired term by appointment by the governor, with consent of the Senate. Any other vacancy shall be filled as provided by law.

(D) Transitional Funding

Appropriations annually from the state general fund for Fiscal Years 1999-2000, 2000-2001, and 2001-2002, for those institutions of higher education supervised and managed in 1998 by each of the management boards of higher education, that is the Board of Supervisors of Louisiana State University and Agricultural and Mechanical College, the Board of Supervisors of Southern University and Agricultural and Mechanical College, and the Board of Trustees for State Colleges and Universities, respectively, shall be no less than the appropriations from the state general fund in Fiscal Year 1998-1999 for those same institutions of higher education regardless of their management boards. Appropriations annually from the state general fund for Fiscal Years 1999-2000, 2000-2001, and 2001-2002, for those institutions in the Louisiana Community and Technical College System shall be no less than the state general fund appropriations in Fiscal Year 1998-1999 for those same institutions regardless of their management boards. Appropriations annually from the state general fund for Fiscal Years 1999-2000, 2000-2001, and 20012002, for postsecondary vocational-technical education shall be no less than the total of all appropriations for such purpose from the state general fund for Fiscal Year 1998-1999. The provisions of this Paragraph shall be null and void for any such fiscal year in which state general fund revenues are less than the state general fund revenues of Fiscal Year 1998-1999 as determined by the Revenue Estimating Conference.

(E) The transfer of any institution of higher education to the Louisiana Community and Technical College System effected on July 1, 1999, pursuant to this Section shall not change the mission of or adversely affect the accreditation of such institution. Acts 1998, 1st Ex. Sess., No. 170, Section 1, approved Oct. 3, 1998, eff. Nov. 5, 1998; Acts 2008, No. 935, Section 1, approved November 4, 2008, effective December 8, 2008.

Section 8. Boards; Membership; Compensation; Congressional District Member

(A) Dual Membership

No person shall be eligible to serve simultaneously on more than one board created by or pursuant to this Article.

(B) Student Membership

The legislature may provide for the membership of one student on the boards created by Sections 5, 6 and 7 of this Article. The term of a student member shall not exceed one year, and no student member shall be eligible to succeed himself. A student member shall have all of the privileges and rights of other board members.

(C) Compensation

A member of a board created by or pursuant to this Article shall serve without pay, but per diem and expenses may be provided by law.

(D) Congressional District Members

In order to implement the provisions of Sub-paragraphs 5(B)(1), 6(B)(1), 7(B)(1), and 7.1(B)(1) of this Article, beginning on January 3, 2013, and beginning every ten years thereafter on the day the members of congress from newly reapportioned congressional districts take office, any vacancy that occurs on the respective board from a congressional district from which there are two or more board members shall be filled by appointment of an individual from a congressional district from which there are less than two members. After the membership includes two members from each congressional district, the next vacancy shall be filled by an appointment from the state at large.

Section 9. Parish School Boards; Parish Superintendents

(A) Boards

The legislature shall create parish school boards and provide for the election of their members.

(B) Superintendents

Each parish board shall elect a superintendent of parish schools. The State Board of Elementary and Secondary Education shall fix the qualifications and prescribe the duties of the parish superintendent. He need not be a resident of the parish in which he serves.

Section 10. Existing Boards and Systems Recognized; Consolidation

(A) Recognition

Parish and city school board systems in existence on the effective date of this constitution are recognized, subject to control and supervision by the State Board of Elementary and Secondary Education and the power of the legislature to enact laws affecting them.

(B) Ouachita Parish and Monroe City School Systems; Board Membership

Only persons residing within the jurisdiction of the Monroe City School Board shall be eligible to vote for or be members of the Monroe City School Board. Only persons residing in that portion of Ouachita Parish outside the jurisdiction of the Monroe City School Board shall be eligible to vote for or be members of the Ouachita Parish School Board. The position of a member of either board shall be vacated when he no longer satisfies the requirements of this Paragraph. Notwithstanding any contrary provision of this constitution, this Paragraph shall become operative upon the election of members to the Ouachita Parish School Board taking office in 1977 or upon the first reapportionment affecting the Ouachita Parish School Board, whichever occurs earlier.

(C) Consolidation

Subject to approval by a majority of the electors voting, in each system affected, in an election held for that purpose, any two or more school systems may be consolidated as provided by law.

Section 11. Appropriations; State Boards

The legislature shall appropriate funds for the operating and administrative expenses of the state boards created by or pursuant to this Article.

Section 12. Appropriations; Higher Education

Appropriations for the institutions of higher education shall be made to their managing boards. The funds appropriated shall be administered by the managing boards and used solely as provided by law.

Section 13. Funding; Apportionment

(A) Free School Books

The legislature shall appropriate funds to supply free school books and other materials of instruction prescribed by the State Board of Elementary and Secondary Education to the children of this state at the elementary and secondary levels.

(B) Minimum Foundation Program

The State Board of Elementary and Secondary Education, or its successor, shall annually develop and adopt a formula which shall be used to determine the cost of a minimum foundation program of education in all public elementary and secondary schools as well as to equitably allocate the funds to parish and city school systems. Such formula shall provide for a contribution by every city and parish school system. Prior to approval of the formula by the legislature, the legislature may return the formula adopted by the board to the board and may recommend to the board an amended formula for consideration by the board and submission to the legislature for approval. The legislature shall annually appropriate funds sufficient to fully fund the current cost to the state of such a program as determined by applying the approved formula in order to insure a minimum foundation of education in all public elementary and secondary schools. Neither the governor nor the legislature may reduce such appropriation, except that the governor may reduce such appropriation using means provided in the act containing the appropriation provided that any such reduction is consented to in writing by two-thirds of the elected members of each house of the legislature. The funds appropriated shall be equitably allocated to parish and city school systems according to the formula as adopted by the State Board of Elementary and Secondary Education, or its successor, and approved by the legislature prior to making the appropriation. Whenever the legislature fails to approve the formula most recently adopted by the board, or its successor, the last formula adopted by the board, or its successor, and approved by the legislature shall be used for the determination of the cost of the minimum foundation program and for the allocation of funds appropriated.

(C) Local Funds

Local funds for the support of elementary and secondary schools shall be derived from the following sources: First: Each parish school board, Orleans Parish excepted, and each municipality or city school board actually operating, maintaining, or supporting a separate system of public schools, shall levy annually an ad valorem maintenance tax not to exceed five mills on the dollar of assessed valuation on property subject to such taxation within the parish or city, respectively. Second: The Orleans Parish

School Board shall levy annually a tax not to exceed thirteen mills on the dollar of the assessed valuation of property within the city of New Orleans assessed for city taxation, and shall certify the amount of the tax to the governing authority of the city. The governing authority shall have the tax entered on city tax rolls. The tax shall be collected in the manner, under the conditions, and with the interest and penalties prescribed by law for city taxes. The money thus collected shall be paid daily to the Orleans Parish School Board. Third: For giving additional support to public elementary and secondary schools, any parish, school district, or sub-school district, or any municipality or city school board which supports a separate city system of public schools may levy an ad valorem tax for a specific purpose, when authorized by a majority of the electors voting in the parish, municipality, district, or sub-district in an election held for that purpose. The amount, duration, and purpose of the tax shall be in accord with any limitation imposed by the legislature.

(D)(1) Municipal and Other School Systems

For the effects and purposes of this Section, the Central community school system and the Zachary community school system in East Baton Rouge Parish, and the municipalities of Baker in East Baton Rouge Parish, Monroe in Ouachita Parish, and Bogalusa in Washington Parish, and no others, shall be regarded and treated as parishes and shall have the authority granted parishes. Consistent with Article VIII of this constitution, relevant to equal educational opportunities, no state dollars shall be used to discriminate or to have the effect of discriminating in providing equal educational opportunity for all students.

(2) Notwithstanding Article III, Sections 12 and 13 and any other provision of this Constitution, in any session of the legislature in which a school system is proposed to be removed from the provisions of this Paragraph including any such proposal effective at the same time as this Subparagraph, the legislature may by law, the effectiveness of which depends on the passage and adoption by the people of such proposition, eliminate any or all relevant statutory provisions without regard to the requirements of such Sections.

Section 14. Tulane University

The Tulane University of Louisiana in New Orleans is recognized as created and to be developed in accordance with Act No. 43 approved July 5, 1884.

Section 15. Members of State Board of Elementary and Secondary Education; beginning and end of terms

In order to effectuate the terms of office as provided in Article VIII, Section 3(B), the successors in office to the elected members whose terms end in 1980 and 1982 shall be elected for terms which shall end at noon on the second Monday in March in 1984, and thereafter the successors in office to those members shall be elected and shall take office at the same time as the governor. The successor in office to the elected member whose term ends in 1984 shall be elected for a term which shall end at noon on the second Monday in March in 1988, and thereafter the successor in office to that member shall be elected and shall take office at the same time as the governor. The successors in office to the appointed members whose terms end in 1980 and 1982 shall be appointed for terms which shall end at noon on the second Monday in March in 1984, and thereafter the successors in office to those members shall be appointed for terms which shall be concurrent with the term of the governor making the appointment. The successor in office to the appointed member whose term ends in 1984 shall be appointed for a term which shall end at noon on the second Monday in March in 1988, and thereafter the successors in office to that member shall be appointed for terms which shall be concurrent with the term of the governor making the appointment.

Section 16. Public Hospitals

Notwithstanding any provision of this Article to the contrary, the legislature may provide by law for the supervision, operation, and management of public hospitals and their programs by the Board of Regents or by any board having powers of management over public institutions of higher education created by this constitution or pursuant to this Article. Such laws may include but shall not be limited to laws providing for the submission and approval of capital and operating budgets, appropriations and expenditures, the supervision, management, and oversight of the hospitals and their programs, and legislative review and disapproval of related rules. This Section shall not apply to institutions and programs operated or managed prior to January 1, 1997, by any higher education management board created by this Article.

ARTICLE IX: NATURAL RESOURCES

Section 1. Natural Resources and Environment; Public Policy

The natural resources of the state, including air and water, and the healthful, scenic, historic, and esthetic quality of the environment shall be protected, conserved, and replenished insofar as possible and consistent with the health, safety, and welfare of the people. The legislature shall enact laws to implement this policy.

Section 2. Natural Gas

(A) Public Policy; Regulation

Natural gas is declared to be affected with a public interest. Notwithstanding any provision of this constitution relative to the powers and duties of the Public Service Commission, the legislature shall provide by law for regulation of natural gas by the regulatory authority it designates. It may designate the Public Service Commission as the regulatory authority.

(B) Pipelines

No intrastate natural gas pipeline or gas gathering line shall be connected with an interstate natural gas pipeline, and no interstate natural gas pipeline shall be connected with an intrastate natural gas pipeline, without a certificate of public convenience and necessity issued as provided by law after application for the connection and hearing thereon.

Section 3. Alienation of Water Bottoms

The legislature shall neither alienate nor authorize the alienation of the bed of a navigable water body, except for purposes of reclamation by the riparian owner to recover land lost through erosion. This Section shall not prevent the leasing of state lands or water bottoms for mineral or other purposes. Except as provided in this Section, the bed of a navigable water body may be reclaimed only for public use.

Section 4. Reservation of Mineral Rights; Prescription

(A) Reservation of Mineral Rights

The mineral rights on property sold by the state shall be reserved, except when the owner or person having the right to redeem buys or redeems property sold or adjudicated to the state for taxes. The mineral rights on land, contiguous to and abutting navigable water-bottoms reclaimed by the state through the implementation and construction of coastal restoration projects shall be reserved, except when the state and the landowner having the right to reclaim or recover the land have agreed to the disposition of mineral rights, in accordance with the conditions and procedures provided by law.

(B) Prescription

Lands and mineral interests of the state, of a school board, or of a levee district shall not be lost by prescription except as authorized in Paragraph C.

(C) Exception

The legislature by act may direct the appropriate parish authority in Terrebonne Parish to transfer title and ownership as to certain lands near Bayou Dularge in Section 16 of Township 20 South, Range 16 East, which due to an error in the original governmental survey completed around 1838 until recently were thought to be within Section 9, to those persons who have possessed the property under good faith and just title for a minimum of ten years or to those who have acquired from them, reserving the mineral rights as just and sole compensation for the transfer. Consistent with the provisions of Article XIII, Section 3, the notice requirements of Article III, Section 13 are satisfied for an act passed as a companion to the act setting forth this Paragraph.

Section 5. Public Notice; Public Bidding Requirements

No conveyance, lease, royalty agreement, or unitization agreement involving minerals or mineral rights owned by the state shall be confected without prior public notice or public bidding as shall be provided by law.

Section 6. Tidelands Ownership

Revenues and royalties obtained from minerals located beyond the seaward boundary of the state belong to the state.

Section 7. Wildlife and Fisheries Commission

(A) Members; Terms

The control and supervision of the wildlife of the state, including all aquatic life, is vested in the Louisiana Wildlife and Fisheries Commission. The commission shall be in the executive branch and shall consist of seven members appointed by the governor, subject to confirmation by the Senate. Six members shall serve overlapping terms of six years, and one member shall serve a term concurrent with that of the governor. Three members shall be electors of the coastal parishes and representatives of the commercial fishing and fur industries, and four shall be electors from the state at large other than representatives of the commercial fishing and fur industries, as provided by law. No member who has served six years or more shall be eligible for reappointment.

(B) Duties; Compensation

The functions, duties, and responsibilities of the commission, and the compensation of its members, shall be provided by law.

Section 8. Forestry

(A) Forestry; Acreage Taxes

Forestry shall be practiced in the state, and the legislature may enact laws therefor. It may authorize parish governing authorities to levy acreage taxes, not to exceed two cents per acre, for the purposes of this Section. The provisions of this constitution exempting homesteads from taxation shall apply to forestry acreage taxes.

(B)(1) Forestry Commission

The practice of forestry is placed under the Louisiana Forestry Commission. The commission shall be in the executive branch and shall consist of seven members. The head of the Department of Forestry at Louisiana State University and Agricultural and Mechanical College and the director of the Wildlife and Fisheries Commission shall serve ex officio as members. The governor shall appoint the remaining five members, subject to confirmation by the Senate, for overlapping terms of five years, as provided by law.

(2) No person who has served as an appointed member of the commission for more than two and one-half terms in three consecutive terms shall be appointed to the commission for the succeeding term. This Subparagraph shall not apply to any person appointed to the commission prior to the effective date of this Subparagraph, except that it shall apply to any term of service of any such person that begins after such date.

(C) State Forester

The commission shall appoint a state forester. He shall be a graduate of an accredited school of forestry and have at least four years of forestry experience, as provided by law.

Section 9. First Use Tax Trust Fund.

(A)(1) Creation

The First Use Tax Trust Fund is hereby created and established in the state treasury as a special and irrevocable trust fund for the deposit of the proceeds, and interest derived therefrom, of the first use tax imposed by law in 1978 or thereafter and any other tax imposed by law which would have the effect of imposing any new or alternative tax on uses of those resources subject to the tax levied by the first use tax. The treasurer shall pay into the state general fund, from the total proceeds of the first use tax, as imposed by law in 1978 or thereafter such amounts as are necessary to fully reimburse the state general fund for tax credits granted in 1978 against that tax pursuant to Part I-B of Chapter 6 of Title 47 of the Louisiana Revised Statutes. The remainder of such tax proceeds shall be credited to the following accounts within the First Use Tax Trust Fund and shall not be deposited into the Bond Security and Redemption Fund or the general fund.

(2) Distribution; debt accounts

Seventy-five percent of the proceeds, and interest derived therefrom, shall be deposited into the following accounts:

(a) Initial Proceeds Account

From this portion of the initial proceeds of the tax, the sum of five hundred million dollars shall be maintained in an account within the First Use Tax Trust Fund in the state treasury to be known as the "Initial Proceeds Account". Monies in the Initial Proceeds Account shall be invested, and the investment earnings shall accrue to that account. Except for investment and except as provided in Paragraph (C), monies on deposit in the Initial Proceeds Account shall not be used. If the balance of the Initial Proceeds Account at any time is less than five hundred million dollars, then an amount from the next proceeds of the tax shall be credited to the Initial Proceeds Account until there is a balance therein of five hundred million dollars.

(b) Debt Retirement and Redemption Account

All proceeds of this portion of the tax over and above the amount required to be maintained in the Initial Proceeds Account shall be maintained in an account in the First Use Tax Trust Fund to be known as the "Debt Retirement and Redemption Account". Monies in the Debt Retirement and Redemption Account shall be invested and the investment earnings shall accrue to that account. Except for investment, monies on deposit in the Debt Retirement and Redemption Account shall be used only to purchase, in advance of maturity, on the open market any outstanding obligations of the state, or to call, pay or redeem in advance of maturity any outstanding bonds, notes or other evidence of state debt, or both. No purchase or redemption of state debt shall occur with the monies unless the purchase or redemption results in interest savings to the state. The methods used for retiring such future debt shall be determined by the state treasurer, with concurrence of two-thirds of the members of the State Bond Commission acting in open session.

(3) Distribution; conservation account

Twenty-five percent of the proceeds, and interest derived therefrom, shall be deposited into the following account:

(a) Barrier Islands Conservation Account

Twenty-five percent of the proceeds of the tax shall be maintained in an account in the First Use Tax Trust Fund to be known as the "Barrier Islands Conservation Account". Monies in the Barrier Islands Conservation Account shall be invested and the investment earnings shall accrue to that account. Except for investment, monies on deposit in the Barrier Islands Conservation Account shall be used exclusively to fund capital improvement projects designed to conserve, preserve and maintain the barrier islands, reefs, and shores of the coastline of

Louisiana. Only such capital improvements contained in the comprehensive capital budget adopted by the legislature each year shall be funded.

(B) Investments

The state treasurer shall invest all monies on deposit in the accounts established under Paragraph (A) in accordance with the law governing the investment of idle funds of the state.

(C) Use of Investment Earnings of Initial Proceeds Account

If in the judgment of the state treasurer the best interest of the state would be served, and only if the Debt Retirement and Redemption Account is depleted or otherwise not funded, the treasurer may, with concurrence of two-thirds of the members of the State Bond Commission, acting in open session, expend the investment earnings which have accrued in excess of five hundred million dollars in the Initial Proceeds Account for any purpose for which the Debt Retirement and Redemption Account may be used.

(D) The funds deposited in the First Use Tax

Trust Fund shall be considered escrowed and shall not be used for the purposes enumerated herein until the proceeds of the first use tax are determined to be available for such uses by the treasurer with concurrence of two-thirds of the members of the State Bond Commission, acting in open session. During the time these funds are escrowed such funds may be ordered remitted upon final action by a court of last resort, with the interest earned thereon, as provided by law, if the tax is held to be invalid as to any taxpayer who has paid the tax.

Section 10. Louisiana Investment Fund for Enhancement

(A) The Louisiana Investment Fund for Enhancement is established as a special fund in the state treasury. All revenues received by the state from the production of oil and gas within the state shall be deposited in the state treasury and credited to the Bond Security and Redemption Fund in accordance with the provisions of Article VII, Section 9, and shall be remitted to the political subdivisions of the state pursuant to Article VII, Section 4. In each fiscal year out of the funds remaining in the Bond Security and Redemption Fund, after a sufficient amount has been allocated for the payment of obligations secured by the full faith and credit of the state which become due and payable within the fiscal year, the treasurer shall credit an amount equal to the windfall revenues from oil and gas price deregulation to the Louisiana Investment Fund for Enhancement.

(B) As used in this Section, "windfall revenues from oil and gas price deregulation" means those revenues received by the state in a fiscal year which are in excess of the base for that particular fiscal year, as calculated in accordance with this Paragraph. The base for fiscal year 1981-1982 shall be the estimated level of collections for oil, gas, and other severance taxes and from oil and gas production royalties in fiscal year 1980-1981, which for the purposes hereof shall be one billion eighty-five million dollars, calculated as follows:

(1) Seven hundred sixty million dollars from oil, gas, and other severance taxes; and

(2) Three hundred twenty-five million dollars from oil and gas royalty payments, excluding bonuses and rentals. In each subsequent fiscal year, the state treasurer shall calculate the windfall revenues from oil and gas price deregulation for that fiscal year by determining a new base as follows: The base for the previous fiscal year shall be multiplied by the most recent annual change in the consumer price index and then the product shall be added to the base for the previous fiscal year.

(C) The state treasurer shall invest the monies in the Louisiana Investment Fund for Enhancement in the manner provided by law. Interest from the investment shall be credited to the general fund.

(D) Monies credited to the Louisiana Investment Fund for Enhancement may be expended only pursuant to an appropriation enacted by the vote of two-thirds of the elected members of each house of the legislature.

(E) The legislature shall have the authority to enact any legislation with regard to the Louisiana Investment Fund for Enhancement not inconsistent with the provisions of this Section.

ARTICLE X: PUBLIC OFFICIALS AND EMPLOYEES

PART I. STATE AND CITY CIVIL SERVICE

Section 1. Civil Service Systems

(A) State Civil Service

The state civil service is established and includes all persons holding offices and positions of trust or employment in the employ of the state, or any instrumentality thereof, and any joint state and federal agency, joint state and parochial agency, or joint state and municipal agency, regardless of the source of the funds used to pay for such employment. It shall not include members of the state police service as provided in Part IV of this Article or persons holding offices and positions of any municipal board of health or local governmental subdivision.

(B) City Civil Service

The city civil service is established and includes all persons holding offices and positions of trust or employment in the employ of each city having over four hundred thousand population and in every instrumentality thereof. However, paid firemen and municipal policemen may be excluded if a majority of the electors in the affected city voting at an election held for that purpose approve their exclusion. The election shall be called by the municipal governing authority within one year after the effective date of this constitution.

Section 2. Classified and Unclassified Service

(A) Classified Service

The state and city civil service is divided into the unclassified and the classified service. Persons not included in the unclassified service are in the classified service.

(B) Unclassified Service

The unclassified service shall include the following officers and employees in the state and city civil service:

(1) elected officials and persons appointed to fill vacancies in elective offices;

(2) the heads of each principal executive department appointed by the governor, the mayor, or the governing authority of a city;

(3) city attorneys;

(4) registrars of voters;

(5) members of state and city boards, authorities, and commissions;

(6) one private secretary to the president of each college or university;

(7) one person holding a confidential position and one principal assistant or deputy to any officer, board, commission, or authority mentioned in (1), (2), (4), or (5) above, except civil service departments;

(8) members of the military or naval forces;

(9) teaching and professional staffs, and administrative officers of schools, colleges, and universities of the state, and bona fide students of those institutions employed by any state, parochial, or municipal agency;

(10) employees, deputies, and officers of the legislature and of the offices of the governor, lieutenant governor, attorney general, each mayor and city attorney, of police juries, school boards, assessors, and of all offices provided for in Article V of this constitution except the offices of clerk of the municipal and traffic courts in New Orleans;

(11) commissioners of elections, watchers, and custodians and deputy custodians of voting machines;

(12) railroad employees whose working conditions and retirement benefits are regulated by federal agencies in accordance with federal law; and

(13) the director, deputy director, and all employees of the Governor's Office of Homeland Security and Emergency Preparedness. Additional positions may be added to the unclassified service and those positions may be revoked by rules adopted by a commission.

Section 3. State Civil Service Commission

(A) Composition

The State Civil Service Commission is established and shall be domiciled in the state capital. It shall be composed of seven members who are electors of this state, four of whom shall constitute a quorum. At least one appointed member shall be from each congressional district. In order to implement this requirement, every ten years beginning on the day the members of congress from newly reapportioned congressional districts take office, any vacancy that occurs on the commission shall be filled from a congressional district from which there is no commission member. Only when the membership includes a member from each congressional district may a vacancy be filled by an appointment from the state at large.

(B)(1) Appointment

The members shall be appointed by the governor, as hereinafter provided, for overlapping terms of six years.

(2) No person who has served as a member of the commission for more than two and one-half terms in three consecutive terms shall be appointed to the commission for the succeeding term. This Subparagraph shall not apply to any person appointed to the commission prior to the effective date of this Subparagraph, except that it shall apply to any term of service of any such person that begins after such date.

(C) Nominations

The presidents of Centenary College at Shreveport, Dillard University at New Orleans, Louisiana College at Pineville, Loyola University at New Orleans, Tulane University of Louisiana at New Orleans, and Xavier University at New Orleans, after giving consideration to representation of all groups, each shall nominate three persons. The governor shall appoint one member of the commission from the three persons nominated by each president. One member of the commission shall be elected by the classified employees of the state from their number as provided by law. A vacancy for any cause shall be filled by appointment or election in accordance with the procedure or law governing the original appointment or election, and from the same source. Within thirty days after a vacancy occurs, the president concerned shall submit the required nominations. Within thirty days thereafter, the governor shall make his appointment. If the governor fails to appoint within thirty days, the nominee whose name is first on the list of nominees automatically shall become a member of the commission. If any nominating authority fails to submit nominees in the time required, or if one of the named institutions ceases to exist, the governor shall make the appointment to the commission.

Section 4. City Civil Service Commission

(A) Creation; Membership; Domicile

A city civil service commission shall exist in each city having a population exceeding four hundred thousand. The domicile of each commission shall be in the city it serves. Each commission shall be composed of five members, who are electors of the city, three of whom shall constitute a quorum. The members shall serve overlapping terms of six years as hereinafter provided.

(B) New Orleans; Nomination and Appointment

In New Orleans, the presidents of Dillard University, Loyola University, Tulane University of Louisiana, and Xavier University, after giving consideration to representation of all groups, each shall nominate three persons. In addition, the employees in the classified service of the city of New Orleans shall nominate three persons in the classified service of the city of New Orleans by means of an election called for that purpose. The municipal governing authority shall appoint one member of the commission from the three persons nominated by each nominating authority.

(C) Other Cities; Nomination and Appointment

In each other city subject to this Section, the presidents of any five institutions of higher education in the state, selected by the governing authority of the respective city, each shall nominate three persons, after giving consideration to representation of all groups. The municipal governing authority shall appoint one member of the commission from the three persons nominated by each.

(D) Vacancies

A vacancy shall be filled by appointment in accordance with the procedure for the original appointment and from the same source. Within thirty days after a vacancy occurs, in a seat held by a university nominee, the university president concerned shall submit the required nominations. Within sixty days after this amendment is ratified by the electors of the state of Louisiana, and when a vacancy occurs in a seat held by a nominee nominated by employees in the classified service, there shall be held an election at which the employees in the classified service shall nominate three persons in accordance with this Section. Within thirty days thereafter, the municipal governing authority shall make the appointment. If the municipal governing authority fails to make the appointment within the thirty days, the nominee whose name is first on the list of nominees automatically shall become a member of the commission. If one of the nominating authorities fails to submit nominees in the time required, or if one of the named institutions ceases to exist, the municipal governing authority shall make the appointment.

(E) New Orleans; Implementation of Certain Member

The member appointed from nominations by the classified employees of the city of New Orleans shall be the successor to the member nominated by the president of St. Mary's Dominican College and the initial member so appointed shall take office at the expiration of the term of the member who took office on April 30, 1987.

Section 5. Removal

A member of the state or of a city civil service commission may be removed by the governor or the governing authority, as the case may be, for cause, after being served with written specifications of the charges against him and being afforded an opportunity for a public hearing thereon by the appointing authority.

Section 6. Department of Civil Service; Directors

(A) State Department

A Department of State Civil Service is established in the executive branch of the state government.

(B) City Departments

A department of city civil service shall exist in each city having a population exceeding four hundred thousand.

(C) Directors

Each commission shall appoint a director, after competitive examination, who shall be in the classified service. He shall be the administrative head of his department. Each director shall appoint personnel and exercise powers and duties to the extent prescribed by the commission appointing him.

Section 7. Appointments; Promotions

Permanent appointments and promotions in the classified state and city service shall be made only after certification by the appropriate department of civil service under a general system based upon merit, efficiency, fitness, and length of service, as ascertained by examination which, so far as practical, shall be competitive. The number to be certified shall not be less than three; however, if more than one vacancy is to be filled, the name of one additional eligible for each vacancy may be certified. Each commission shall adopt rules for the method of certifying persons eligible for appointment, promotion, reemployment, and reinstatement and shall provide for appointments defined as emergency and temporary appointments if certification is not required.

Section 8. Appeals

(A) Disciplinary Actions

No person who has gained permanent status in the classified state or city service shall be subjected to disciplinary action except for cause expressed in writing. A classified employee subjected to such disciplinary action shall have the right of appeal to the appropriate commission pursuant to Section 12 of this Part. The burden of proof on appeal, as to the facts, shall be on the appointing authority.

(B) Discrimination

No classified employee shall be discriminated against because of his political or religious beliefs, sex, or race. A classified employee so discriminated against shall have the right of appeal to the appropriate commission pursuant to Section 12 of this Part. The burden of proof on appeal, as to the facts, shall be on the employee.

Section 9. Prohibitions Against Political Activities

(A) Party Membership; Elections

No member of a civil service commission and no officer or employee in the classified service shall participate or engage in political activity; be a candidate for nomination or election to public office except to seek election as the classified state employee serving on the State Civil Service Commission; or be a member of any national, state, or local committee of a political party or faction; make or solicit contributions for any political party, faction, or candidate; or take active part in the management of the affairs of a political party, faction, candidate, or any political campaign, except to exercise his right as a citizen to express his opinion privately, to serve as a commissioner or official watcher at the polls, and to cast his vote as he desires.

(B) Contributions

No person shall solicit contributions for political purposes from any classified employee or official or use or attempt to use his position in the state or city service to punish or coerce the political action of a classified employee.

(C) Political Activity Defined

As used in this Part, "political activity" means an effort to support or oppose the election of a candidate for political office or to support a particular political party in an election. The support of issues involving bonded indebtedness, tax referenda, or constitutional amendments shall not be prohibited.

Section 10. Rules; Investigations; Wages and Hours

(A) Rules

(1) Powers

(a) Each commission is vested with broad and general rule-making and subpoena powers for the administration and regulation of the classified service, including the power to adopt rules for regulating employment, promotion, demotion, suspension, reduction in pay, removal, certification, qualifications, political activities, employment conditions, compensation and disbursements to employees, and other personnel matters and transactions; to adopt a uniform pay and classification plan; to require an appointing authority to institute an employee training and safety program; and generally to accomplish the objectives and purposes of the merit system of civil service as herein established. It may make recommendations with respect to employee training and safety.

(b) Nothing herein shall prevent the legislature from supplementing the uniform pay plans for sworn, commissioned law enforcement officers employed by a bona fide police agency of the state or its political subdivisions and for fire protection officers employed by a port authority, from any available funds of the state, the department, the agency, or the political subdivision, provided that such supplement may be made available only for those sworn, commissioned law enforcement officers employed on a full-time basis who serve the welfare of the public in the capacity of a police officer by providing police services to the general public, by effecting arrests, issuing citations, and serving warrants while patrolling waterways and riverfront areas and for those fire protection officers employed on a full-time basis who provide fire protection services to a port authority.

(2) Veterans

The state and city civil service departments shall accord a five-point preference in original appointment to each person who served honorably in the armed forces of the United States during a war declared by the United States Congress; or in a peacetime campaign or expedition for which campaign badges are authorized; or for at least ninety days after September 11, 2001, for reasons other than training; or during war period dates or dates of armed conflicts as provided by state law enacted by two-thirds of the elected members of each house of the legislature. The state and city civil service departments shall accord a ten-point preference in original appointment to each honorably discharged veteran who served either in peace or in war and who has one or more disabilities recognized as service-connected by the Veterans Administration; to the spouse of each veteran whose physical condition precludes his or her appointment to a civil service job in his or her usual line of work; to the unremarried widow of each deceased veteran who served in a war period, as defined above, or in a peacetime campaign or expedition; or to the unremarried widowed parent of any person who died in active wartime or peacetime service or who suffered total and permanent disability in active wartime or peacetime service; or the divorced or separated parents of any person who died in wartime or peacetime service or who became totally and permanently disabled in wartime or peacetime service. However, only one ten-point preference shall be allowed in the original appointment to any person enumerated above. If the ten-point preference is not used by the veteran, either because of the veteran's physical or mental incapacity which precludes his appointment to a civil service job in his usual line of work or because of his death, the preference shall be available to his spouse, unremarried widow, or eligible parents as defined above, in the order specified. However, any such preference may be given only to a person who has attained at least the minimum score required on each test and who has received at least the minimum rating required for eligibility.

(3) Layoffs; Preference Employees

When a position in the classified service is abolished, or needs to be vacated because of stoppage of work from lack of funds or other causes, preference employees (ex-members of the armed forces and their dependents as described in this Section) whose length of service and efficiency ratings are at least equal to those of other competing employees shall be retained in preference to all other competing employees. However, when any function of a state agency is transferred to, or when a state agency is replaced by, one or more other state agencies, every preference employee in classifications and performing functions transferred, or working in the state agency replaced, shall be transferred to the replacing state agency or agencies for employment in a position for which he is qualified before that state agency or agencies appoint additional employees for such positions from eligible lists. The appointing authority shall give the director written notice of any proposed lay-off within a reasonable length of time before its effective date, and the director shall issue orders relating thereto which he considers necessary to secure compliance with the rules. No rule, regulation, or practice of the commission, of any agency or department, or of any official of the state or any political subdivision shall favor or discriminate against any applicant or employee because of his membership or non-membership in any private organization; but this
shall not prohibit any state agency, department, or political subdivision from contracting with an employee organization with respect to wages, hours, grievances, working conditions, or other conditions of employment in a manner not inconsistent with this constitution, a civil service law, or a valid rule or regulation of a commission.

(4) Effect

Rules adopted pursuant hereto shall have the effect of law and be published and made available to the public. Each commission may impose penalties for violation of its rules by demotion in or suspension or discharge from position, with attendant loss of pay.

(B) Investigations

Each commission may investigate violations of this Part and the rules, statutes, or ordinances adopted pursuant hereto.

(C) Wages and Hours

Any rule or determination affecting wages or hours shall have the effect of law and become effective only after approval by the governor or the appropriate governing authority.

Section 11. Penalties

Willful violation of any provision of this Part shall be a misdemeanor punishable by a fine of not more than five hundred dollars or by imprisonment for not more than six months, or both.

Section 12. Appeal

(A) State

The State Civil Service Commission shall have the exclusive power and authority to hear and decide all removal and disciplinary cases, with subpoena power and power to administer oaths. It may appoint a referee, with subpoena power and power to administer oaths, to take testimony, hear, and decide removal and disciplinary cases. The decision of a referee is subject to review by the commission on any question of law or fact upon the filing of an application for review with the commission within fifteen calendar days after the decision of the referee is rendered. If an application for review is not timely filed with the commission, the decision of the referee becomes the final decision of the commission as of the date the decision was rendered. If an application for review is timely filed with the commission and, after a review of the application by the commission, the application is denied, the decision of the referee becomes the final decision of the commission as of the date the application is denied. The final decision of the commission shall be subject to review on any question of law or fact upon appeal to the court of appeal wherein the commission is located, upon application filed with the commission within thirty calendar days after its decision becomes final. Any referee appointed by the commission shall have been admitted to the practice of law in this state for at least three years prior to his appointment.

(B) Cities

Each city commission established by Part I of this Article shall have the exclusive power and authority to hear and decide all removal and disciplinary cases, with subpoena power and power to administer oaths. It may appoint a referee to take testimony, with subpoena power and power to administer oaths to witnesses. The decision of a commission shall be subject to review on any question of law or fact upon appeal to the court of appeal wherein the commission is located, upon application filed with the commission within thirty calendar days after its decision becomes final.

Section 13. Appropriations

(A) State

The legislature shall make adequate annual appropriations to the State Civil Service Commission and to the Department of State Civil Service to enable them to implement this Part efficiently and effectively. The amount so appropriated shall not be subject to veto by the governor.

(B) Cities

Each city subject to this Part shall make adequate annual appropriations to enable its civil service commission and department to implement this Part efficiently and effectively.

Section 14. Acceptance of Act; Other Cities, Parishes, City and Parish Governed Jointly

(A) Local Option

Each city having a population exceeding ten thousand but not exceeding four hundred thousand, each parish, and each parish governed jointly with one or more cities under a plan of government, having a population exceeding ten thousand, according to the latest official decennial federal census, may elect to be governed by this Part by a majority vote of its electors voting at an election held for that purpose. The election shall be ordered and held by the city, the parish, or the city-parish, as the case may be, upon

(a) the adoption of an ordinance by the governing authority calling the election; or

(b) the presentation to the governing authority of a petition calling for such an election signed by electors equal in number to five percent of the registered voters of the city, the parish, or the city-parish, as the case may be.

(B) Acceptance

If a majority of the electors vote to adopt this Part, its provisions shall apply permanently to the city, the parish, or the city-parish, as the case may be, and shall govern it as if this Part had originally applied to it. In such case, all officers and employees of the city, the parish, or the city-parish, as the case may be, who have acquired civil service status under a civil service system established by legislative act, city charter, or otherwise, shall retain that status and thereafter shall be subject to and be governed by this Part and the rules and regulations adopted under it.

(C) Rejection

If a majority of the electors vote against the adoption of this Part, the question of its adoption shall not be resubmitted to the voters of the political subdivision within one year thereafter.

Section 15. City, Parish Civil Service System; Creation; Prohibition

Nothing in this Part shall prevent the establishment by the legislature, or by the respective parish governing authority, of a parish civil service system in one or more parishes, applicable to any or all parish employees, except teaching and professional staffs and administrative officers of schools, or the establishment by the legislature or by the respective municipal governing authority of a municipal civil service system in one or more municipalities having a population of less than four hundred thousand, in any manner now or hereafter provided by law. However, paid firemen and paid municipal policemen in a municipality operating a regularly paid fire and police department and having a population exceeding thirteen thousand, and paid firemen in all parishes and in fire protection districts, are expressly excluded from such a civil service system. Nothing in this Part shall permit inclusion in the local civil service of officials and employees listed in Section 2 of this Article. No law enacted after the effective date of this constitution establishing a civil service system applicable to one or more parishes or to one or more municipalities having a population of less than four hundred thousand shall be effective in any parish or in any municipality until approved by ordinance adopted by the governing authority of the parish or municipality.

PART II. FIRE AND POLICE CIVIL SERVICE

Section 16. Establishment of System

A system of classified fire and police civil service is created and established. It shall apply to all municipalities having a population exceeding thirteen thousand and operating a regularly paid fire and municipal police department and to all parishes and fire protection districts operating a regularly paid fire department.

Section 17. Appointments and Promotions

Permanent appointments and promotions in municipal fire and police civil service shall be made only after certification by the applicable municipal fire and police civil service board under a general system based upon merit, efficiency, fitness, and length of service as provided in Article XIV, Section 15.1 of the Constitution of 1921, subject to change by law enacted by two-thirds of the elected members of each house of the legislature.

Section 18. Prior Provisions

Except as inconsistent with this Part, the provisions of Article XIV, Section 15.1 of the Constitution of 1921 are retained and continued in force and effect as statutes. By law enacted by two-thirds of the elected members of each house, the legislature may amend or otherwise modify any of those provisions, but it may not abolish the system of classified civil service for such firemen and municipal policemen or make the system inapplicable to any municipality having a population exceeding thirteen thousand according to the latest decennial federal census or to any parish or fire protection district operating a regularly paid fire department. However, in a municipality having a population exceeding four hundred thousand, paid firemen and municipal policemen shall be included if a majority of the electors therein voting at an election held for that purpose approve their inclusion. Such an election shall be called by the governing authority of the affected city within one year after the effective date of this constitution.

Section 19. Exclusion

Nothing in Part I of this Article authorizing cities or other political subdivisions to be placed under the provisions of said Part by election, act of the legislature, or ordinance of the local governing authority shall authorize the inclusion in a city civil service system of firemen and policemen in any municipality having a population greater than thirteen thousand but fewer than four hundred thousand and operating a regularly paid fire and municipal police department or in any parish or fire protection district operating a regularly paid fire department. Such firemen and policemen are expressly excluded from any such system.

Section 20. Political Activities

Article XIV, Section 15.1, Paragraph 34 of the Constitution of 1921 is retained and continued in force and effect.

PART III. OTHER PROVISIONS

Section 21. Code of Ethics

The legislature shall enact a code of ethics for all officials and employees of the state and its political subdivisions. The code shall be administered by one or more boards created by the legislature with qualifications, terms of office, duties, and powers provided by law. Decisions of a board shall be appealable, and the legislature shall provide the method of appeal.

Section 22. Dual Employment and Dual Officeholding

The legislature shall enact laws defining and regulating dual employment and defining, regulating, and prohibiting dual officeholding in state and local government.

Section 23. Compensation of Elected Public Officials; Reduction

The compensation of an elected public official shall not be reduced during the term for which he is elected.

Section 24. Impeachment

(A) Persons Liable

A state or district official, whether elected or appointed, shall be liable to impeachment for commission or conviction, during his term of office of a felony or for malfeasance or gross misconduct while in such office.

(B) Procedure

Impeachment shall be by the House of Representatives and trial by the Senate, with senators under oath or affirmation for the trial. The concurrence of two-thirds of the elected senators shall be necessary to convict. The Senate may try an impeachment whether or not the House is in session and may adjourn when it deems proper. Conviction upon impeachment shall result in immediate removal from office. Nothing herein shall prevent other action, prosecution, or punishment authorized by law.

Section 25. Removal by Suit; Officials Subject

For the causes enumerated in Paragraph (A) of Section 24 of this Article, the legislature shall provide by general law for the removal by suit of any state, district, parochial, ward, or municipal official except the governor, lieutenant governor, and judges of the courts of record.

Section 25.1. Removal by Suit; State, District, Parochial, Ward, or Municipal Employees

Notwithstanding any provision of this Article to the contrary, the legislature shall provide by general law for the removal of any state, district, parochial, ward, or municipal employee, whether classified or unclassified, from his position of employment, for conviction, during his employment, of a felony as defined by law. "Conviction", as used in this Section, means a conviction that is final and all appellate review of the original trial court proceedings is exhausted.

Section 26. Recall

The legislature shall provide by general law for the recall by election of any state, district, parochial, ward, or municipal official except judges of the courts of record. The sole issue at a recall election shall be whether the official shall be recalled.

Section 27. Filling of Vacancies.

(A) Gubernatorial Appointment; Election

If no other provision therefor is made by this constitution, by statute, by local government charter, by home rule charter or plan of government, or by ordinance, the governor may fill a vacancy occurring in any elective office. When a vacancy occurs in the office and the unexpired portion of the term exceeds one year, the vacancy shall be filled at an election, as provided by law, and the appointment shall be effective only until a successor takes office.

(B) Qualifications

Nothing in this Section shall change the qualifications for any office, and every appointee must be otherwise eligible to hold the office to which appointed.

Section 28. Definition of Vacancy

A vacancy, as used in this Constitution, shall occur in the event of death, resignation, removal by any means, or failure to take office for any reason.

Section 29. Retirement and Survivor's Benefits

(A) Public School Employees

The legislature shall provide for retirement of teachers and other employees of the public educational system through establishment of one or more retirement systems. Membership in such a retirement system shall be a contractual relationship between employee and employer, and the state shall guarantee benefits payable to a member or retiree or to his lawful beneficiary upon his death.

(B) Other Officials and Employees

The legislature shall enact laws providing for retirement of officials and employees of the state, its agencies, and its political subdivisions, including persons employed jointly by state and federal agencies other than those in military service, through the establishment of one or more retirement systems. Membership in any retirement system of the state or of a political subdivision thereof shall be a contractual relationship between employee and employer, and the state shall guarantee benefits payable to a member of a state retirement system or retiree or to his lawful beneficiary upon his death.

(C) Retirement Systems; Change; Notice

No proposal to effect any change in existing laws or constitutional provisions relating to any retirement system for public employees shall be introduced in the legislature unless notice of intention to introduce the proposal has been published, without cost to the state, in the official state journal on two separate days. The last day of publication shall be at least sixty days before introduction of the bill. The notice shall state the substance of the contemplated law or proposal, and the bill shall contain a recital that the notice has been given.

(D) Compensation for Survivors of Law Enforcement Officers and Firemen

The legislature shall establish a system, including the expenditure of public funds, for compensating the surviving spouses and dependent children of law enforcement officers, firemen, and personnel, as defined by law, who die, or who died after June 30, 1972, as a result of injury sustained in the performance of official duties or in the protection of life or property while on or off duty.

(E) Actuarial Soundness

(1) The actuarial soundness of state and statewide retirement systems shall be attained and maintained and the legislature shall establish, by law, for each state or statewide retirement system, the particular method of actuarial valuation to be employed for purposes of this Section.

(2) For public retirement systems whose benefits are guaranteed by this constitution as is specified in Paragraphs (A) and (B) of this Section:

(a) The legislature shall, by law, determine and set all required contributions to be made by members. However, until the unfunded accrued liability referenced in (c) below is eliminated, this determination and setting shall not cause the ratio of employee contributions to total contributions, on the basis of each particular plan or classification within each particular retirement system, to exceed such ratio as it existed on January 1, 1987. Upon elimination of the unfunded accrued liability referenced in (c) below, this determination and setting shall not cause a member's contribution to exceed an amount contributed on his behalf as an employer contribution.

(b) The legislature shall, in each fiscal year, by law, provide an amount necessary to fund the employer portion of the normal cost, which shall be determined in accordance with the method of valuation established under (1) above. (c) The legislature shall, in each fiscal year, by law, provide for the amortization of the unfunded accrued liability existing as of June 30, 1988, which shall be determined in accordance with the method of valuation selected in (1) above, by the year 2029, commencing with Fiscal Year 1989-1990.

(d) Amounts provided for under (b) and (c) above are hereby guaranteed payable, each fiscal year, to each retirement system covered herein. If, for any fiscal year, the legislature fails to provide these guaranteed payments, upon warrant of the governing authority of the retirement system, following the close of said fiscal year, the state treasurer shall pay the amount guaranteed directly from the state general fund.

(3) For statewide public retirement systems not covered by Paragraphs (A) and (B) of this Section, the legislature shall determine all required contributions to be made by members, contributions to be made by employers, and dedicated taxes required for the sound actuarial maintenance of the systems, including the elimination of the unfunded accrued liability as of the end of the 1988-1989 Fiscal Year, under the method of valuation selected under (1) above, by the year 2029, commencing with Fiscal Year 1989-1990.

(4) For all state and statewide public retirement systems, neither the state nor the governing authority of such system shall take any action that shall cause the actuarial present value of expected future expenditures of the retirement system to exceed or further exceed the sum of the current actuarial value of assets and the actuarial present value of expected future receipts of the retirement system, except with respect to the following:

(a) Normal business operating expenses of the retirement system.

(b) Capital outlay expenditures of the retirement system.

(c) Management of investments of the retirement system.

(d) Cost-of-living increases to retirees, as provided by law, provided the retirement system is approaching actuarial soundness as provided by law, and the granting of such increase does not cause an increase in the actuarially required contribution rate.

(5) All assets, proceeds, or income of the state and statewide public retirement systems, and all contributions and payments made to the system to provide for retirement and related benefits shall be held, invested as authorized by law, or disbursed as in trust for the exclusive purpose of providing such benefits, refunds, and administrative expenses under the management of the boards of trustees and shall not be encumbered for or diverted to any other purpose. The accrued benefits of members of any state or statewide public retirement system shall not be diminished or impaired.

(F) Benefit Provisions; Legislative Enactment

Benefit provisions for members of any public retirement system, plan, or fund that is subject to legislative authority shall be altered only by legislative enactment. No such benefit provisions having an actuarial cost shall be enacted unless approved by two-thirds of the elected members of each house of the legislature. Furthermore, no such benefit provision for any member of a state retirement system having an actuarial cost shall be approved by the legislature unless a funding source providing new or additional funds sufficient to pay all such actuarial cost within ten years of the effective date of the benefit provision is identified in such enactment. This Paragraph shall be implemented as provided by law.

(G) Forfeiture of Retirement Benefits; Felony Convictions

The receipt of a public retirement benefit shall be expressly conditioned upon the rendition of honorable service by the public official or employee. Notwithstanding any provision of this constitution or of any home rule charter to the contrary, the legislature may provide for the forfeiture of all or part of the benefits from a public retirement system, plan, or fund in this state by any person who holds or held any public office or employment and who is convicted of a felony associated with and committed during his service in such public office or employment. The legislature may provide for the application of all or part of any forfeited benefits to the unfunded accrued liability of the system, plan, or fund. The provisions of this Paragraph shall be applied only to persons employed, re-employed, or elected on or after January 1, 2013. The provisions of this Paragraph shall be applied only to benefits earned on or after January 1, 2013.

Section 29.1. Part-time Public Officials

(A) Except as provided in Paragraph

(B) the following elected or appointed officials are hereby deemed to be part-time public servants who, based on such part-time service, shall not participate in, or receive credit for service in, any public retirement system, fund, or plan sponsored by the state of Louisiana or any instrumentality or political subdivision thereof:

(1) Any legislator or any member of a school board, levee board, police jury, or parish council.

(2) Any member of a city council, city-parish council, or town council or any alderman or any constable.

(3) Any member of a board or commission established by the state of Louisiana or any instrumentality or political subdivision thereof unless authorized by law enacted by two-thirds of the elected members of each house.

(4) Any person holding or serving in any other elected or appointed position or office defined to be part-time public service by law enacted by two-thirds of the elected members of each house.

(B) The provisions of Paragraph (A) shall not apply to any person who is serving on January 1, 1997, in any elected or appointed position set forth in Paragraph (A) and who is also a member on January 1, 1997 of a retirement system covering that position.

(C) The provisions of this Section shall not apply to participation in the Louisiana Public Employees Deferred Compensation Plan, or its successor.

(D) This Section shall become effective on January 1, 1997.

Section 30. Oath of Office

Every official shall take the following oath or affirmation: "I, . . ., do solemnly swear (or affirm) that I will support the constitution and laws of the United States and the constitution and laws of this state and that I will faithfully and impartially discharge and perform all the duties incumbent upon me as . . ., according to the best of my ability and understanding, so help me God."

PART IV. STATE POLICE SERVICE

Section 41. State Police Service

(A) Service Established

The state police service is established and includes all regularly commissioned full-time law enforcement officers employed by the Department of Public Safety and Corrections, office of state police, or its successor, who are graduates of the state police training academy course of instruction and are vested with full state police powers, as provided by law, and persons in training to become such officers.

(B) Implementation

The provisions of this Part IV shall become effective on January 1, 1991; however, prior to that date members of the State Police Commission shall be selected and take office and shall adopt rules and take actions necessary to implement this Part on January 1, 1991.

Section 42. Classified and Unclassified Service

(A) Classified Service

The state police service is divided into the unclassified and the classified service. Persons not included in the unclassified service are in the classified service.

(B) Unclassified Service

The State Police Commission shall determine those positions which shall be in the unclassified service and may provide that any such position shall become classified.

Section 43. State Police Commission

(A) Composition

The State Police Commission is established and shall be domiciled in the state capital. It shall be composed of seven members who are electors of this state, four of whom shall constitute a quorum. At least one appointed member shall be from each congressional district. No appointed member shall concurrently serve on another board or commission whose purpose is similar to that of the State Police Commission. In order to implement this requirement, every ten years beginning on the day the members of congress from newly reapportioned congressional districts take office, any vacancy that occurs on the commission shall be filled from a congressional district from which there is no commission member. Only when the membership includes a member from each congressional district may a vacancy be filled by an appointment from the state at large.

(B)(1) Appointment

The members shall be selected, as hereinafter provided, for terms of six years, after initial terms of one year, two years, three years, four years, five years, and six years for the appointed members, as designated by the governor, and six years for the elected member.

(2) No person who has served as a member of the commission for more than two and one-half terms in three consecutive terms shall be appointed or elected to the commission for the succeeding term. This Subparagraph shall not apply to any person appointed or elected to the commission prior to the effective date of this Subparagraph, except that it shall apply to any term of service of any such person that begins after such date.

(C) Nominations

The presidents of Centenary College at Shreveport, Dillard University at New Orleans, Louisiana College at Pineville, Loyola University at New Orleans, Tulane University of Louisiana at New Orleans, and Xavier University at New Orleans, after giving consideration to representation of all groups, each shall nominate three persons. The governor shall appoint one member of the commission from the three persons nominated by each president. One member of the commission shall be elected by the classified state police officers of the state from their number as provided by law. A vacancy for any cause shall be filled by appointment or election in accordance with the procedure or law governing the original appointment or election, and from the same source. Within thirty days after a vacancy occurs, the president concerned shall submit the required nominations. Within thirty days thereafter, the governor shall make his appointment. If the governor fails to appoint within thirty days, the nominee whose name is first on the list of nominees automatically shall become a member of the commission. If any nominating authority fails to submit nominees in the time required, or if one of the named institutions ceases to exist, the governor shall make the appointment to the commission.

(D) Removal

An appointed member of the commission may be removed by the governor for cause after being served with written specifications of the charges against him and being afforded an opportunity for a public hearing thereon by the governor.

Section 44. Director

The commission shall appoint a director and such personnel as shall be necessary to carry out its duties.

Section 45. Appointments; Promotions

Permanent appointments and promotions in the classified state police service shall be made only after certification by the director under a general system based upon merit, efficiency, fitness, and length of service, as ascertained by examination which, so far as practical, shall be competitive. The number to be certified shall not be less than three; however, if more than one vacancy is to be filled, the name of one additional person eligible for each vacancy may be certified. The commission shall adopt rules for the method of certifying persons eligible for appointment, promotion, reemployment, and reinstatement and shall provide for appointments defined as emergency and temporary appointments if certification is not required.

Section 46. Appeals

(A) Disciplinary Actions

No person who has gained permanent status in the classified state police service shall be subjected to disciplinary action except for cause expressed in writing. A classified state police officer subjected to such disciplinary action shall have the right of appeal to the commission. The burden of proof on appeal, as to the facts, shall be on the appointing authority.

(B) Discrimination

No classified state police officer shall be discriminated against because of his political or religious beliefs, sex, or race. A classified state police officer so discriminated against shall have the right of appeal to the commission. The burden of proof on appeal, as to the facts, shall be on the state police officer.

Section 47. Prohibitions Against Political Activities

(A) Party Membership; Elections

No member of the commission and no state police officer in the classified service shall participate or engage in political activity; be a candidate for nomination or election to public office except to seek election as the classified state police officer serving on the State Police Commission; or be a member of any national, state, or local committee of a political party or faction; make or solicit contributions for any political party, faction, or candidate; or take active part in the management of the affairs of a political party, faction, candidate, or any political campaign, except to exercise his right as a citizen to express his opinion privately, to serve as a commissioner or official watcher at the polls, and to cast his vote as he desires.

(B) Contributions

No person shall solicit contributions for political purposes from any classified state police officer or use or attempt to use his position to punish or coerce the political action of a classified state police officer.

(C) Political Activity Defined

As used in this Part, "political activity" means an effort to support or oppose the election of a candidate for political office or to support a particular political party in an election. The support or opposition of a candidate seeking election as the classified state police officer member of the State Police Commission, issues involving bonded indebtedness, tax referenda, or constitutional amendments shall not be prohibited.

Section 48. Rules; Investigations; Wages and Hours

(A) Rules

(1) Powers

The commission is vested with broad and general rulemaking and subpoena powers for the administration and regulation of the classified state police service, including the power to adopt rules for regulating employment, promotion, demotion, suspension, reduction in pay, removal, certification, qualifications, political activities, employment conditions, compensation and disbursements to employees, and other personnel matters and transactions; to adopt a uniform pay and classification plan; to require an appointing authority to institute an employee training and safety program; and generally to accomplish the objectives and purposes of the merit system of state police service as herein established. It may make recommendations with respect to employee training and safety.

(2) Veterans

The director shall accord a five-point preference in original appointment to each person honorably discharged, or discharged under honorable conditions from the armed forces of the United States who served in the Vietnam Era from July 1, 1958 through May 7, 1975, except the period of July 1, 1958 through August 4, 1964, shall apply only to those who served within the area known as the Vietnam Theater; or during a war declared by the United States Congress; or in a peacetime campaign or expedition for which campaign badges are authorized; or for at least ninety days after September 11, 2001, for reasons other than training; or during war period dates or dates of armed conflicts as provided by state law enacted by two-thirds of the elected members of each house of the legislature. The director shall accord a ten-point preference in original appointment to each honorably discharged veteran who served either in peace or in war and who has one or more disabilities recognized as service-connected by the Veterans Administration; to the spouse of each veteran whose physical condition precludes his or her appointment to the state police service; to the unremarried widow of each deceased veteran who served in a war period, as defined above, or in a peacetime campaign or expedition; or to the unremarried widowed parent of any person who died in active wartime or peacetime service or who suffered total and permanent disability in active wartime or peacetime service; or the divorced or separated parents of any person who died in wartime or peacetime service or who became totally and permanently disabled in wartime or peacetime service. However, only one ten-point preference shall be allowed in the original appointment to any person enumerated above. If the ten-point preference is not used by the veteran, either because of the veteran's physical or mental incapacity which precludes his appointment to the classified state police service or because of his death, the preference shall be available to his spouse, unremarried widow, or eligible parents as defined above, in the order specified. However, any such preference may be given only to a person who has attained at least the minimum score required on each test and who has received at least the minimum rating required for eligibility.

(3) Layoffs; Preference Employees

When a position in the classified state police service is abolished, or must be vacated because of stoppage of work from lack of funds or other causes, preference employees (ex-members of the armed forces and their dependents as described in this Section) whose length of service and efficiency ratings are at least equal to those of other competing employees shall be retained in preference to all other competing employees. However, when any function of the state police is transferred to, or when the state police is replaced by, one or more other state agencies, every preference employee in classifications and performing functions transferred, or working in the state police, shall be transferred to the replacing state agency or agencies for employment in a position for which he is qualified before that state agency or agencies appoint additional employees for such positions from eligible lists. The appointing authority shall give the commission written notice of any proposed lay-off within a reasonable length of time before its effective date, and the commission shall issue orders relating thereto which it considers necessary to secure compliance with the rules. No rule, regulation, or practice of the commission, of any agency or department, or of any official of the state shall favor or discriminate against any applicant or employee because of his membership or nonmembership in any private organization; but this shall not prohibit the Department of Public Safety and Corrections, office of state police, or its successor, from contracting with an employee organization with respect to wages, hours, grievances, working conditions, or other conditions of employment in a manner not inconsistent with this constitution, law, or a valid rule or regulation of the commission.

(4) Effect

Rules adopted pursuant hereto shall have the effect of law and be published and made available to the public. The commission may impose penalties for violation of its rules by demotion in or suspension or discharge from position, with attendant loss of pay.

(B) Investigations

The commission may investigate violations of this Part and the rules, statutes, or ordinances adopted pursuant hereto.

(C) Wages and Hours

Any rule or determination affecting wages or hours shall have the effect of law and become effective only after approval by the governor and subject to appropriation of sufficient funds by the legislature.

Section 49. Penalties

Willful violation of any provision of this Part shall be a misdemeanor punishable by a fine of not more than five hundred dollars or by imprisonment for not more than six months, or both.

Section 50. Appeal

The State Police Commission shall have the exclusive power and authority to hear and decide all removal and disciplinary cases, with subpoena power and power to administer oaths. It may appoint a referee to take testimony, with subpoena power and power to administer oaths to witnesses. The decision of the commission shall be subject to review on any question of law or fact upon appeal to the court of appeal wherein the commission is located, upon application filed with the commission within thirty calendar days after its decision becomes final.

Section 51. Appropriations

The legislature shall make adequate appropriations to the State Police Commission to enable it to implement this Part efficiently and effectively. The amount so appropriated shall not be subject to veto by the governor.

ARTICLE XI: ELECTIONS

Section 1. Election Code

The legislature shall adopt an election code which shall provide for permanent registration of voters and for the conduct of all elections.

Section 2. Secret Ballot; Absentee Voting; Preservation of Ballot

In all elections by the people, voting shall be by secret ballot. The legislature shall provide a method for absentee voting. Proxy voting is prohibited. Ballots shall be counted publicly and preserved inviolate as provided by law until any election contests have been settled. In all elections by persons in a representative capacity, voting shall be viva-voce.

Section 3. Privilege from Arrest

While going to and returning from voting and while exercising the right to vote, an elector shall be privileged from arrest, except for felony or breach of the peace.

Section 4. Prohibited Use of Public Funds

No public funds shall be used to urge any elector to vote for or against any candidate or proposition, or be appropriated to a candidate or political organization. This provision shall not prohibit the use of public funds for dissemination of factual information relative to a proposition appearing on an election ballot.

Section 5. Registrar of Voters

The governing authority of each parish shall appoint a registrar of voters in the manner provided by law. The compensation, removal from office for cause, bond, powers, qualifications, and functions of the registrar shall be provided by law. Upon qualifying as a candidate for other public office, a registrar shall forfeit his office. No law shall provide for the removal from office of a registrar by the appointing authority.

ARTICLE XII: GENERAL PROVISIONS

Section 1. State Capital

The capital of Louisiana is the city of Baton Rouge.

Section 2. Civilian-Military Relations

The military shall be subordinate to the civil power.

Section 3. Right to Direct Participation

No person shall be denied the right to observe the deliberations of public bodies and examine public documents, except in cases established by law.

Section 4. Preservation of Linguistic and Cultural Origins

The right of the people to preserve, foster, and promote their respective historic linguistic and cultural origins is recognized.

Section 5. Successions; Forced Heirship and Trusts

(A) The legislature shall provide by law for uniform procedures of successions and for the rights of heirs or legatees and for testate and intestate succession. Except as provided in Paragraph (B) of this Section, forced heirship is abolished in this state.

(B) The legislature shall provide for the classification of descendants, of the first degree, twenty-three years of age or younger as forced heirs. The legislature may also classify as forced heirs descendants of any age who, because of mental incapacity or physical infirmity, are incapable of taking care of their persons or administering their estates. The amount of the forced portion reserved to heirs and the grounds for disinherison shall also be provided by law. Trusts may be authorized by law and the forced portion may be placed in trust.

Section 6. Lotteries; Gaming, Gambling, or Wagering

(A) Lotteries

(1) The legislature may provide for the creation and operation of a state lottery and may create a special corporation for that purpose whose employees shall not be subject to state civil service. The net proceeds from the operation of the lottery shall be deposited in a special fund created in the state treasury entitled the Lottery Proceeds Fund. Amounts deposited in the fund shall not be appropriated for expenditure in the same calendar year in which they are received. The legislature shall annually appropriate from the fund only for the purposes of the minimum foundation program and no more than five hundred thousand dollars for services related to compulsive and problem gaming as may be provided by law.

(2) A law providing for the creation and operation of a state lottery, once enacted, may be modified only by a law enacted by two-thirds of the elected members of each house but may be repealed in its entirety by a law enacted by a majority thereof. If such a law has been repealed, the legislature thereafter may provide for the creation and operation of a state lottery only by law enacted by two-thirds of the elected members of each house.

(3) No state general funds may be expended for the primary purpose of inducing persons to participate in the lottery. However, state general funds may be expended for the purpose of reasonably informing the public solely about the following factors pertaining to the operation and administration of the lottery:

(a) The type or types of lottery to be conducted.

(b) The price or prices of tickets or shares in the lottery.

(c) The numbers and sizes of prizes.

(d) The approximate odds of winning.

(e) The manner of payment.

(f) Frequency and time of awarding of prizes.

(g) Location of sites for sale of tickets or shares and sites of determination of winners and awarding of prizes.

(4) No political subdivision of the state shall authorize or conduct a lottery. (B) Gambling. Gambling shall be defined by and suppressed by the legislature.

(C) Gaming, Gambling, or Wagering Referendum Elections

(1)(a) No law authorizing a new form of gaming, gambling, or wagering not specifically authorized by law prior to the effective date of this Paragraph shall be effective nor shall such gaming, gambling, or wagering be licensed or permitted to be conducted in a parish unless a referendum election on a proposition to allow such gaming, gambling, or wagering is held in the parish and the proposition is approved by a majority of those voting thereon.

(b) No form of gaming, gambling, or wagering authorized by law on the effective date hereof shall be licensed or permitted to be conducted in a parish in which it was not heretofore being conducted, except licensed charitable gaming which may be conducted in any parish provided it is conducted in compliance with the law, pursuant to a state license or permit unless a referendum election on a proposition to allow such gaming, gambling, or wagering is held in the parish and the proposition is approved by a majority of those voting thereon.

(2) No new license or permit shall be issued for the conducting of riverboat gaming, gambling, or wagering operations or activities at a berth or docking facility in a parish in which such gaming, gambling, or wagering is then being conducted, unless a referendum election on a proposition to allow such additional gaming, gambling, or wagering operations or activities has been held in the parish and the proposition has been approved by a majority of those voting thereon. In addition, no license or permit regardless of when issued shall be reissued, amended, or replaced to authorize the holder to conduct riverboat gaming, gambling, or wagering operations or activities at a berth or docking facility different from that authorized in the license or permit, unless a referendum election on a proposition to allow such gaming, gambling, or wagering operations or activities has been held in the parish in which the proposed berth or docking facility is located and the proposition has been approved by a majority of those voting thereon.

(3) The legislature may at any time repeal statutes authorizing gaming, gambling, or wagering.

(4) Notwithstanding Article III, Section 12, or any other provision of this constitution, the legislature by local or special law may provide for elections on propositions relating to allowing or prohibiting one or more forms of gaming, gambling, or wagering authorized by legislative act.

Section 7. Parish Expense

The state shall reimburse a parish in which a state penal institution is located for expenses the parish incurs arising from crime committed in the institution or by an inmate thereof.

Section 8. Welfare, Unemployment Compensation, and Health

The legislature may establish a system of economic and social welfare, unemployment compensation, and public health.

Section 8.1. Workers' Compensation

(A) Authorization

(1) Notwithstanding any other provision of this constitution to the contrary, and subject to the conditions contained in this Section, the legislature by law may create a private, nonprofit corporation to provide workers' compensation insurance and to deliver related services as provided by law.

(2) Once the full faith and credit of the state for the payment of the corporation's legal obligations is extinguished, and the corporation provides security, as required by law, to hold the state harmless from all claims arising from any legal obligation of the corporation to which the full faith and credit of the state is applicable, including all costs associated therewith:

(a) This private corporation may not be dissolved or otherwise terminated by the repeal of the statutes enabling its creation or by the passage of other legislation providing for its dissolution or termination.

(b) Exclusive power to dissolve or otherwise terminate the corporation shall rest solely with the commissioner of insurance or the corporation's policyholders. Such dissolution or termination shall be in accordance with law.

(c) The corporation shall not be sold or converted to a domestic stock insurer, nor shall ownership or control be transferred.

(d) The corporation shall not be subject to any legislation directed exclusively at the corporation which impairs the corporation's ability to provide a competitive market for workers' compensation insurance to Louisiana employers.

(e) Upon the failure of the corporation to maintain security as required herein and as certified by the commissioner of insurance, the provisions of sub-sub-paragraphs (a), (b), (c), and

(d) shall be null.

(B)(1) Loan, Pledge, or Donation by State

Notwithstanding any other provision of this constitution to the contrary, the funds, credit, property, or things of value of the state may be loaned, pledged, or donated to or for the corporation under terms, conditions, or procedures to be provided by law with specific applicability to the corporation. However, any cash or negotiable instrument advanced to the corporation by the state shall be a loan and may not be donated by the state.

(2) Full Faith and Credit

The corporation may rely on the full faith and credit of the state of Louisiana for the payment of legal obligations, for a period of five years or until such time as the United States Department of Labor approves United States Longshore and Harbor Worker's Compensation Act coverage by the corporation without such security, whichever occurs later.

(C) Board of Directors

(1) The board of directors for a corporation established pursuant to the authorization contained in Paragraph A of this Section shall consist of twelve members as follows:

(a) One person from a list of three names submitted by the Louisiana American Federation of Labor and Congress of Industrial Organizations, or by a successor organization representative of organized labor to be designated by the legislature in the event that the Louisiana American Federation of Labor and Congress of Industrial Organizations ceases to exist.

(b) One person from a list of three names submitted by the Louisiana Association of Business and Industry, or by a successor organization representative of organized business to be designated by the legislature in the event that the Louisiana Association of Business and Industry ceases to exist.

(c) Four persons, all residents of Louisiana, each of whom represents a for-profit business, provided that at least one of these persons represents a business with ten or fewer employees, one of these persons represents a business with at least eleven but not more than fifty employees, one of these persons represents a business with over fifty employees, and one of these persons represents a business with over one hundred employees.

(d) A member of the Senate who has management experience in a for-profit business, who shall be a nonvoting ex officio member.

(e) A member of the House of Representatives who has management experience in a for-profit business, who shall be a nonvoting ex officio member.

(f) One person, from a list of three submitted by the board of directors of the Louisiana Workers' Compensation Corporation, who is an agent licensed by the Department of Insurance to sell workers' compensation insurance in Louisiana and who possesses executive level experience in the field of workers' compensation insurance.

(g) Two persons, each from a list of three submitted by the board of directors of Louisiana Workers' Compensation Corporation, who are residents of the state of Louisiana and who shall represent the interest of the citizens of the state at large.

(h) Repealed.

(i) The insurance commissioner or his designee, who shall be a nonvoting ex officio member.

(2) The governor shall appoint the charter members to the board, except that the president of the Senate shall appoint the Senate member and the speaker of the House shall appoint the House of Representatives member.

(3) The legislature shall provide by law for staggered terms of board members. Those who hold policies issued by the corporation will elect the successors to the four charter members representing for-profit businesses. The president of the Senate shall appoint the successors to the charter Senate member and the speaker of the House of Representatives shall appoint the successors to the charter House of Representatives member. The governor shall continue to appoint all other members as initially provided.

(4) All gubernatorial appointees shall be confirmed by the Senate in conformity with the procedures of Article IV, Section 5(H) of this constitution.

(D) Corporation Property Separate

The corporation shall not be a state agency. The property and assets of the corporation shall not be state property, shall not be subject to appropriation by the legislature, shall not be deposited in the state treasury, and shall consist of all premiums collected from underwriting worker's compensation risks, all reserves to pay future claims and all interest earned upon any monies invested by the corporation, any properties or securities acquired through the use of monies belonging to the corporation, all earnings of such property or securities, and all other monies received by the corporation from any other source.

(E) Solvency

The corporation shall adopt actuarially sound rates and underwriting policies that insure the corporation's solvency.

(F) Guaranty Fund

The corporation shall be exempt from participation in and shall not join or contribute financially to or be entitled to the protection of any plan, pool, association, or guaranty fund or insolvency fund authorized or required pursuant to the Insurance Code. However, upon the extinguishment of the full faith and credit guarantee of the state, the corporation shall no longer be exempt from participation in, contribution to, and protection under the insurance guaranty association fund created and operating under R.S. 22:1375 et seq., of the Insurance Code. The corporation's participation in, contribution to, and protection under the insurance guaranty association fund shall be on a prospective basis only. This prospective participation, contribution, and protection shall only apply to claims arising from injuries occurring after the extinguishment of the full faith and credit guarantee.

Section 9. Exemptions From Seizure and Sale

The legislature shall provide by law for exemptions from seizure and sale, as well as waivers of and exclusions from such exemptions. The exemption shall extend to at least fifteen thousand dollars in value of a homestead, as provided by law.

Section 10. Suits Against the State

(A) No Immunity in Contract and Tort

Neither the state, a state agency, nor a political subdivision shall be immune from suit and liability in contract or for injury to person or property.

(B) Waiver in Other Suits

The legislature may authorize other suits against the state, a state agency, or a political subdivision. A measure authorizing suit shall waive immunity from suit and liability.

(C) Limitations; Procedure; Judgments

Notwithstanding Paragraph (A) or (B) or any other provision of this constitution, the legislature by law may limit or provide for the extent of liability of the state, a state agency, or a political subdivision in all cases, including the circumstances giving rise to liability and the kinds and amounts of recoverable damages. It shall provide a procedure for suits against the state, a state agency, or a political subdivision and provide for the effect of a judgment, but no public property or public funds shall be subject to seizure. The legislature may provide that such limitations, procedures, and effects of judgments shall be applicable to existing as well as future claims. No judgment against the state, a state agency, or a political subdivision shall be exigible, payable, or paid except from funds appropriated therefor by the legislature or by the political subdivision against which the judgment is rendered.

Section 11. Continuity of Government

The legislature shall provide for orderly and temporary continuity of state government, in periods of emergency, until normal processes of government can be reestablished in accordance with the constitution and laws of the state; and, except as otherwise provided by this constitution, for the prompt and temporary succession to the powers and duties of public offices when incumbents become unavailable to perform their functions.

Section 12. Corporations; Perpetual or Indefinite Duration; Dissolution; Perpetual Franchises or Privileges

Neither the state nor any political subdivision shall grant a perpetual franchise or privilege; however, the legislature may authorize the organization of corporations for perpetual or indefinite duration. Every corporation shall be subject to dissolution or forfeiture of its charter or franchise, as provided by general law.

Section 13. Prescription Against State

Prescription shall not run against the state in any civil matter, unless otherwise provided in this constitution or expressly by law.

Section 14. Administrative Agency Codes

Rules, regulations, and procedures adopted by all state administrative and quasi-judicial agencies, boards, and commissions shall be published in one or more codes and made available to the public.

Section 15. Defense of Marriage

Marriage in the state of Louisiana shall consist only of the union of one man and one woman. No official or court of the state of Louisiana shall construe this constitution or any state law to require that marriage or the legal incidents thereof be conferred upon any member of a union other than the union of one man and one woman. A legal status identical or substantially similar to that of marriage for unmarried individuals shall not be valid or recognized. No official or court of the state of Louisiana shall recognize any marriage contracted in any other jurisdiction which is not the union of one man and one woman.

Section 16. Patient's Compensation Fund

(A) Authorization

Notwithstanding any other provision of this constitution to the contrary, the legislature may establish a private custodial fund to be designated the "Patient's Compensation Fund". Any deposits into a fund established pursuant to this Section are not public monies, but are self-generated, private monies to be held in trust by a board created by the legislature for the use, benefit, and protection of medical malpractice claimants and the private health care provider members. Pursuant to Article VII, Section 10(J) of this constitution, such funds shall not be defined as state general funds or dedicated funds required for deposit in the state treasury.

(B) Patient's Compensation Fund assets

The assets of a fund, when established pursuant to this Section, shall not be state property, shall not be subject to appropriation by the legislature, and shall not be required for deposit in the state treasury pursuant to Article VII, Section 9(A) of this constitution. Assets of such a fund shall consist of all surcharges collected from health care provider members and filing fees collected from claimants, all reserves to pay future claims, all interest earned upon any monies invested by the board, any securities acquired through the investment of fund monies, all earnings on such securities, and all other monies and assets deposited into the fund.

(C) Guaranty fund

Any such fund created pursuant to this Section shall be exempt from participation in and shall not join or contribute financially to or be entitled to the protection of any plan, pool, association, or guaranty fund or insolvency fund.

(D) Full faith and credit

No fund nor board that may be created pursuant to this Section may rely on the full faith and credit of this state for the payment of legal obligations.

(E) State general funds

Any such fund or board created pursuant to this Section shall not be entitled to an appropriation of state general funds without a specific appropriation approved by the legislature.

ARTICLE XIII: CONSTITUTIONAL REVISION

Section 1. Amendments

(A)(1) Procedure

An amendment to this constitution may be proposed by joint resolution at any regular session of the legislature, but the resolution shall be prefiled, at least ten days before the beginning of the session or as provided in Subparagraph (2) of this Paragraph, in accordance with the rules of the house in which introduced. An amendment to this constitution may be proposed at any extraordinary session of the legislature if it is within the objects of the call of the session and is introduced in the first five calendar days thereof. If two-thirds of the elected members of each house concur in the resolution, pursuant to all of the procedures and formalities required for passage of a bill except submission to the governor, the secretary of state shall have the proposed amendment published once in the official journal of each parish within not less than thirty nor more than sixty days preceding the election at which the proposed amendment is to be submitted to the electors. Each joint resolution shall specify the statewide election at which the proposed amendment shall be submitted. Special elections for submitting proposed amendments may be authorized by law.

(2) Any joint resolution proposed at a regular session of the legislature which effects any change in constitutional provisions relating to any retirement system for public employees shall be prefiled no later than five o'clock in the evening of the forty-fifth calendar day prior to the first day of session.

(B) Form of Proposal

A proposed amendment shall have a title containing a brief summary of the changes proposed; shall be confined to one object; and shall set forth the entire article, or the sections or other subdivisions thereof, as proposed to be revised or only the article, sections, or other subdivisions proposed to be added. However, the legislature may propose, as one amendment, a revision of an entire article of this constitution which may contain multiple objects or changes. A section or other subdivision may be repealed by reference. When more than one amendment is submitted at the same election, each shall be submitted so as to enable the electors to vote on them separately.

(C) Ratification

If a majority of the electors voting on the proposed amendment approve it, the governor shall proclaim its adoption, and it shall become part of this constitution, effective twenty days after the proclamation, unless the amendment provides otherwise. A proposed amendment directly affecting not more than five parishes or areas within not more than five parishes shall become part of this constitution only when approved by a majority of the electors voting thereon in the state and also a majority of the electors voting thereon in each affected parish. However, a proposed amendment directly affecting not more than five municipalities, and only such municipalities, shall become part of this constitution only when approved by a majority of the electors voting thereon in the state and also a majority of the electors voting thereon in each such municipality.

Section 2. Constitutional Convention

Whenever the legislature considers it desirable to revise this constitution or propose a new constitution, it may provide for the calling of a constitutional convention by law enacted by two-thirds of the elected members of each house. The revision or the proposed constitution and any alternative propositions agreed upon by the convention shall be submitted to the people for their ratification or rejection. If the proposal is approved by a majority of the electors voting thereon, the governor shall proclaim it to be the Constitution of Louisiana.

Section 3. Laws Effectuating Amendments

Whenever the legislature shall submit amendments to this constitution, it may at the same session enact laws to carry them into effect, to become operative when the proposed amendments have been ratified.

ARTICLE XIV: TRANSITIONAL PROVISIONS

PART I.

Section 1. Board of Regents

On the effective date of this constitution, each member of the Louisiana Coordinating Council for Higher Education appointed by the governor whose term has not expired shall become a member of the Board of Regents until his respective term expires. The governor shall appoint additional members required to complete the membership of the board in accordance with and to effectuate Article VIII, Section 5.

Section 2. Board of Supervisors of Louisiana State University and Agricultural and Mechanical College

On the effective date of this constitution, each member of the Board of Supervisors of Louisiana State University and Agricultural and Mechanical College whose term has not expired shall become a member of the Board of Supervisors of Louisiana State University and Agricultural and Mechanical College until his term expires. The governor shall appoint additional members required in accordance with and to effectuate Article VIII, Section 7.

Section 3. Board of Supervisors of Southern University

At the next session of the legislature following the effective date of this constitution, the governor shall submit to the Senate for its consent the names of his appointees to the Board of Supervisors of Southern University and Agricultural and Mechanical College in accordance with and to effectuate Article VIII, Section 7.

Section 4. State Board of Elementary and Secondary Education; Board of Trustees for State Colleges and Universities

On the effective date of this constitution, each member of the State Board of Education whose term has not expired may elect to become a member of either the State Board of Elementary and Secondary Education or the Board of Trustees for State Colleges and Universities. He shall serve until the expiration of the term for which he was elected. The legislature shall provide by law the procedures by which this right shall be exercised, the secretary of state notified of those elections which must be held, and the governor notified of the appointments which must be made to complete the membership of the boards. The elections and appointments shall be made in accordance with and to effectuate Article VIII, Sections 3 and 6.

Section 5. Boards; New Appointments

In making new appointments to a board created by Sections 5, 6, or 7 of Article VIII, the governor shall consider appropriate representation on the board by alumni of the institutions under the control of the board.

Section 6. Mandatory Reorganization of State Government

The legislature shall allocate, within not more than twenty departments, the functions, powers, duties, and responsibilities of all departments, offices, agencies, and other instrumentalities within the executive branch, except those allocated by this constitution. The allocation, which shall not be subject to veto by the governor, shall become operative not later than December 31, 1977.

Section 7. Legislative Sessions

The legislature shall provide, by rule or otherwise, for a recess, during the 1975 and 1976 regular annual sessions, which shall be for at least eight calendar days immediately after the first fifteen calendar days of the session.

Section 8. Civil Service Commission; State; Cities

(A) State Commission

Each person who, on the effective date of this constitution, is a member of the State Civil Service Commission shall continue in such position for the remainder of the term to which he was appointed. Within thirty days after the effective date of this constitution, the president of Xavier University of Louisiana shall submit three names to the governor for appointment to the commission as provided in Article X, Section 3. Within ninety days after the effective date of this constitution, one member of the commission shall be elected by the classified employees of the state from their number as provided by law. The term of these appointees shall be six years. Within thirty days after the expiration of the term of the present member nominated by the president of Louisiana State University and Agricultural and Mechanical College, the president of Dillard University shall submit three names to the governor for appointment to the commission as provided in Article X, Section 3. The term of this appointee shall be six years.

(B) City Commission

Each person who, on the effective date of this constitution, is a member of the New Orleans City Civil Service Commission shall continue in such position for the remainder of the term to which he was appointed. Within thirty days after the effective date of this constitution, the presidents of St. Mary's Dominican College and Xavier University of Louisiana each shall submit three names to the governing body of the city for appointment to the commission as provided in Article X, Section 4. Within thirty days after the expiration of the term of the present member nominated by the governing body of the city, the president of Dillard University shall submit three names to the governing body of the city for appointment to the New Orleans City Civil Service Commission as provided in Article X, Section 4. The term of these appointees shall be six years.

Section 9. Civil Service Officers; Employees; State; Cities

Upon the effective date of this constitution, all officers and employees of the state and of the cities covered hereunder who have status in the classified service shall retain said status in the position, class, and rank that they have on such date and shall thereafter be subject to and governed by the provisions of this constitution and the rules and regulations adopted under the authority hereof.

Section 10. Offshore Mineral Revenues; Use of Funds

Funds derived from offshore mineral leases and held in escrow under agreement between the state and the United States pending settlement of the dispute between the parties shall be deposited in the state treasury when received. Upon such settlement, these funds and the interest from their investment, except the portion otherwise allocated or dedicated by this constitution, shall be used by the state treasurer to purchase, retire, or pay in advance of maturity the existing bonded indebtedness of the state or shall be invested for that purpose. If any of these funds cannot be so expended within one year, the legislature may appropriate annually, for capital improvements or for the purchase of land, ten percent of the remaining funds, not to exceed ten million dollars in one year.

Section 11. Prescription; Tidelands Taxes

No state, district, parish, or other tax, license, fee, or assessment of any kind, and interest charges and penalties attaching thereto, which are imposed, due, or collectible on any property, minerals or the severance thereof, or due or payable by any person, firm, or corporation on any business operation or activity within the tidelands area in dispute between the state and the United States and within the state's historic gulfward boundary three leagues from coast, as established and defined by the Act of Congress of April 8, 1812, which admitted this state into the Union, and as redefined in Louisiana Act No. 33 of 1954,1 shall prescribe until three years after the thirty-first day of December in the year in which the controversy existing between the United States and this state over the state gulfward boundary is finally resolved and settled in accordance with law. However, no interest charge or penalty shall be assessed or collected on any such tax, license, fee, or assessment if it is paid within one year after the thirty-first day of December in the year in which the controversy is finally resolved and settled.

Section 12. Forfeitures Prior to 1880

Whenever any immovable property has been forfeited or adjudicated to the state for nonpayment of taxes due prior to January 1, 1880, and the state did not sell or dispose of it or dispossess the tax debtor or his heirs, successors, or assigns prior to the adoption of the Constitution of 1921, it shall be presumed conclusively that the forfeiture or adjudication was irregular and null or that the property has been redeemed. The state and its assigns shall be estopped forever from claiming any title to the property because of such forfeiture or adjudication.

Section 13. Effective Date of Property Tax Provisions

Section 18 and Section 20 of Article VII shall become effective January 1 of the year following the end of three years after the effective date of this constitution. Until that date, the provisions of the Constitution of 1921 governing matters covered by those Sections shall continue to apply, notwithstanding any contrary expiration date stated in any provision thereof concerning the veterans' homestead exemption.

PART II.

Section 14. Limitation on Transitional Provisions

Nothing in this Part shall be construed or applied in such a manner as to supersede or invalidate, or limit or change the meaning of any provision of the foregoing Articles of this constitution, but only to provide for an orderly transition from the Constitution of 1921.

Section 15. Existing Officials

A person holding an office by election shall continue to exercise his powers and duties until his office is abolished, his successor takes office or the office is vacated, as provided by law. A person holding an office by appointment shall continue to exercise his powers and duties until his office is abolished, his term ends, or he is removed or replaced under the provisions of this constitution or by law. Each public body shall continue to exercise its powers and duties until changed as provided by this constitution or by law.

Section 16. Provisions of 1921 Constitution Made Statutory

(A) Provisions Continued as Statutes

Subject to change by law or as otherwise provided in this constitution, and except as any of them conflicts with this constitution, the following provisions of the Constitution of 1921 are continued as statutes, but restricted to the same effect as on the effective date of this constitution: 1. Article IV, Sections 2(c), 12-b, and 12-c. 2. Article V, Sections 2, 7, 18, 20, and 21. 3.

Article VI, Sections 1, 1(A-1), 11.1, 19, 19.2, 19.3, 19.4, 22(l), 23 except any dedications contained therein, 23.1, 26, 28, 31, 32, 33, 35, 36.1, and 39. 4. Article VI-A, Sections 1 through 14, except any dedications therein contained. 5. Article VII, Sections 7, 8, 9, 12.1, 13, 20, 21, 28, 31, 31.1, 31.2, 33, 46 through 51, 51(a), 52, 53, 55, 80, 81, 82, 83, 85, 89 through 92, and 94 through 97. 6. Article IX, Section 4. 7. Article X, Sections 1, 2, 6, 7, 9, 10A, 15, 16, and 23; except any dedications contained therein. 8. Article X-A, Sections 3 and 4. 9. Article XII, Sections 18, 19 through 22, 25, and 26. 10. Article XIV, Sections 3(b), 3(d) (first), 6, 10, 12, 14, 19, 21, 23, 23.1 through 23.43, 24, 24.2 through 24.23, 25, 25.1, 26 through 28, 30, 30.1, 30.3, 30.4, 30.5, 31, 31.3, 31.6, 31.7, 32, 33, 34, 35, 36, 37.1, 38, 38, 38.1, 39, 39.1, 43, 44, 44.1, 45, 47, and 48. 11. Article XV, Sections 1, 3, and 4. 12. Article XVI, Sections 1, 4, 6, 7, 8, and 8(a). 13. Article XVII, Sections 3 and 4. 14. Article XVIII, Sections 4, 8, and 13. 15. Article XIX, Sections 6, 19, 19(a), 20, and 27.

(B) Arrangement

The provisions made statutory in this Article shall be arranged in proper statutory form and recommendations made for additional laws and modifications as provided in R.S. 24:201 through 256, or as otherwise provided by law.

Section 17. Provisions of Constitution of 1921 Repealed

Except to the extent provided in this Article and except as retained in Articles I through XIII of this constitution, the provisions of the Constitution of 1921 are repealed.

Section 18. Existing Laws

(A) Retention

Laws in force on the effective date of this constitution, which were constitutional when enacted and are not in conflict with this constitution, shall remain in effect until altered or repealed or until they expire by their own limitation.

(B) Expiration of Conflicting Law

Laws which are in conflict with this constitution shall cease upon its effective date.

Section 19. Ports; Transition to Statutes

All provisions of Article VI, Sections 16, 16.1, 16.2, 16.3, 16.4, 16.5, 16.6, 17, 29, 29.1, 29.2, 29.3, 29.4, 33.1, 34 and Article XIV, Section 30.2 of the Constitution of 1921 shall become statutes subject to amendment or repeal only as provided in Article VI, Section 43 of this constitution.

Section 20. Public Service Commission

At its next extraordinary or regular session, the legislature shall divide the state into five single-member districts as required by Article IV, Section 21(A) and shall provide for a special election at which the two additional members of the commission shall be elected, the initial term to be served by each, and other matters necessary to effectuate said Section 21(A).

PART III.

Section 21. References to 1921 Constitution

Whenever reference is made in this constitution to the Constitution of 1921, it shall mean the Louisiana Constitution of 1921, as amended.

Section 22. Effect of Titles

No title or sub-title, heading or sub-heading, marginal note, index, or table printed in or with this constitution shall be considered or construed to be a part of this constitution, but to be inserted only for convenience in reference.

Section 23. Continuation of Actions and Rights

All writs, actions, suits, proceedings, civil or criminal liabilities, prosecutions, judgments, sentences, orders, decrees, appeals, rights or causes of action, contracts, obligations, claims, demands, titles, and rights existing on the effective date of this constitution shall continue unaffected. All sentences as punishment for crime shall be executed according to their terms.

Section 24. Protection of Existing Taxes

All taxes, penalties, fines, and forfeitures owing to the state or any political subdivision levied and collectible under the Constitution of 1921 and valid laws enacted thereunder shall inure to the entity entitled thereto.

Section 25. Impairment of Debt Obligations Prohibited

Nothing in this constitution shall be construed or applied in such a manner as to impair the obligation, validity, or security of any bonds or other debt obligations authorized under the Constitution of 1921.

Section 26. Constitution Not Retroactive

Except as otherwise specifically provided in this constitution, this constitution shall not be retroactive and shall not create any right or liability which did not exist under the Constitution of 1921 based upon actions or matters occurring prior to the effective date of this constitution.

Section 27. Legislative Provisions

(A) President of Senate

The lieutenant governor in office on the effective date of this constitution shall continue to serve as president of the Senate until his term expires in 1976.

(B) First Session

The provisions of Article III of this constitution shall become effective for the first session of the legislature to be held in 1975 and each session thereafter. However, in 1976, the legislature shall convene in regular session at twelve o'clock noon on the second Monday in May, at which time the members elected at the statewide election in 1976 shall take office; otherwise, the legislature shall conduct that session as provided in Article III of this constitution.

(C) Legislative Auditor

The legislative auditor shall continue to exercise the powers and perform the functions set forth in Article VI, Section 26(2) of the Constitution of 1921 until otherwise provided by law.

(D) Legislative Reapportionment

The requirement for legislative reapportionment in Section 6 of Article III of this constitution shall apply to the reapportionment of the legislature following the decennial census of 1980, and thereafter.

Section 28. Judiciary Commission

The members of the judiciary commission in office on the effective date of this constitution shall serve until the expiration of their terms. Within thirty days after the effective date of this constitution, the additional two citizen members shall be selected as required by Article V, Section 25. A lawyer member, as thereby required, shall be selected to succeed the judge of a court of record other than a court of appeal whose term as a member of the commission first expires. Thereafter, when a vacancy occurs, the successor to the position shall be selected in accordance with Article V, Section 25.

Section 29. Repealed.

Section 30. Commissioner of Elections

The commissioner of elections, as provided by Article IV, first elected under this constitution shall be elected to take office in 1976. The custodian of voting machines in office on the effective date of this constitution shall continue to exercise the functions of that office, without change, until the expiration of his term.

Section 31. Pardon Board

Until a pardon board is appointed under the terms of this constitution, the lieutenant governor, attorney general, and presiding judge of the sentencing court shall continue to serve as a board of pardons.

Section 32. Levee Districts; Compensation for Property

The provisions of Article XVI, Section 6 of the Constitution of 1921 shall be continued as a statute, subject to change by the legislature, and the amount of compensation therein required to be paid for property used or destroyed for levee or levee drainage purposes shall be paid as provided in Section 6 of Article XVI of the Constitution of 1921 until the legislature enacts a law to effectuate Article VI, Section 42 of this constitution. Section 33. Suits Against the State; Effective Date Section 33. The provisions of Article XII, Section 10 waiving the immunity of the state, its agencies, or political subdivisions from suit and liability in contract or for injury to person or property only shall apply to a cause of action arising after the effective date of this constitution.

Section 34. Exemption from Seizure and Sale

The provisions of Article XI of the Constitution of 1921 shall be continued as a statute until the legislature enacts the law required by Article XII, Section 9 of this constitution, but the amount of the exemption shall be fifteen thousand dollars in value until otherwise fixed by law.

Section 35. Effective Date

This constitution shall become effective at twelve o'clock midnight on December 31, 1974. The secretary of state shall promulgate the results of the election by publication in the official state journal on the thirtieth day prior thereto; however, he shall announce the results of the election within thirty days after the date of the election at which the constitution is submitted to the people.

Section 36. Effect of Adoption

Notwithstanding any contrary provision of any law or the prior constitution, this constitution when approved by the electors of this state shall be the Constitution of the State of Louisiana upon the effective date as provided in Section 35 of this Article. Section 37. Severability Clause Section 37. If any provision of this constitution is declared invalid for any reason, that provision shall not affect the validity of the entire constitution or any other provision thereof.

www.ingramcontent.com/pod-product-compliance
Lightning Source LLC
Chambersburg PA
CBHW052240220526
45471CB00001B/128